T0142260

Machine Translation: Technologies and Applications

Volume 2

This book series tackles prominent issues in MT at a depth which will allow these books to reflect the current state-of-the-art, while simultaneously standing the test of time. Each book topic will be introduced so it can be understood by a wide audience, yet will also include the cutting-edge research and development being conducted today.

Machine Translation (MT) is being deployed for a range of use-cases by millions of people on a daily basis. Google Translate and FaceBook provide billions of translations daily across many language. Almost 1 billion users see these translations each month. With MT being embedded in platforms like this which are available to everyone with an internet connection, one no longer has to explain what MT is on a general level. However, the number of people who really understand its inner workings is much smaller.

The series includes investigations of different MT paradigms (Syntax-based Statistical MT, Neural MT, Rule-Based MT), Quality issues (MT evaluation, Quality Estimation), modalities (Spoken Language MT) and MT in Practice (Post-Editing and Controlled Language in MT), topics which cut right across the spectrum of MT as it is used today in real translation workflows.

More information about this series at http://www.springer.com/series/15798

Bernard Scott

Translation, Brains and the Computer

A Neurolinguistic Solution to Ambiguity
and Complexity in Machine Translation

 Springer

Bernard Scott
Tarpon Springs, FL, USA

ISSN 2522-8021   ISSN 2522-803X   (electronic)
Machine Translation: Technologies and Applications
ISBN 978-3-030-09538-3   ISBN 978-3-319-76629-4   (eBook)
https://doi.org/10.1007/978-3-319-76629-4

Printed on acid-free paper

This Springer imprint is published by the registered company Springer International Publishing AG part
of Springer Nature.
The registered company address is: Gewerbestrasse 11, 6330 Cham, Switzerland

Gratefully Dedicated
A. M. D. G.

Any intelligent fool can make things bigger and more complex. It takes a touch of genius – and a lot of courage – to move in the opposite direction.

– Albert Einstein

Preface

This book is about Machine Translation (MT) and the classic problems associated with this language technology. It is intended for anyone who wonders what if anything might be done to relieve these difficulties. For linguistic, rule-based systems, we attribute the cause of these difficulties to language's ambiguity and complexity and to their interplay in logic-driven processes. For non-linguistic, data-driven systems, we attribute translation shortcomings to the very lack of linguistics. We then propose a demonstrable way to relieve these drawbacks in both instances.

Throughout the book, we present a variety of translations by several of the most prominent linguistic, statistical and neural net MT systems in use today. Our object in doing this is to illustrate both the relative strengths and weaknesses of the various technologies these systems embody. The book's principal intent, however, is not to promote one particular translation system over against others (not even the one the author worked on for thirty years, described herein as Logos Model), but rather to examine the deeper and more critical question of the mechanisms that underlie the translation act itself, and to illustrate what can be done to optimize these mechanisms in a translation machine. We hold this to be the more fundamental issue that needs to be addressed if the classic problems associated with MT are to be solved, and consistent, high-quality machine output is ever to be realized.

Because the linguistic processes of the brain are singularly free of the classic difficulties that beset the machine, we have looked to the brain for possible guidance. We describe a working translation model (Logos Model) that has taken its inspiration from key assumptions about psycholinguistic and neurolinguistic function. We suggest that this brain-based mechanism is effective precisely because it bridges both linguistically-driven and data-driven methodologies. In particular, we show how simulation of this cerebral mechanism has freed this one MT effort, Logos Model, from the all-important, classic problem of complexity when coping with the ambiguities of language. Logos Model accomplishes this by a data-driven process that does not sacrifice linguistic knowledge, but that, like the brain, integrates linguistics within a data-driven process. As a consequence, we suggest that the brain-like mechanism simulated in this model has the potential to contribute to further advances in MT in all its technological instantiations.

These admittedly are controversial claims, and we recognize that the reader may be inclined to dismiss them out of hand, especially given the fact that the model being described, Logos Model, had its origins more than 45 years ago in the earliest days of MT. How, one will ask, can technology from so far back in time offer anything of interest to present-day MT? That is certainly a legitimate question, but it is one we trust this book will answer.

As readers work their way through this book, they will see that we are showing Logos Model at its best, seemingly at times at the expense of other translation systems. Our purpose in writing this book, however, has *not* been to prove that Logos is a better translation system. In terms of the general output quality of many MT systems nowadays, no such claim could be defended. Our purpose rather has been quite different, namely, to demonstrate that the technology underlying Logos Model offers a demonstrable solution to the problem that complexity poses for MT. As we argue throughout this book, complexity is the one issue that is most apt to limit the ultimate potential of any MT system, whether linguistic, statistical or neural. And we attempt to show that Logos Model, originally designed as it was to address the complexity problem, may offer a workable answer. Logos Model translations shown in this book are meant to demonstrate that the model must be doing something right in that regard, something that we trust would be of interest to MT developers generally. Allow me to repeat the point. Logos Model translations in this book are *not* intended to prove that Logos is a better system, only that underlying Logos Model technology may have something of genuine interest to offer. It is hoped that the MT community will understand this, and that the empirical data, arguments and personal testimony we have presented will be considered in constructive spirit intended.

One final matter. Translations shown in this book by Google Translate, Microsoft's Bing Translator, SYSTRANet, PROMT Translator and LISA Lab's neural MT system were carried out in the 2016–2017 timeframe. Readers should be aware that these translations do not necessarily represent output of these systems subsequent to this 2016–2017 timeframe. Readers will note that output from Google Translate and Bing Translator had to be marked as either statistical or neural, since both the Google and Microsoft systems transitioned to neural net technology in late 2016 as this book was being written.

Tarpon Springs, FL, USA   Bernard Scott

Acknowledgements

The following individuals, among still others, are responsible for having turned the concepts of this book into a working system.

Linguists
Kutz Arrieta
Anabela Barreiro
Mary Lou (Christine) Faggione
Claudia Gdaniec
Brigitte Orliac
Karen (Liz) Purpura
Patty Schmid
Steve Schneiderman
Sheila Sullivan
Monica Thieme

Systems
Charles Byrne (Logos co-founder)
Daniel Byrne
Jonathan Lewis
Oliver Mellet
Barbara Tarquinio
Kevin Wiseman
Theresa Young

Corporate
Cecilia Mellet
Robert Markovits
Arnold Mende
James Linen
Charles Staples
Hans Georg Forstner

Special thanks to Anabela Barreiro and Fernando Batista (INESC-ID) without whose assistance this book would not have been possible. And much appreciation for helpful suggestions by two anonymous reviewers.

Permissions

All figures in this book were created by the author except for those listed below, used with permissions indicated:

Fig. 4.3 Permission granted by Dr. Francis Wong

Fig. 4.5 Permission granted by National Institute of Health under GNU Free Document License (GFDL)

Fig. 4.6 Permission granted by Oxford University Press

Fig. 5.1 Permission granted by Elsevier

Postscript Fig. 5G-1 Permission granted by World Scientific Publishing

Fig. 8.1 Permission granted by the Association of Computational Linguistics (ACL)

Fig. 8.2 Permission granted by Christoph Bugmer under GNU Free Document License (GFDL)

Fig. 8.4 Permission granted by Elsevier

Contents

Part II

Part I

Chapter 1
Introduction

Abstract This chapter illustrates some of the errors that translation machines may make in processing natural language. That these translation errors would never have been made by human translators raises the question as to why this is so. What is the translator's brain doing in its handling of language that is different from the machine? Is the brain processing language in ways that have yet to be understood? Could it be that neuroscience has overlooked evidence of a cerebral language process that is different from what cognitive science and neurolinguistics have traditionally proposed for the brain? What would such a hitherto under-recognized process look like and might it be simulatable in a translation machine? These questions constitute the topic of this book.

MOST READERS ARE AWARE that Alan Turing, at the very outset of the computer age, had suggested these new number-crunching machines ought also be able to do things like play chess and translate languages. Turing was prescient about chess, but as we know his predictions about computers and language have never been fully realized. Turing inspired many to try, but as the record shows, the history of the computer's struggles with language is long and legendary. And while telling progress has been made since the inclusion of statistics and neural net technology into the effort, huge, unsolved problems remain, making the goal of consistent, high-quality MT seem as illusive as ever. After so many decades of trying and never quite getting there, one has to wonder whether there is not something about language itself that is ultimately intractable.

Michael Halliday (2003) noted that language is among the most complex phenomena in the universe. To a non-linguist his statement must seem greatly overblown. After all, language cannot be that complex if children acquire it so readily, virtually without even trying. The world is filled with natural phenomena that seem far more complex than language, and more difficult to grasp. Weather is a good example, things like avalanches and earthquakes are another. But there's a difference here. The complexities of nature are invariably regular and law-like, even if the factors are non-linear and almost impossible to pin down. The complexity of language seems of an entirely different kind.

© Springer International Publishing AG, part of Springer Nature 2018
B. Scott, *Translation, Brains and the Computer*, Machine Translation:
Technologies and Applications 2, https://doi.org/10.1007/978-3-319-76629-4_1

It is tempting to think otherwise of course, to treat language as essentially regulated by rules. After all, isn't that what grammar is all about, the regularities of language? To be sure, that's true, but the language that grammarians typically deal with is different from the language that the translation machine (or the brain) has to deal with; it has usually been purged of the ambiguities and irregularities that make for the troublesome character of raw language. By contrast, the language fed to the computer is ambiguous, complex, and often as not, irksomely resistant to rules. Just like the language, we might add, that gets input to the brain. What's so interesting about this is that none of these aspects of language that so bother the machine seem to trouble the brain in the least. Do we know why this is so?

It is easy to understand why Chomsky reduced linguistics to the simpler, more manageable level of syntax. And why his influence led linguistics and computational linguists after him to deal with language in terms of abstract, univocal symbols (N, V, PREP, etc., with word class subcategories). Chomsky's reduction is what made literal language suddenly amenable to generalized treatment and the formulation of axiomatic rules. MT couldn't have gotten off the ground were it not for this reduction. Apart from syntax, how else was one to deal with language in a generalized way?

But for all the supposed gains of Chomsky's syntax-based approach to language, it must be remembered (as statistical MT reminds us) that the language the translation machine must cope with comprises strings of literal words, vast quantities of them, not just a handful of syntactic symbols. And these literal words, apart from some context, often have no univocal meaning or even fixed grammatical function. Formal grammars are generally not obliged to deal with words at this equivocal level, but translation machines most certainly are. One might observe here that so are the brains of human translators.

To illustrate what the translation machine (and the brain) is typically confronted with, let's imagine a string of words, *w1, w2, w3*, etc., that constitutes an input sentence in English. Imagine that one of these words happens to be the morpheme *sound*. Out of context, neither the machine (nor the brain) has any idea what the morpheme *sound* signifies. Is it a noun, a verb, an adjective? If the context tells us that *sound* is a noun, there is still much a translation agent needs to figure out. Does *sound* as a noun denote something you hear, something used in a medical practice, or maybe a body of water?

If *sound* turns out to be a noun that denotes audible phenomena, should it be transferred in German, for example, as *Ton* (for *sound* in general); *Geräusch* (as in a strange *sound*); or *Klang*, (as in the *sound* of music). Obviously, in all these cases, the context holds the key, but that only raises a more troublesome issue. How does a translation machine get at something as nebulous as context? How does the translator's brain? And, most troublesome of all, what happens when the context itself is equivocal in some way, as it very often is? It is not hard to understand why a machine, whether driven by rules, statistics, or some other mechanism, will have its difficulties. It is less clear why brains are normally free of these problems.

To illustrate our point about the difficulties for the machine, consider the string of short sentences in (1). Notice that the morpheme **sound** occurs variously in all of its parts of speech.

(1) *John's heart is **sound**. John's heart **sounds** healthy. The **sound** of the heart **sounds** normal.*

We had these short sentences translated into German by the most prominent of present-day phrase-based statistical systems, Google Translate,[1] and also by the oldest and most well known linguistic system, SYSTRANet.[2] Output is given in (1) (i) and (1)(ii) below. Errors are underlined. Oddly, errors are curiously rampant for such simple sentences.

<u>Translation by Google SMT Translate[3]</u>
(1)(i) *Johns Herz ist **gesund**. Johns Herz <u>**töne**</u> gesund. Der Klang <u>Herz</u> <u>**töne**</u> normal.*

<u>Translation by SYSTRANet</u>
(1)(ii) *Johns Herz ist **<u>Ton</u>**. Johns Herz <u>**töne**</u> gesund. Der Ton der <u>Herz</u> <u>**töne**</u> normal.*

<u>Commentary</u>
In the first sentence of (1)(i), the statistical system nicely renders the predicate adjective ***sound*** with the German adjective ***gesund*** (*healthy*). In the first sentence of (1)(ii), the linguistic system misresolves the predicate adjective ***sound*** to a noun (***Ton***). In the second sentence of (1)(i) and (1)(ii), both systems misresolve the string *John's heart **sounds*** to a noun phrase instead of correctly recognizing it as a subject-predicate construction. Similar misresolutions of ***sound*** occur in the third sentence of both systems.[4]

That two such well-established translation systems should mishandle simple sentences like these is both surprising and telling. Surprising because both systems are generally able to translate much more difficult sentences quite well; telling because stumbles like this in the simplest of sentences, after many years of development, suggest some inherent difficulty underlies the process. Are such deficiencies signs of underlying weakness, or are they merely indications that work still needs to be done? Doubtless the latter will always be the case, but such errors may well suggest a deeper problem.

---

[1] In November, 2016, Google released a new neural MT version (GNMT) of Google Translate. Except where otherwise noted, a number of the Google translations in this book predate this release. See Postscript 6-B of Chap. 6 for the GNMT versions of Google Translate's SMT translations shown in this book.

[2] SYSTRAN is now said to be a hybrid linguistic/statistical system. Historically, its foundation is linguistic and algorithmic in nature.

[3] Google Translate's new GNMT output for the third sentence in (1) is now correct: *Der **Klang** des Herzens **klingt** normal.*

[4] Logos Model translation of (1) is syntactically correct: *Johns Herz ist **solid**. Johns Herz **klingt** gesund. Das **Geräusch** des Herzens **klingt** normal.*

No one can deny that shortcomings are intrinsic to MT, in all its stages and all its approaches. The long history of MT corroborates this clearly enough. In MT, output errors are a way of life, whether one's approach is linguistic, statistical or neural. And certainly, the developers of these systems can fix this particular problem, and the countless other output errors lined up behind it waiting to be dealt with. There's little doubt about that. The real issue is not whether a particular issue can be fixed. The real question is what happens when new fixes begin at times to undo old fixes, requiring them to be re-fixed, and this keeps happening until the cumulative process becomes harder and harder to maintain? Are the above errors a sign this might already be happening? We cannot know of course, but whatever the case, complexities like this are always lurking in the wings, threatening to frustrate progress.

Here's another question. Why is it that human translators never make these sorts of errors? What keeps them from virtually ever misresolving a part of speech? The quick answer of course is that translators have brains and machines do not. Language after all is a product of the brain, part and parcel of its cognitive life. But that quick answer merely begs the question why this is so. What is the brain doing that frees it from such blunders? Are its linguistic mechanisms data-driven or rule-driven, as the different schools tend to argue? Or is the brain possibly doing something that the machine is inherently incapable of, something so complex as to defy our programming capabilities, or possibly even our understanding? Perhaps, but to my knowledge no cognitive scientist or neuroscientist has ever suggested as much.

Cognitive scientists like Stephen Pinker (1994) tend to suggest to the contrary that linguistic brain function is best understood by symbol manipulation in accordance with Universal Grammar, i.e., by processes typical of the computer. And neuropsychologists like Angela Friederici, among a host of others, conduct their language research in the syntax-oriented, Universal Grammar framework.[5] Many neuroscientists have published neuroimage-based studies supporting a syntax-first, grammar-driven view of language processing in the brain, more or less in keeping with Chomsky's perspectives on language.

But other takes on brain function are also possible. For example, neuroscientists also recognize that data-driven word associations, frequencies and patterns play an important role in cognitive operations, especially in the learning and use of language. This is basically the perspective of this book. And certainly, the exhaustive, data-driven explorations of raw language that underlie statistical MT (SMT) are what account for its remarkable success, and for the improvements in hybridized, rule-based MT (HMT). Data-driven processes are also behind the immense promise apparent in the emerging neural MT (NMT) technology.

From a strictly historical perspective, then, it seems that we are left with only two recognized ways of processing language for translation purposes: processes that are either rule-driven or data-driven. And these ways seem to apply whether this process-

---

[5] The work of Optiz and Friederici (e.g., 2003) is a good example of this, as may be seen in Chap. 5.

ing is postulated for brain or machine. On one side we have the (by now) classical theory that holds that language processing must be driven by computer-like manipulations of symbols, which means at the abstract, syntactic level. Its proponents in computer science, cognitive science and neuroscience don't see how language can be dealt with in any other generalized way. (See fuller discussion of this issue in Chap. 5).

On the other side, in contrast to this theory, we have the practical evidence of various data-driven systems, among them SMT, NMT, and Logos Model described in this book. The successes of these systems demonstrate that language can be translated fairly effectively by a process driven not by rules of grammar but by patterns and frequencies extracted from the data of raw language itself.

It is tempting to think that a data-driven, non-linguistic approach is effective precisely because it might be closer to actual brain function. But even if that should partly be the case, data-driven MT remains deficient, as their developers freely acknowledge, and that deficiency has to do with linguistic competence. Something is still lacking in the data-driven process that the brain is able to do.[6]

So we continue to be left with the question how the brain processes language. Why does the brain not exhibit any of MT's manifest shortcomings? Why, for instance, would the translator's brain never make the resolution errors seen in (1)(i) and (1)(ii)? It is clear the translator's brain is doing something not yet accounted for in theory or in practice, neither by data-driven SMT and NMT nor by the rule-driven approaches of linguistic systems. Does anyone at all have a clue what this cerebral mechanism amounts to? Are there perhaps neurological data that might suggest what this brain function might actually look like (e.g., evidence that may have been overlooked or wrongly interpreted by neuropsychologists in the past)?

No one of course can expect a definitive answer to our question; neuroscience will not be coming up anytime soon (if ever) with a settled understanding of linguistic function in the brain. But suppose, for a moment, that neurological data do exist that suggest the brain really could be handling language differently than has been surmised. Such data could be suggestive, even if not definitive. And suppose, furthermore, that this suggestive cerebral process could be modeled in a machine so that this under-recognized cerebral operation might be tested and persuasively demonstrated. Suppose, most importantly, that this brain-based computer model were to show itself capable of dealing with language's ambiguities in a way that, for the very first time in any MT system, does not incur the usual complexity costs. What would it mean if this were so, if we had an MT process that was free from complexity in its dealings with ambiguity, free from the one factor that (in our view) most limits the MT process?

If it should turn out that the brain actually has this insufficiently recognized, complexity-free mechanism, and if indeed a computer model could be made to demonstrably persuade that this mechanism is simulatable in a machine, might it not mean that a way was now in hand that could free MT endeavors of the one thing

---

[6] What remains to be answered is the question of how one is to deal with language in a generalized way without doing as Chomsky did, i.e., without reducing language to syntax. This is the question this book attempts to answer, as it has a critical bearing on the underlying linguistic competence of any MT system.

that most constrains its success, viz., the growing complexity of these systems as they mature and strive for greater and greater improvement? Wouldn't it mean that fixes and improvements without end might now be implemented without incurring these complexity costs? If all this were so, wouldn't it suggest that machine output of human quality might now be ultimately foreseeable? Alan Turing saw no reason why such a thing ought not be possible. Nor did we who spent decades in developing and testing Logos Model as described in this book, naïve as this may sound.[7]

Admittedly, the above narrative is apt to strike the reader as far-fetched, if not utterly fanciful. After all, MT has been pondered and worked on from virtually every conceivable angle for over 50 years now. Are we to believe that some telling, beneficial clue from the brain has been overlooked? Are we to believe that simulation of an unappreciated brain mechanism could conceivably open up new, unforeseen vistas for MT? That must hardly seem likely, and yet that is the reason we have undertaken to write this book. We present both theory and evidence for precisely these assertions. We of course must leave it to our readers to make what they will of its findings and claims.

To illustrate something of the potential strength of Logos Model in a very small matter, consider the sentence in (2) and the French and German translations that follow. Sentence (2) once again involves the morpheme *sound*, and has been artificially contrived so as to allow *sound* to occur in all three of its parts of speech in a single sentence.

(2)   The **sounds** of his heart **sound sound**.

We translated sentence (2) into German and French by the statistical and linguistic MT systems identified below, this time including output from Logos Model. Errors are underlined.

Translation by Google SMT Translate[8]
(2)(i)   Die **Klänge** <u>des</u> Herzens **<u>Ton Ton.</u>**
(2)(ii)   Les **sons** de son cœur **sonnent** <u>sonore</u>.

Commentary
In the German translation in (2)(i), only the first instance of the morpheme *sound* is handled correctly, viz., its noun sense. In the second instance, the verb sense of *sound* is misresolved to a noun (*Ton*). In the third instance, the adjectival sense of *sound* is also misresolved to a noun (*Ton*). By contrast, in the French translation in (2)(ii), all syntactic functions of *sound* are resolved correctly. The adjective *sonore* however incorrectly renders *sound* as *sonerous*.

---

[7]In Sect. 8.4 THE HIPPOCAMPUS AND CONTINUAL LEARNING of Chap. 8, we discuss a paper by Kumaran et al. (2016) that describes a previously unrecognized power for *semantic* generalization in the hippocampus, and the relevance that this unappreciated cerebral mechanism has for AI's deep learning (and, in our view, more specifically for MT).

[8]Google Translate's new neural MT (GNMT) translation of (2) into German shows some improvement: (2)(i) *Die **Klänge** seines Herzens **klingen**____*. The French translation however is poorer:

Translation by Microsoft's Bing SMT Translator[9]

(2)(iii)   *Die **Klänge** <u>des</u> Herzens **<u>klingt sound</u>**.*

(2)(iv)   *Les **sons** de son <u>bruit sonore du coeur</u>.*

Commentary

In the German translation in (2)(iii), **sound** both as noun and verb are resolved correctly. However, the verb **klingt** is singular and should be plural (**klingen**). For some reason, **sound** as adjective is left untranslated. In the French translation in (2)(iv), the verb and adjectival functions of **sound** are both misresolved, completely destroying the translation.[10]

Translation by SYSTRANet

(2)(v)   *Die **Töne** seines <u>Herz</u> **<u>tontones</u>**.*

(2)(vi)   *Les **bruits** de son **<u>bruit</u>** <u>de</u> **<u>bruit</u>** <u>cardiaque</u>.*

Commentary

In the German translation in (2)(v), **sound** as both verb and adjective are misresolved, completely ruining the translation. In the French translation in (2)(vi), the verb and adjectival functions of **sound** are also both misresolved.

Translation by Logos Model

(2)(vii)   *Die **Geräusche** seines Herzens **klingen solid**.*

(2)(viii)   *Lessons de son coeur **semblent solides**.*

Commentary

In the German in (2)(vii), all parts of speech for **sound** are resolved correctly. In the French in (2)(viii), again, all parts of speech for **sound** are resolved correctly. Note the translation of the verb **sound** as **semblent** (*seem*).

All systems have their strengths and weaknesses. Some are better at one thing, others at another. SMT systems normally do quite well, but not always and not uniformly. NMT systems tend to be better, but again, not always. In (3), below, we focus on another instance where translation depends upon linguistic competence. At issue here is the syntactic function of the morpheme *that*, whether it is a conjunction introducing a *that* clause, or a demonstrative pronoun. Errors are underlined.

---

(2)(ii) *Les **sons** de son <u>**son**</u> <u>du</u> <u>**son**</u> <u>du</u> cœur*. See Postscript 6-B in Chap. 6 for the GNMT versions of Google SMT output shown here and there throughout this book.

[9] In late 2016 Microsoft also incorporated neural net technology into its Bing Translator. Bing Translator translations shown in this book are either from the SMT or NMT version, and are marked accordingly.

[10] Bing Translator's new neural net system appears to have regressed in its translation of (2), both in the German and French: (2)(iii) *Der **Klang** seines Herzens **<u>Klang klingt</u>*** (2)(iv) *Les **sons** de son cœur <u>**son**</u>*.

(3)   *He said **that** was not the case at all.*

<u>Translation by SYSTRANet and Logos Model</u>
(3)(i)   *Il a dit que___ n'était pas le cas du tout.*

<u>Translation by Microsoft's Bing SMT translator</u>
(3)(ii)   *Il a dit que ce n'était pas du tout le cas.*

Commentary

Both of the linguistic systems that we tested (SYSTRANet and Logos Model) mistakenly treated the demonstrative pronoun ***that*** as a conjunction, as shown by the underlining in (3)(i). So too did Google Translate (SMT translation, not shown). The exception was the translation by Microsoft's Bing translator in (3(ii)). Both the SMT and NMT versions of Bing translator correctly interpreted the morpheme ***that*** as a demonstrative pronoun (***ce***), and properly inserted the conjunction (***que***) missing in the English sentence. (French, unlike English, does not allow the ***that*** conjunction to be elided.) The excellent translation in (3)(ii) by Microsoft's Bing translator clearly suggests a significant degree of linguistic competence underlying both the SMT and NMT versions of this system.

Language being what it is, all systems are bound to stumble over unanticipated constructions of one kind or other. The question is not whether systems make mistakes but whether and to what extent these mistakes can be addressed, one after the other, endlessly, without these fixes causing new problems. The ability to absorb fixes without end seems to be the only legitimate measure of a system's potential. In short, if a translation model can absorb corrections and improvements literally without limit, and can do so without the complication of new logic fighting older logic, i.e., without the sort of complications that eventually arrest growth beyond a certain point, then it is fair to say that there are very few limits to what such a system can ultimately be made to accomplish. And theoretically, one day such a system would have the prospect of passing the classic Turing test as it might be applied to MT: machine output consistently indistinguishable from human translation.

After half a century of effort, there still seems to be no prospect of ever realizing this original ideal. In fact, one barely speaks of it any more. But need that be the case? We already see signs of potential breakthroughs in the recent merging of statistical and neural net technologies. The newly emerging neural MT technology (NMT) has already overcome some of the linguistic shortcomings of SMT, as we shall show in later chapters. But as we have already seen, problems still remain to be solved.

The present book seeks to further these positive developments by suggesting an entirely different kind of neural model, one with more of a psycholinguistic and neurolinguistic basis, the effectiveness of which we hope to demonstrate as we proceed. We will suggest that by combining the best elements of all these technologies, linguistic, statistical, and neural, a final breakthrough in the quality of MT output may yet become possible.

References

Halliday MAK (2003) In: Webster J (ed) On language and linguistics: collected works of M.A.K. Halliday. Continuum, London/New York

Kumaran D, Hassabis D, McClelland JL (2016) What learning systems do intelligent agents need? Complementary learning systems theory updated. Trends Cogn Sci 20(7):512. https://doi.org/10.1016/j.tics.2016.05.004. Accessed 12 Jan. 2017

Optiz B, Friederici AD (2003) Interactions of the hippocampal system and the prefrontal cortex in learning language-like rules. NeuroImage 19:1730–1737. https://doi.org/10.1016/S1053-8119(03)00170-8. Accessed 25 Jan. 2016

Pinker S (1994) The language instinct. William Morrow and Co., New York

Chapter 2
Background

Abstract This Chapter describes the exceptional circumstances that brought Logos Model MT into existence in 1969, and details the difficulties that confronted this pioneer development effort. Chief among the difficulties was the lack of proven models to guide the design and development of a workable MT system, causing Logos developers to turn for inspiration to assumptions about the processes taking place in human translation. Logos Model is contrasted in broad terms with statistical translation models, with which it shares certain resemblances. The eventual Logos Model translation process is then briefly described. The Chapter concludes with an overview of the basic assumptions about human translation processes that shaped Logos Model and that accounted for its early successes in the nascent MT world. The Chapter concludes with reflections about the nature and origin of language and grammar, all of which had a bearing on Logos Model design, development and performance. The advent of neural net MT is noted and the promise of this new development is briefly characterized.

2.1 Logos Model Beginnings

THIS BOOK REPORTS ON ITS AUTHOR'S DECADES of immersion in the issues of language acquisition and language translation, both by humans and by machine. The work was begun in 1969 at a small commercial R&D center in the U.S.A., and was initially motivated by an urgent, national need for volumes of translation that human translators could not possibly satisfy, a need I believed I could address by machine. The need had to do with the Vietnamese conflict taking place at the time, and the federal government's announced decision to turn the fighting and all its associated military equipment over to the South Vietnamese, making it their conflict, not ours. But there was a problem. To implement this decision, thousands of training and maintenance manuals had to be translated into Vietnamese, and in those days there were hardly any Vietnamese translators in the country to do that work. That is how I and a small team of co-workers became involved. We were to try and meet

© Springer International Publishing AG, part of Springer Nature 2018
B. Scott, *Translation, Brains and the Computer*, Machine Translation:
Technologies and Applications 2, https://doi.org/10.1007/978-3-319-76629-4_2

that need with the computer; in effect, to prepare a machine to do what human translators would do if they were available, but were not.

Given the national circumstance, the pressure on us for a successful outcome far exceeded what would normally be asked of a research enterprise. We were obliged to deal with scores upon scores of linguistic puzzles of a purely academic nature, and then almost immediately come up with practical solutions that worked in a machine. With a group of co-workers under my direction, often working up to twelve hours a day, we had to train a computer to analyze English sentences and do this well enough to generate equivalent sentences of equal quality in the Vietnamese target. This took place over 45 years ago, and all of this language work had to be accomplished by some as yet unestablished computer process that we had to conceive, model and implement. This process, of course, was known even then as machine translation.

In 1969 when our work began, there was literally no translation model to guide us, not a single one. We were pretty much on our own. The human brain is able to translate easily enough, but in 1969 neuroscience offered no consensus regarding how the brain dealt with language, least of all a cerebral process that might be imitated in a computer. And as for the computer, only a few years earlier the National Academy of Sciences had concluded in its investigative ALPAC Report[1] that good quality translation by machine was not feasible, not by any technology known to the state of the art. This negative conclusion soon became received wisdom echoed in virtually every university and research center around the world. MT efforts worldwide were abandoned. In effect, this meant we had no positive model of any kind to guide our efforts.

I knew of these negative judgments, of course, but couldn't bring myself to agree with them. I had a philosophy background in epistemology, some language training, some experience with manual translation (Vietnamese, Russian, French, German)[2], plus work experience with computers; for some reason the combination led me to think I could meet this requirement. I recall reasoning that if the brain can process language, one ought be able to find a way to simulate that process, certainly in an area of language as limited as technical translation.

All one had to do was try and figure out what the mind (and the underlying brain) must be doing when it decodes a single sentence it has just heard or read. Not a simple assignment, obviously, but I was naïve enough, and maybe hard-pressed enough, to try and do just that. I conceived some half-formed notions about what might be going on in the brain as translators cope with the input of a sentence, notions more in the order of intuitive hunches than worked-out ideas. Still, they were strong hunches, and in a bold moment I told some key people in government I felt I could solve their translation problem. Given the national need, the government, its

---

[1] A report by the Automatic Language Advisory Committee published by the National Academy of Science in 1966.

[2] During earlier service in the Air Force, the author worked as Vietnamese, Russian and French linguist.

well-founded skepticism aside, decided it had little choice but to give me a chance. All I had to do now was to prove these hunches were right, and make it happen.[3]

I formed a little company for this purpose, Logos Corporation, and with a small, well-motivated team we took on this task, working purely inductively, day in and day out, looking at thousands upon thousands of mistranslated target sentences as they came rolling off the printer, and asking ourselves the academic question—what was it that the computer needed to understand not only about English and Vietnamese but about language itself to get these mistranslations right the next time through? The issues often had to do with the seemingly intractable ambiguities of natural language and with questions of how one was to resolve them. For example, how is the machine to decide when it encounters the word *contact* whether it is a noun or a verb? How can it differentiate the scope of the adjectives in phrases like *fresh air and sunshine* in one case, and *smart boys and girls* in another? How does it know whether a simple comma separates words in a phrase, one phrase from another, or entire clauses? Clearly, proper translation depends upon getting these matters right time after time. What sort of machine intelligence is needed to do that?

Just as basically, we had to figure out how to do this without the machine (or, more specifically, the mind that instructs the machine) getting tangled up in the mounting complexities of logic that would be called for. How is something as rich and stubbornly irregular as natural language to be corralled by logic? Without a suitable model to draw upon, we had to figure out on our own what sort of linguistic smarts the machine needed to have. We had to figure out how that linguistic intelligence was to be represented in a computer, and then how the computer was to store, and most critically of all, how it was to apply this linguistic know-how to the input stream.

Early on we realized that even more important than linguistics was this computational dilemma that confronted us. We kept finding that language was maddeningly ambiguous at all levels—lexical and structural—and disambiguation at any of these levels required lots of intelligence on the part of the machine. But therein lay the dilemma. The more developers tried to effect disambiguation algorithmically, the more complex the requisite logic would become. The complexity of the logic was not a problem for the machine, but it was for the human mind that had to create and keep track of that logic. We realized almost right from the start that everything depended upon our doing this in a correct computational way for the sake of our own cognitive limitations. We could see that our cognitive powers were going to be challenged to the limit if we sought to create pre-established logic adequate to cope with streams of unpredictable input.

Human sentence processing of course experiences none of these problems. The brain disambiguates sentences effortlessly, without even being aware that it is doing so, and seems not the least bit troubled by complexity, certainly not in the normal course of coping with language. Why was this? Could we learn something from it? The breakthrough for us occurred when I came to appreciate that the cerebral

---

[3] Everett Pyatt, the early government advocate of our effort, was criticized for *"chasing after fool's gold"* (personal communication). Pyatt later became Assistant Secretary of the Navy.

handling of language had to be essentially data-driven, not logic-driven, it had to be declarative in nature, not procedural, pattern-based, not rule-based. We devised a way to imitate this imagined, data-driven process and because of it, *mirabile dictu*, problems of cognitive complexity were never an issue for us. Out of the trials of this effort arose the intellectual understanding and attendant translation mechanism described in the chapters that follow.

Our English-Vietnamese MT project turned out to be an unqualified success. The post-edited translations we produced were well received by the South Vietnamese in the field and therefore by our government. In fact, an official U.S. Department of Defense report in 1973 stated that the Logos English-Vietnamese system had now demonstrated the feasibility of large-scale, productive MT, thus reversing the 1966 conclusions of the National Academy of Science's ALPAC Report.[4] Our Vietnamese translations were judged by the South Vietnamese military to be from good to excellent, the difference being a function of the quality of the original English source.

The success of the project reassured us we were doing something right. It even suggested that the positive results of our undertaking might in some degree have validated our conjectures about human sentence processing. That of course was wishful thinking. It will be some time, if ever, before neuroscience fully understands how the brain's faculty for language really works. Our hunches will always remain just that, although we report in subsequent chapters on a degree of neurolinguistic support for these early intuitions.

2.2   The Advent of Statistical MT

Our little company kept on with its research and development for almost three decades, adding languages and refining the underlying intellectual model. Logos Model eventually became a world-class system producing cost-effective translations for commercial firms and government entities in the U.S., Canada, and a number of European countries.[5] However, this favorable state of affairs was not to last. It ended at the start of the present century when the market became intrigued with the new approach to MT that came to be known as statistical MT (SMT). By then SMT had begun producing quality translations that were done more quickly and at less cost. And in many cases (but by no means all), translations done by phrase-based SMT in particular were frequently as good as if not better than those Logos Model could

---

[4] Personal communication to the author by Everett Pyatt, stating that this judgment appeared in the official (classified) Annual Report in 1973 of the then Director of Defense Research and Engineering (DDR&E), John S. Foster, Jr. Pyatt was attached to the Joint Chiefs of Staff at the time of this communication.

[5] See Postscript 2-A for a brief note on the history of the commercial system.

produce.[6] And that generally remains true today with regard to OpenLogos, the publically available, open-source copy of the commercial version of Logos Model.[7] Let me just say here that this book recommends Logos Model to the MT community for a different reason than just its translation quality, one which we trust will become meaningful in the pages that follow.

At first glance, the translation methods of SMT and Logos Model would seem to be radically at odds, the one being grounded in statistical data, the other in linguistic understanding. But they have one very critical feature in common: the translation process in both is bottom-up, essentially driven by patterns of language rather than by some pre-established body of rules.[8] In effect, the translation process of both is driven by the raw data of language rather than by some form of supervening logic.[9]

2.2.1 Pattern-Based Processes in SMT and Logos Model

Both Logos Model and phrase-based SMT rely on stored (learned) language patterns rather than on procedures (rules) in effecting translation. In the case of SMT, aligned source and target patterns are automatically extracted during system training from huge volumes of bilingual corpora. In the case of Logos Model, the pattern pairs are handcrafted through linguists' exposure to texts. In both cases, the process yields many thousands of commonly occurring source language patterns paired with target equivalents (most probable equivalents, in SMT). Captured patterns should all be grammatically legitimate, but the non-linguistic methods of phrase-based SMT provide no way of judging grammaticality, so it is not unusual for captured phrases to be agrammatical in both source and target.

With SMT, aligned source and target word strings are stored in a translation table and this table is accessed in the manner of dictionary lookup during the translation process.[10] Since the order of extracted target strings still reflects source word order,

---

[6] Barreiro et al. (2014). In the Google Translate-Logos Model translation exercises described in this 2014 study, output for English-German favored Logos Model. But the case was just the opposite in the Romance language pairs.

[7] Logos Corporation ceased operations at the turn of the century but a near equivalent copy of the commercial system continues to be available as OpenLogos, an open-source version of the commercial product, produced by DFKI in Germany. OpenLogos however has never undergone further development.

[8] It is a misnomer to call Logos Model rule-based, although it is often associated with rule-based systems because virtually all other *linguistic* MT systems have been rule-based.

[9] Evans (2014). This author states that *cognitive* linguists generally agree that the brain's linguistic processes are pattern-based, not rule-driven.

[10] Some neural MT models have begun to employ *continuous* processes that by-pass this initial alignment phase of SMT. See Kalchbrenner and Blunsom (2013).

the extracted target elements must then be reordered in accordance with a statistically induced target language model. Reordered, n-gram target chunks thus get formed into a pruned list of conditional, candidate target sentences.[11] Finally, selection is made of the one sentence from that list of candidate translations computationally found to be most probable (generated via maximum likelihood estimation).

This word-ordering process remains a point of weakness in SMT, but in general, where translation tables and language models are comprehensive, and where source and target languages enjoy basically similar word order, the translations normally turn out reasonably well.[12]

Of the three principal functions in any act of *literal* translation, namely, (a) transfer of source words and phrases into apt target equivalents; (b) generation of suitable target word order for these transfers; and (c) insuring proper morphological agreement among constituents in the resultant target sentence, it is clear that SMT only excels in (a). Since transfers have been extracted from huge amounts of contemporary text on the basis of probability, their tendency to greater aptness is the principal advantage SMT has over non-statistical systems, and is the chief reason why SMT has become an unparalleled tool for gisting. Take for example the idiomatic translation that SMT gives for the adjectival clause in (1)(i), below.

(1)   *Strange as it may seem,* he did not accept the promotion.

German Translation by Google SMT Translate

(1)(i)   *So seltsam es scheinen mag,....*

The principal weaknesses of SMT is that such systems have no explicit way of insuring proper linguistic correlation between the extracted chunks that make up the target sentence. Translation models based on n-gram technology are inherently limited in their effectiveness, as becomes evident in translation functions (b) and (c). In the case of translation function (b), viz., generating appropriate target word order, we see in (1)(ii) that Google SMT Translate had problems with word order in the main clause of (1).[13] Errors are underlined.

---

[11] Language models in Google Translate's SMT system were derived from two trillion tokens of unlabeled monolingual text, yielding models comprising 300 million n-grams where n = 5 (Brants et al. 2007).

[12] Koehn (2011, 305) suggests that for pairs like German-English, reordering requires annotating of words with part-of-speech tags and rules for their manipulation.

[13] Google's GNMT Translate now translates the main clause of (1) correctly, but renders the initial adjectival clause literally rather than idiomatically as its SMT system nicely did in 1(i). Microsoft's Bing NMT Translator mistranslates the main clause of sentence (1): *Seltsam, wie es scheinen mag, hat er nicht akzeptieren, die Promotion.* Ironically, the earlier SMT version of Bing Translator (unshown) translated (1) correctly.

(1)   Strange as it may seem, *he did not accept the promotion.*

German Translation by Google SMT Translate

(1)(ii)   ... *er wollte* nicht *akzeptieren, die Förderung.*

Commentary

Translation should read ... *wollte er die Förderung nicht akzeptieren.*

In the case of translation function (c), SMT often has trouble effecting morphological agreement among sentence constituents. For example, in the translation of (2) in (2)(i), disagreement is between subject and predicate with respect to number. Errors are underlined.

(2)   *The **individuals** who **sold** their house **want** to purchase my house.*

German Translation by Google SMT Translate

(2)(i)   *Die **Personen**, die ihr Haus **verkauft möchte** mein Haus **zu** kaufen.*

Commentary

The translation should read ...***verkauften, möchten**....* to reflect the plural subject. Linguistically-based SYSTRANet and Logos Model translated (2) correctly (unshown).

In (3) and (3)(i), the morphological disagreement is with respect to gender. The error is underlined

(3)   *His eldest **daughter** was **married** last week.*

French Translation by Google SMT Translate

(3)(i)   *Sa **fille** aînée était **marié** la semaine dernière.*

Commentary

Translation should read ... *était **mariée**....* to agree with the feminine subject *fille*. The linguistic systems translated (3) correctly.

Table 2.1, below, summarizes strengths and weaknesses of the methodologies, and suggests how the strengths of one methodology might complement the weaknesses of another.[14]

---

[14] Every indication is that NMT technology is beginning to solve the morphology problem that has plagued SMT. For example, Google GNMT Translate now translates both (2) and (3) correctly. Bing NMT Translator also renders (2) and (3) correctly.

Table 2.1 *Breakdown of translation functions, suggesting how the two methodologies might complement each other*

Translation function	Statistical methodology	Linguistic methodology
(a) Transfers	Stronger	Weaker
(b) Word order	Weaker	Stronger
(c) Morphology	Weaker	Stronger

2.3   Overview of Logos Model Translation Process

As stated, Logos Model translation process is also pattern-based, as in SMT and NMT. And the patterns in Logos Model are also stored in dictionary-like tables. But there are huge differences in what these Logos Model patterns look like. We briefly characterize them below, along with a short account of how these patterns are used to effect translation.

First of all, stored patterns in Logos Model are not sequences of *literal* word strings but sequences of abstract, semantico-syntactic, symbolic representations known as SAL words. (SAL stands for Semantico-syntactic Abstraction Language.) It is also important to understand that, in Logos Model, the input stream is likewise represented as a string of SAL words. This conversion of literal input to SAL expression takes place at the beginning, during lexical lookup. The consequent representational homogeneity between SAL input and stored SAL patterns is a distinguishing feature of Logos Model.

SAL is a taxonomic language, a second-order language (somewhat akin to hypernyms) to which natural language words easily map. Input terms like *bench, table, shelf, ledge, highchair* would all be represented in the lexicon by the more abstract SAL word *support surface*, shown in Table 2.2, below. These SAL input terms would be available for matching against a corresponding stored SAL constituent at any of its taxonomic levels.

To summarize, both stored patterns and input stream are expressed as SAL strings, and constituent-matching between input stream and stored patterns can occur at any called-for taxonomic level.

Note that stored SAL patterns are more properly called pattern-rules because each stored SAL pattern has associated with it an activation component. The activation (rule) component of a pattern-rule gets executed when a SAL input string matches on it, in dictionary-lookup fashion. (Pattern-matching, not rules, is what propels this translation process.) This activation component performs a great variety of functions connected with source analysis, both locally and sentence-wide, including tests for constraint satisfaction, pattern rewriting, parse formation, etc.[15] In addition, the pattern-rule may optionally link to a target component that accomplishes commensurate functions for the target language sentence that is in the process of being generated.

---

[15] The character of this parse is linear rather than that of a traditional parse tree. This will be clarified in Chaps. 4 and 6 and in the discussion in Chap. 8 on Logos Model's remote kinship with recursive, convolutional, deep neural nets.

Table 2.2 *Example of SAL Representation.* Both input stream and internally-stored patterns are expressed in the Semantico-syntactic Abstraction Language known as SAL

TAXONOMIC SEMANTICO-SYNTACTIC REPRESENTATION for words like *table, shelf, ledge, highchair, floor,* etc.	
(i)	*N(COsupp)* – SAL subset term for concrete, support surface nouns
(ii)	*N(COfunc)* – SAL set term for concrete, functional nouns
(iii)	*N(CO)* – SAL superset term for concrete nouns
(iv)	*N* – SAL syntactic (part-of-speech) symbol for any noun

Table 2.3 *Principal translation steps of Logos Model.* Stored SAL patterns all have an activation component (rule) that accounts for operations F and G, with optional links to a target-action component that performs operation H, leading to target generation in Step I	OVERVIEW OF ANALYSIS AND GENERATION
	A – CAPTURE INPUT SENTENCE
	B – PERFORM LEXICAL LOOKUP
	C– CONVERT INPUT TO SAL STRING
	D – MATCH SAL STRING TO STORED SAL PATTERN-RULES
	E – RESOLVE PART OF SPEECH AND STRUCTURAL AMBIGUITIES
	F – RESOLVE SEMANTIC AMBIGUITIES
	G – CREATE PARSE
	H – CREATE EQUIVALENT TARGET PARSE
	I – GENERATE TARGET OUTPUT

Table 2.3, above, identifies the principal operations performed for source analysis and target generation, listed in the sequence in which they occur. Note that D and E generally occur simultaneously, i.e. that resolutions by E are an automatic function of the matching in D. All translation steps are briefly described below.

Translation Steps in Table 2.3

A. Capture Input Sentence. To illustrate, let's envision an input sentence containing the string *revolving credit*.
B. Perform Lexical Lookup. We assume that *revolving credit* is not found as a unit in the lexicon, but as separate words.
C. Convert Input to SAL String. Conversion of literal words to SAL expressions is accomplished by lexical lookup. The term *revolving*, for example, was found to have three parts of speech: intransitive verb, transitive verb, and participial adjective. The term *credit* has two: noun and transitive verb. SAL expressions for these terms are in Table 2.4.
D. Match SAL String to Stored SAL Pattern-Rules. The SAL input string is segmented into search arguments that, theoretically, can be as long as the sentence

Table 2.4 *Conversion of literal words to SAL words during lexical look-up.* Lexicon is purposely limited to three parts of speech for a given entry. Words like *revolving* that entail more than three parts of speech are dealt with by pattern-rules later in the process

---

revolving ➜ *VI(MO-around; ing)*—i.e., intransitive verb whose SAL superset code is *motional*, and whose SAL set code is *around*, signifying it governs prepositions *around* or *about*. The form of the verb is *ing*.

➜ *VT(OBTR-undiff; ing)*—i.e., verb whose SAL superset code is objective transitive, and whose set code is undiff. Form is *ing*.

➜ *VADJ(MO-around; pres)*—i.e., intransitive participial adjective whose SAL superset code is intransitive and whose SAL set code is *around*. Form code signifies present participle.

credit ➜ *VT(PREVX-with; inf)*—i.e., transitive verb whose SAL superset is preverbal complex and whose SAL set code is *with-of-for* (e.g., *credit x with v'ing, accuse x of v'ing; criticize x for v'ing*, etc.). Form is infinitive.

➜ *N(MA-fina; sg)*—i.e., a noun whose superset code is *mass*, and whose set code is *financial*, e.g., *money, stock, credit*, etc. Form is singular.

---

itself. Separate arguments are fashioned to accommodate all the various string permutations caused by words with multiple parts of speech.

E. <u>Resolve Part-of-Speech and Structural Ambiguities</u>. POS ambiguity is resolved automatically by the matchup of one of these search argument permutations with a stored pattern-rule, one having greater weight than competing pattern-rules (and that might want to resolve it differently). The stored pattern-rule's weight is basically a function of its length and semantico-syntactic specificity, but other weight factors may apply, including satisfaction of various constraints. A typical constraint entails tests of the state of the clause current at the time of the match. If, for example, the test indicates that the clause has already been found to have a verb, then a stored pattern whose intent is to resolve to verb would normally not be allowed to fire and therefore would be kept from resolving a noun/verb homograph incorrectly.

Homograph resolution is not always so simple and may require further contextual clues. We illustrate this in (4) involving the ambiguous morpheme ***revolving***.

(4)   *There are many* **X** *of* ***revolving credit***.

To resolve ***revolving*** here to either a verb or a verbal adjective, the matching pattern-rule has to be sensitive to the semantics of *X*, as in (5) and (6).

(5)   *There are many* **ways** *of* ***revolving credit***.
(6)   *There are many* **types** *of* ***revolving credit***.

The ambiguous morpheme ***revolving*** in (5) gets resolved automatically to a verb by virtue of a matchup between the search argument permutation, where ***revolving*** is a *possible* verb, and a stored pattern-rule of corresponding semantico-syntactic values that confirms ***revolving*** as a verb, as illustrated below.

Search Argument Permutation for ways of *revolving credit*
Where revolving is a Possible Verb
N(ABmeth; pl) PREP(of) VT(OBTR; ing) N(MAfina; sg)

Stored Pattern-Rule, Resolving *revolving* to a Verb
N(ABverbl, any) PREP(of, for,to,in) VT(any; ing) N(any, any)

Note that this single stored pattern-rule disambiguates *credit* as well as *revolving*, just by virtue of this dictionary-like matchup. Note also that this stored pattern-rule is far more abstract and more general than the input pattern that matched on it, a circumstance that is very often the case. But the main point to understand is that all unresolved homographs in an input string get to be resolved automatically just by virtue of a matchup with a stored pattern-rule that best corresponds. As a result of the match, all alternative search argument permutations are discarded (that might have allowed words to be resolved differently). And all this is accomplished without the mediation of transition network logic or metarules of any kind.

In (7), below, Google SMT Translate and Bing SMT Translator mistakenly see *revolving credit* as a noun phrase rather than as a clausal complement, possibly because *revolving credit* was stored as a phrase in the translation table. Output for the two statistical systems is in (7)(i). Output for Logos Model is in (7)(ii). Errors are underlined.

(7)   *There are no new **methods** for **revolving credit**.*

Translation by Google SMT Translate[16] and Bing SMT Translator
(7)(i)   *Il n'y a pas de nouvelles **méthodes** de **crédit renouvelable**.*

Translation by Logos Model
(7)(ii)   *Il n'y a pas de nouvelles **façons** de **faire tourner le crédit**.*

Commentary
Logos Model correctly resolves *revolving credit* to an infinitive clause complementing *façons*. All other systems incorrectly treated this expression as a noun phrase (these others are unshown). Logos Model's transfer *faire tourner* is correct both syntactically and semantically.

F. Resolve Semantic Ambiguities (as far as possible). While abstract semantico-syntactic information is employed in most stages of a Logos Model parse (as for example in the scoping of adjectives), Logos Model has a special store of context-sensitive pattern-rules that provide for the semantic resolution and transfer of *literal* words with multiple meanings, chiefly verbal elements, as in (8) and (9).[17]

---

[16] Google's new neural-net version of Google Translate (GNMT) now translates (7) with correct syntax: *Il n'existe pas de nouvelles **méthodes** de **renouvellement du crédit**.*

Translations by Logos Model

(8)   *The seller **raised** the price.*

(8)(i)   *Le vendeur **a augmenté** le prix.*

(9)   *The landlord **raised** the temperature.*

(9)(i)   *Le propriétaire **a fait remonter** la température.*

G. Create Source Parse. The output of previous Step E is a syntactically disambigu-
   ated SAL string. This eventually allows for an appropriate parse node to be created for the NP constituent **methods for revolving credit**. Logos Model's parse is
   created incrementally, over a series of processing steps, in deterministic, bottom-
   up fashion. The parse is linear rather than in tree form. Clauses are identified;
   nested clauses are removed for separate processing, leaving behind a trace; all
   phrases within clauses are concatenated and syntactically identified.
H. Create Equivalent Target Parse. A target parse is created parallel to source parse
   creation, in quasi tree-to-tree fashion.
I. Generate Target Output. Logos Model translations in (10)(i) and (11)(i), below,
   illustrate the sort of morphological and syntactic transformations that have to be
   effected by target components in the course of analysis. Note how, in each case,
   the tense of the main clause is properly transmitted to the *dass* clause.

Translations by Logos Model

(10)   *They **do** not **expect** him to **return**.*

(10)(i)   *Sie **erwarten** nicht, dass er **zurückkehrt**.*

(11)   *They **did** not **expect** him to **return**.*

(11)(i)   *Sie **erwarteten** nicht, dass er **zurückkehrte**.*

To summarize, source analysis in Logos Model is driven by the input stream
itself, re-expressed as a SAL string. It would be correct to say that the SAL input
string itself constitutes the algorithm that drives what happens in source analysis.
The relatively simpler work of target generation in turn, feeding off this input-driven
source analysis, is accomplished by linked functions that, node by node, generate a
target equivalence of the source parse.

   This summary of the translation process given here is necessarily simplified but
nonetheless represents an accurate, skeletal overview of how Logos Model translates
a text, sentence by sentence. We hold that in some rudimentary way this Model

---

[17]These semantically oriented rules are accessed in a Semantic Table called SEMTAB. Logos
Model does *not* have provision for handling multiple senses of common nouns, one of the most
difficult challenges facing linguistically based systems. (A linguist who worked on the European
Community's MT system in the 1990s told us they had written 700 rules to handle the transfers of
a single source noun.) However, see Postscript 4-B in Chap. 4 for a conceptual Logos Model solution that was considered for this problem, one that was never implemented.

mimics basic assumptions about input-driven, psycholinguistic processes of the mind, processes that entail stored, abstract patterns of language reacting to patterns of language input. As stated, in Logos Model all internal procedures relating to parse formation for both source and target are tied to input-driven processes.

There are several advantages associated with this pattern-based approach of Logos Model. One is that stored patterns in Logos Model can keep growing in number (as in a dictionary) without incurring complexity issues. In effect, complexity as a consequence of knowledge-base growth is not likely to ever become a factor limiting improvability. Another advantage is that the size of its stored pattern-rules has distinctly sublinear implications on computer throughput, much as dictionary size little affects the processing costs of lexical lookup. Both rely upon effective indexing.

2.4 Psycholinguistic and Neurolinguistic Assumptions

Initially, the conceptual model underlying Logos Model was based on little more than hunches and intuitions about heuristic mental processes, and how simulation of these processes might be exploited in the computer. It would take several decades before these brain-machine intuitions would become more explicit and arguably be seen as validated by the performance of a world-class translation system predicated upon these hunches. As we try to show in the pages that follow, these psycholinguist and neurolinguistic assumptions, only half-understood at the time, were nevertheless precisely what enabled this Model to cope with the two key problems developers face in processing natural language, (i) the linguistic ambiguity problem and (ii) the complexity problem that arises in dealing with (i).[18]

In what follows we review these assumptions, first in psycholinguistic terms and then more generally in neurolinguistic terms.

2.4.1 First Assumption

The mind does not employ an algorithm or anything resembling a pre-established rule of thumb (whether learned or hardwired) when processing natural language sentences. Not normally. Processing of language by the mind is opportunistic; a given sentence is processed by the mind/brain reacting to it with all needed cognitive resources in play. It is probably correct to say that the principal instrument of human sentence processing is cognitive memory. This means that the human brain, on hearing an utterance, does not perk up and start manipulating the words of that utterance, but instead is itself manipulated by these words (at least initially, while the process remains preconscious, which is most of the time).

---

[18] Most of the matters we address regarding ambiguity and complexity concern source analysis.

This also means that since no two people have the same cognitive associations, no two people process a sentence in quite the same way. That process becomes more common only if the two are asked to step back and formally analyze (parse) the sentence. Prior to that consciously analytic operation, individuals operate preconsciously and in their own way, which is to say on the basis of their own individual cognitive resources and linguistic experience.

In neurolinguistic terms, this manipulation consists of the input stream activating neuronal cells (or circuits of such cells) whose specialization corresponds to the data of the input stream. This neuronal activation in turn produces correspondingly appropriate responses by other circuitry, a process that goes on until a state of cerebral equilibrium has been attained. That equilibrium is tantamount to saying that the meaning of the linguistic stream just input to the brain has been superficially understood. The cogitation that may happen after that, of course, is another matter entirely.

2.4.2   Second Assumption

The mind integrates semantics and syntax at all stages of sentence processing. In terms of the First Assumption, this means that the mind does not normally decompose words into separate and distinct syntactic and semantic stimuli. Indeed, there is no reason to think that such decomposition ever takes place in preconscious processes. Logos Model reflects this assumption by treating semantics and syntax as two extremes of a semantico-syntactic continuum, every aspect of which is available at every stage of analysis.[19]

2.4.3   Third Assumption

The mind abhors complexity and relieves itself of complexity overload by the mechanism of abstraction, reducing multiple distinct things to some one common thing whenever semantically possible. It may be reasoned that an individual mind is typically not in equilibrium until it has achieved optimal complexity-reduction consistent with its capabilities, a presumption that likely holds true of the mind's handling of natural language sentences as well. Furthermore, it would be reasonable to expect that the mind's operational bias towards abstraction would be reflected in the structure and organization of the brain, a conjecture which seems to be borne out by the architecture of the brain's basic cell—the neuron. The prototype model of this cell, with its multiple dendrites (for input) and single axon (with collaterals) for

---

[19]The case is otherwise of course whenever the decoding process becomes conscious and deliberate, as for example when the preconscious mind stumbles over a sentence and has virtually to parse it in order to untangle its import.

output is routinely spoken of as an integration circuit and from our perspective may be thought of as an abstracting circuit. The neuron's architecture therefore would appear intrinsically suited to serve bottom-up parse reductions. Logos developers have also assumed, with cause, that human sentence processing entails a comparable reduction of semantic content to higher levels of abstraction. There is evidence that the mind makes use of second-order concepts in processing natural language, demonstrable particularly in second language acquisition, as illustrated in Chap. 3. Cerebral reliance on abstraction constitutes the assumption that underlies the SAL representation language.

Now let us conclude this Chapter with some personal reflections about language in general.

2.5   On Language and Grammar

In our view, language originally arose because the earliest homo sapiens, dwelling as they did in a social context, had something to say to those around them, and collectively developed the necessary means for doing so. This would seem to be a sufficient explanation for the appearance of language. Of course, what the "means" are that enable language remain controversial. In an informal talk, Chomsky once described a pair of deaf twins whose parents decided not to teach them sign language by way of encouraging them to read lips. These twins nevertheless developed a sign language of their own so they could communicate in privacy with each other. Chomsky cited the example as clear evidence for his theory of language as a uniquely innate faculty (Goldin-Meadow and Mylander 1990). But one could just as easily hold, with cognitive linguists, that the twins invented language because of thoughts that were going around in their heads, thoughts that they wanted to express, and that their basic intelligence afforded them the necessary means for doing so. Having something to say seems to be the more fundamental or originating grounds for language.[20] That is what is truly innate; language in homo sapiens flows from that. (See Fig. 2.1.)

The deeper question, of course, is whether thought itself is linguistically structured. Does thought have syntax? Is there such a language as *mentalese*, and if so, what is its relationship to natural language?[21] It is difficult to more than theorize about this. Our guess is that having something to say must necessarily entail conceptual relationships, but does not yet involve lexicon and grammar, semantics and syntax, as linguists understand these matters. Nor need mentalese involve the brain regions associated with language per se, not until the fuller means to express thought are acquired empirically through sociolinguistic exposure. We are not aware of any studies that link spontaneous thought to specific cerebral regions associated with language.

---

[20] Of course, linguistic exposure in turn will condition thought itself, as Sapir and Whorf have argued.

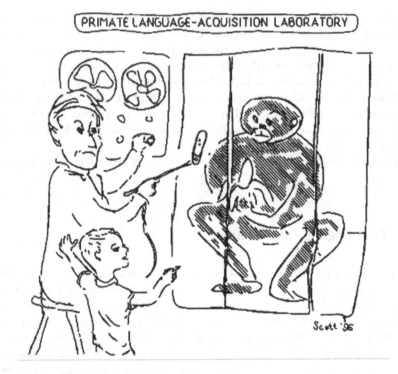

Fig. 2.1 *"Hey, Dad, maybe Chimsky can't talk because he has nothing to say!"*

2.5.1   The Origin and Nature of Grammar

Grammar (morphology and syntax) sprang into existence as arbitrary, sociolinguistic conventions arrived at by a social group for the simple and straightforward purpose of avoiding ambiguity. In short, grammar arose inductively out of the social need for conventions and habits that minimized miscommunication.[22] Each social group evolves its own set of rules to that end, rules constrained by competing considerations both of efficiency and felicity of style. This would explain why there are so many different sorts of grammars in the world, and why each of them seems to enjoy a certain rightness with respect to efficiency and aptness, as if the rules came to be honed by collective usage and taste. But what these variegated grammars share in common is their social purpose to aid and abet efficient linguistic expression, each social group doing so in its own inductively arrived at way. To me, this social need for unambiguous expression seems a sufficient basis for the appearance and nature of grammar. This implies that having a grammar, having rules of inflection and word

---

[21] See Postscript 2-B for discussion of mentalese.

order, etc., is never optional. Obviously, it cannot be. But the existence of grammar in every language does not necessarily imply that their origin must be due to some innate, uniquely linguistic substrate of the brain, no more than, say, the use of fire for cooking signifies innate know-how. Both are a function of innate intelligence. A sufficient explanation could be that grammars are due to social intelligence satisfying both collective need and the law of least effort. This latter point would account for the simplifications that took place in the evolution of Latin to Italian or Old English to modern English.

2.5.2 Language, Grammar and Associative Memory

Despite the demur of the generativist tradition, Logos Model comports with those who hold that language and its grammars are just specialized functions of basic conceptual intelligence in humans (as held for example in Langacker's *Cognitive Grammar* (Langacker 2008)), i.e., having to do with memory associations engaged in seeing connections, similarities, differences, discerning analogies, making judgments, analyzing, grouping, ordering, characterizing, and above all, wishing to communicate, all basic acts of intelligence. In the understanding that went into Logos Model, all of these functions belonged under the rubric of associative memory. In our view, associative memory can be argued as a principal mechanism for encoding and decoding of language.

Proponents of Universal Grammar of course will never agree with any of this. UG maintains that there is an innate faculty for the handling of syntax, and that rules for structure are a distinct, generative faculty with its own separate and distinct anatomical basis. Most tellingly, UG holds that syntax alone is what turns thoughts into language. There is of course a place for syntax and (rules) in the brain's handling of language, but one questions whether the UG hypothesis (for that's what it is) offers a correct account of language processes either in the brain or the computer.

It is inarguable that structure is an essential part of human language, that without structure natural language could not exist. But it seems that when it comes to the place of syntax in the linguistic spectrum, UG may have it backwards. It is absolutely true, no sentence can be uttered that does not entail syntax, but the shape of the sentence is also determined by the semantic intention that gives rise to it; the syntax of a sentence is in the service of its meaning, its semantic purpose. That is incontrovertible also. So if all that is true, if syntax is in the service of semantic intention, one wonders why one would make syntax the central focus of language study. Most probably because syntax is easy to generalize upon, and semantics is not, and much of linguistics since Chomsky had become an exercise in the formulation of principles and rules.

Here's a simple translation exercise that illustrates how syntax is a function of semantics, how a sentence takes its shape from meaning. Below are two German source sentences, (12) and (13), that signify the same thing semantically, but have radically opposed syntax. Note that the order of subject and object in (13) is the reverse of (12). The inverted word order of (13) is odd but entirely acceptable in German, given an appropriate context of emphasis. Despite the syntactic differences in the German, the English translations for (12) and (13) are the same, as they should be, as shown in (14). The point here is that the shape of the English translation in (14) had to be determined on the basis of the semantics in the German of (13), not of its syntax.[23]

(12)   *Meine **Mutter** liebt diese **Farbe**.*
(13)   *Diese **Farbe** liebt meine **Mutter**.*
        Translation of both (12) and (13) by Bing SMT Translator and
                                Logos Model
(14)   *My **mother** loves this **color**.*[24]

Commentary[25]

Interestingly, Mircrosoft's Bing SMT Translator gets the translation of (13) right, suggesting that this statistical system is *"linguistically informed"* to a significant degree, as Microsoft claims. Apart from Bing SMT Translator and Logos Model, all the other MT systems tested translated (13) on the basis of its German word order, getting the English syntax wrong therefore.[26]

2.5.3   *In Principio Erat Verbum*

Semantically speaking, what makes a sentence a sentence is the predication it makes about some notion, circumstance, entity, or relation, or some combination thereof. Without at least an implied verb there cannot be a meaningful utterance. Sentences built around such predications express states, actions or relationships pertinent to the referenced notions or entities, etc. If the verb expresses a state, notion or activity focusing on its subject, the verb is generally considered intransitive. Verbs that are transitive are transitive in different degrees. Verbs like *learn, study*, as in *John is learning French*, are minimally transitive in that the effect of the verb falls back on

---

[22] No doubt considerations of felicity of style also entered importantly into the formulation of grammatical convention, but matters of style and felicity would be secondary to the more fundamental need to avoid misunderstanding.

[23] See Haupt et al. (2008) for an obliquely related comprehension study of short German sentences with object-subject ambiguities and object-initial structures.

[24] Given suitable context of course, the German sentence could possibly mean that this color suits my mother. Out of context, however, neither man nor machine would be expected to interpret it that way.

[25] See Postscript 2-C for depiction of how (13) is processed by Logos Model to produce (14).

[26] Curiously, the new neural net version of Bing Translator also translates (13) incorrectly.

its subject, not its object, making the verb reflexive (i.e., partially intransitive). With verbs like *fight, engage,* the effect is more or less reciprocal to both subject and object. Verbs like *hammer* and *paint* are maximally transitive, the effect being entirely on their object.[27]

Apart from verbs in their customary part of speech, other parts of speech may have verbal meaning. Process nouns are one obvious example, among other deverbals such as participial adjectives and gerunds. But even purely descriptive adjectives such as *shady, delightful, greedy* express verbal effects. And descriptive adjectives not so obviously derived from verbs nevertheless can be said to express verbal states of being, as e.g., *healthy*. Prepositions too generally imply verbs and often function as verb surrogates, as in *a book **on** the table* (***lying on** the table*), and in *the music **of** Bach* (***composed by** Bach*).

Less obvious are the implicit verbs in English compound noun phrases, as illustrated below in (13), (14) and (15).

(13)   *kitchen sink*
(14)   *silver bracelet*
(15)   *wine glass*

In (13) we understand that the *sink* is situated in the *kitchen*. In (14), we understand that the *bracelet* is made of *silver*. In (15) we understand that the *glass* is for the purpose of holding *wine*.

Detecting the implied verb here can be crucial to correct translation. In French, for example, (13) would be translated as in (13)(i), below. This *N2 de N1* pattern is the default way most English *N1 N2* compounds are transferred in French. But this default transfer pattern would not be correct for (14) and (15), as evidenced below in (14)(i) and (15)(i).

(13)(i)   *évier **de** cuisine*
(14)(i)   *bracelet **en** argent*
(15)(i)   *verre **à** vin*

In (14)(i) and (15(i) the French default preposition ***de*** is inappropriate because (we argue) the verbal relationships that are implied in these cases invite a different preposition to serve as verb surrogate.

Let me conclude this discussion with an indication of how the SAL representation language would allow Logos Model to deal with (14) and (15). As we explained earlier, these noun compounds are dealt with not as literal strings but as SAL strings, as shown below.

(14)(ii)   *silver bracelet* → *N1(MAmat) N2(COfunc)* → *functional*
            device (made of) *material* → *bracelet **en** argent*

---

[27] This topic of verb types in Logos Model is graphically illustrated in Part II.

(15)(ii)   *wine glass* ➔ *N1(MAliqu) N2(COrecep)* ➔ *receptacle*
            (for holding) *liquid* ➔ *verre à vin*

Commentary

In (14)(ii), the same SAL pattern would allow phrases like *silk tie, glass vase, aluminum chair* to be similarly rendered, e.g., *cravate en soie, vase en verre, chaise en aluminum,* respectively. A variant of rule (15)(ii) would render a phrase like *flower vase* as *vase à fleurs,* i.e., receptacle (for holding) plants. Note that without rule (15)(ii), the default treatment of *N1 N2* as *N2 de N1* would have incorrectly rendered *wine glass* in (15) with the meaning *glass of wine,* i.e., *glass* filled with *wine.*

Problems with exceptions to English *N1 N2* pattern-rules caused Logos linguists to desist from implementation, pending further research. For example, *lead pencil* should be rendered idiomatically as *crayon à papier,* not *crayon en mine.* Such exceptions were too troublesome to warrant implementation, but the principle of implied verbs between paired nouns is interesting and seems worthy of further study.

2.6   A Note About Neural MT (NMT)

For the past 5 years or so, statistically oriented, hierarchical, neural network MT has made its appearance from various "deep learning" centers around the world.[28] Intriguing breakthroughs in neural MT (NMT) at such centers as Google Deep Mind, Microsoft's deep learning lab in China, and LISA Lab at the University of Montreal are showing prospects of overcoming many of the limitations of phrase-based SMT, particularly so in the case of recursive, convolutional NMT models that perform bottom-up parsing.[29,30]

Several such NMT models have shown themselves able to overcome, in part, the morphology agreement problem endemic to SMT. For example, see below the translation of (16) produced in (16)(i) by University of Montreal's LISA Lab. Note how the inflections of both verbs in (16)(i) agree with their feminine, plural subject. In (16)(ii), Bing NMT Translator gets both number and gender correct only for the

---

[28] In *Proceedings of MT Summit XV* (2015), eds. Yaser Al-Onaizan and Will Lewis, papers on NMT dominate MT presentations for the first time.

[29] Bengio (2009). LISA Lab's NMT model is bidirectional, the first pass working from right to left, affording the second, left to right pass a degree of top-down intelligence about the entire sentence. See *Proceedings of MT Summit XV* (2015), eds. Yaser Al-Onaizan and Will Lewis.

[30] Castilho et al. (2017) report that NMT outperformed SMT in six of 12 language pairs in formal translation exercises.

main verb, which nevertheless is an improvement over its earlier SMT output (not shown). Google GNMT Translate, however, continues to have serious problems with morphology in (16)(iii). Errors are underlined.

> (16)   *The two watches we **lost** were **found**.*
>
>   Translation by LISA Lab's NMT system
> (16)(i)   *Les deux montres que nous avons **perdues** ont été **trouvées**.*
>
>   Translation by Microsoft's Bing NMT Translator
> (16)(ii) *Les deux montres que nous avons **perdus** ont été **trouvées**.*
>
>   Translation by Google GNMT Translate
> (16)(iii) *Les deux montres que nous avons **perdu** ont été **retrouvés**.*

Commentary

Despite residual errors in NMT output, it is clear that these neural systems are beginning to cope better with the agreement problem. This is a very positive sign. Not surprisingly, the three linguistic systems (PROMT Translator, SYSTRANet and Logos Model) all handled the morphology issues in (16) correctly (not shown). Of the earlier SMT models tested on (16) (not shown), Google SMT Translate got the morphology right with respect to number but not gender. Microsoft's Bing SMT Translator also had agreement problems with (16).

As we shall explain in subsequent chapters, these NMT models are of particular interest to the present author because of certain key similarities the 45-year-old Logos Model has with NMT. Computationally, the two models could not be more different, but with respect to architecture and basic functionality, these similarities are rather pronounced, suggesting that Logos Model had anticipated fundamental aspects of this promising new direction in translation technology some decades before its time.[31,32]

2.7   Conclusion

The connection NMT makes between the act of translation and the act of learning is a particularly interesting artificial intelligence departure from traditional perspectives on MT. As with SMT, NMT holds that the most rational way to approach language

---

[31] In Chap. 8 we relate Logos Model to this new development in neural net MT.

[32] Scott (1990, 2000, 2003). Partly because of the requirements of corporate secrecy, and partly because of development pressures, nothing at all was published about Logos Model technology for the first twenty years of its existence, and only very little in the public domain after that. It is understandable, therefore, that the claims of this book may be difficult to recognize for readers familiar with the published history of MT.

is to let sentences themselves directly teach us what they are like, without intermediation of any kind. As this book will make clear, the approach to translation in Logos Model is also predicated upon a not dissimilar, data-driven theory of language acquisition, where in effect the system learns to translate natural language sentences directly from the patterns found in language itself, without the necessity of rules to drive the process. Of course the two models differ computationally in how they learn. Another significant difference pertains to representation. The vectors in NMT represent *literal* words and their features numerically. In Logos Model, number-based vectors constitute *symbolic* representations of abstract SAL words and their features.[33]

There is no doubt that Logos Model would have been more effective had we known to employ statistical methods in learning about language, e.g., in better acquiring aligned vocabulary and patterns that make up Logos Model's source and target knowledge stores. By the same token, it is also interesting to speculate on the benefit that might accrue to SMT-NMT if their numerical vectors were reconstrued to represent not just features of literal words but also the more abstract, semantico-syntactic features of SAL words (denoting POS, semantic type, morphology). If a way could be found to do that, one foresees an increase in NMT's powers of generality (with a concomitant lessening of the sparseness problem), and also better handling of long sentences. Most critically, the inclusion of SAL features would introduce a degree of useful semantic knowledge into NMT's data-driven processes.

It is relatively easy to argue, and even to demonstrate, that the two data-driven technologies could benefit from each other. But how a hybridization of symbolic and non-symbolic processes might be accomplished is another matter entirely, one we do not feel capable of addressing in this present work. Perchance some reader may be moved to examine the possibilities.

Postscripts

Postscript 2-A

Logos Model constitutes the technology that underlies both the commercial Logos System that is no longer available and the currently available, open-source variant known as OpenLogos. Further development of Logos Model linguistic knowledge base ended in 2000. The OpenLogos adaptation of the commercial version was accomplished by The German Research Center for Artificial Intelligence (DFKI) in 2005.[34] This adaptation pertained exclusively to systems aspects. With one or two exceptions, all Logos Model translations in this book were run on OpenLogos. OpenLogos has reduced functions (e.g., no translation memory, no source format

---

[33] See Chap. 9 Postscript for illustration of numeric representation in Logos Model.

preservation in target output, no run-time Subject Matter Code options to govern lexical look-up at run time) and its translations, in rare instances, may not be identical with that of the commercial product (for unknown reasons). Logos Model translations in both versions have flaws as well as strengths, much as in any other MT system. We maintain, however, that translation flaws in Logos Model reflect where the system happened to be, development-wise, when work ceased in 2000, and do not imply inherent shortcomings in underlying methodology. Obviously, this is a crucial, distinguishing claim for the approach taken in Logos Model, one we try to make intelligible in the account given in this book.

With the end of American involvement in the Vietnam conflict in 1974, Logos Corporation turned to the development of new language combinations, some of which were then developed into products, others remaining simply as prototypes. For these efforts we received contractual assistance from a variety of sources: from the pre-revolutionary Iranian government for English-Farsi, from IBM and Xerox for English-French, from Siemens for German-English, from Walloon Provence of Belgium for German-French, from Swindell-Dressler for English-Russian, from the Italian government for English-Italian and German-Italian. In conjunction with these efforts, Logos Model was productized and ported from the IBM mainframe to other platforms, including Wang (VS), Sun (UNIX) and Microsoft's Windows.

By the 1980s Logos Corporation had sales offices in Frankfurt, Germany, offering German source to English, French and Italian, and in the US (Boston) and Canada (Montreal), offering English to German, French, Spanish, Italian and Portuguese. In those early days, MT was still a more or less unproven novelty and translators often met it with skepticism. The experience we had with the Canadian government was not untypical. During a sales demonstration of the English-French system, one of the translators asked if he might enter a sentence. He sat down at the terminal and typed in:

> It is quite unusual to find this type of machine in a non-creative environment that **calls for** less specific results and undoubtedly **brings about** a lot of confusion.

Needless to say, the Logos sales representative was relieved as the French translation began to appear on the screen:

> Il est tout à fait inhabituel de trouver ce type de machine dans un environnement non-créatif qui **réclame** des résultants moins spécifique et **provoque** indubitalement beaucoup de confusion.

Translations of this sort are standard fare nowadays, but 35 years ago, as the test sentence suggests, MT was still considered largely unproven. The Canadian government eventually purchased English-French systems for the Department of Foreign Affairs, Trade and Development, the Department of National Defense, and a number of other government entities. One private Canadian translation company used the Logos English-French system to translate tens of thousands of pages documenting all the various systems of a new Canadian frigate. *"There is no doubt,"*

---

[34] http://logos-os.dfki.de

stated Manager Jean Gordon of the Centre d'Expertise at the Canadian Secretary of State, speaking of their experience with the Logos English-French system, *"as long as the source text is well written, the raw translations will be quite good."*

In Germany, Siemens Nixdorf tested the viability of our system by having us translate one of its computer manuals from German into English. Two Logos staff members post-edited the machine's output. Interestingly, one of the post-editors knew very little about computers, and the other had very limited knowledge of German. Despite this, the resultant man-machine combination won Logos a long-standing contract with Siemens Nixdorf. And we were told by Julian Cox, Nixdorf's translation manager, that Logos Model MT motivated technical writers to compose their sentences more thoughtfully, resulting in machine output that required very little post-editing, with consequent savings in translation costs. A similar attention to source language style occurred at the German company Osram upon its acquisition of the American firm, Sylvania. Osram purchased the Logos system to facilitate online communications between the engineers on either side of the Atlantic. We were told engineers soon realized that attention to the quality of the source language paid immediate dividends in the translation quality of their messages.

SAP Germany, an early and long-standing customer, used Logos' German system to translate documents into English and then, after editing the English output, entered it into our English system to produce documentation in French and other languages.

Undoubtedly, MT's greatest attraction was the consistency in usage that MT by nature guarantees, a quality control function particularly needed in large translation projects. Sweden's Ericsson was an example of this. This firm was so pleased with the effect of the Logos system on translation quality, it set up a translation bureau subsidiary to offer MT services to other companies.

Océ Technologies, the Netherland printer company, used the Logos system to translate its text, but Océ had outside translation bureaus do its post-editing. This arrangement guaranteed much sought-after consistency in usage while reducing translation costs.

In the United States, several translation agencies used the Logos System to take on huge translation jobs that other agencies could not handle. One, for General Motors, entailed over 10,000 pages. This is redolent of the very first translation contract that Logos received in its earliest days in 1970, when we translated 10,000 pages of helicopter documentation into Vietnamese, after several manual translation bureaus proved unable to address the government's need. This was done on an emergency basis, even before the English-Vietnamese development effort was completed.

Postscript 2-B

... having something to say must necessarily entail conceptual relationships, but does not yet involve lexicon and grammar, semantics and syntax, as linguists understand these matters.

Mentalese, while very different from external, spoken language, is nevertheless still language, *"the language of thought"* in Pinker's terms, or I-language (for internal language) in Chomsky's terms. According to them, mentalese is far simpler than what we usually understand by the term language. For example, mentalese is unconcerned with word order and even with words themselves. Yet mentalese is the basis for language. According to Pinker (1994, 73), when we learn a spoken language, what we are doing is translating mentalese into a string of ordered words in accordance with a particular sociolinguistic convention. The theories of the Russian psychologist Lev Vygotsky (1934/1986) on *"inner speech"* are relevant here. In his work *Thought and Language* he itemizes the following characteristics of inner language: (a) predominance of private meaning over public meanings; (b) abbreviation of syntax, e.g., where the subject or object is understood and never made explicit; (c) agglutination of multiple, complex concepts into a single abstract concept that has no conventional counterpart in public discourse. At the extreme, he envisions inner speech as *"thinking in pure meanings,"* i.e., conceptually, without the literalness, morphology and structure of so-called external language.

Postscript 2-C

Brief overview of how Logos Model effects its translation of (13).

> (13)   *Diese Farbe liebt meine Mutter.*
> (14)   *My mother loves this color.*

1. The literal German input string in (13) gets re-expressed as a SAL string during lexical lookup at the very start of source analysis.
2. As source analysis proceeds through its various stages (through pipeline modules or hidden layers, depending on the metaphor being used), this SAL input string gets progressively re-written (concatenated) to eventually look like (13)(i). To keep things simple, the SAL string in (13)(i) is shown in clear English, not in SAL symbols.

<u>German input string (13) re-expressed as a SAL Input String</u>
(13)(i)   *NP1(non-agentive) VT NP2(agentive)*

VT in (13)(i) stands for any transitive verb. The agentive, non-agentive designations for the two *NP's* are derived from the SAL taxonomy for the head nouns in each case.

There are actually seven possible representation levels in a stored SAL pattern by which an input element may be represented and dealt with at any one time. These are: (i) set of POSs; (ii) POS; (iii) tagset of SAL elements within a POS; (iv) SAL superset; (v) SAL set (vi) SAL subset; (vii) literal string. For obvious reasons, the principle is always to deal with input at the abstraction level consistent with acceptable results, i.e., as near to literal as necessary and as abstract as otherwise possible.

3. SAL input string (13)(i) matches on a stored SAL pattern-rule having a commensurate SAL pattern, shown below in (13)(ii). Note that the *agentive* designation for *NP2* in 13(ii), below, represents a tagset that comprises a list of agentive-like SAL supersets. This matching function is effected automatically; a process driven by the input pattern itself, not by some metarule or other form of intermediate, procedural logic. Moreover, the stored rule is never looked at if it is not potentially relevant, no more than are entries in a properly indexed lexicon looked at if not potentially relevant.

<u>Stored Pattern Rule together with Rewrite</u>
(13)(ii)   *NP1(non-agentive) VT NP2(agentive)* ➔ *NP2 VT NP1*

4. As a consequence of this match, the action portion of the pattern-rule links to a target action, and this target action, taking its clue from the semantics of the German source pattern, then transforms the German syntax into appropriate English target order preparatory to the final, literal translation.

In sum, the matchup of pattern-rule (13)(ii) with SAL input string (13)(i) occurs because both entail a transitive verb with the agent of the verb following rather than preceding the verb. That's the anomaly (from the point of view of English) that this particular pattern-rule was designed to detect and deal with, doing so at the highest effective level of abstraction possible. In effect, the stored pattern-rule shown in (13)(ii) allows the literal German input string in (13)(i), and virtually any German sentence with reversed, subject-object word order, to be rendered in correct English order, as illustrated in (14) above, doing so purely on the basis of semantics.

References

Al-Onaizan Y, Lewis W (eds) (2015) Proceedings of MT Summit XV
Barreiro A, Monti J, Orliac B, Arrieta K, Batista WF, Trancoso I (2014) Linguistic evaluation of support verb constructions by OpenLogos and Google Translate. In: Proceedings, language resources and evaluation. Reykjavik, Iceland, pp 26–31

Bengio Y (2009) Learning deep architectures for AI. Found Trends in Mach Learn 2(1):1–127

Brants T, Popat A, Peng Xu, Och F, Dean J (2007) Large language models in machine translation. In: Proceedings of the 2007 joint EMNLP-CoNLL conference. Prague, Czech Republic.

Castilho S, Moorkens J, Gaspari F, Calisto I, Tinsley J, Way A (2017) Is neural machine translation the New State of the art? Prague Bull Math Linguist 108:109–120

Evans V (2014) The language myth: why language is not an instinct. Cambridge University Press, Cambridge

Goldin-Meadow S, Mylander SC (1990) Beyond the input given. The child's role in the acquisition of language. Language 66:323–355

Haupt FS, Schlesewsky M, Roehm D, Friederici A, Bornkessel-Schlesewsky I (2008) The status of subject-object reanalysis in the language comprehension architecture. J Mem Lang 59(1):54–96

Kalchbrenner N, Blunsom P (2013) Recurrent convolutional neural networks for discourse compositionality. In: Proceedings of the 2013 workshop on continuous vector space models and their compositionality. Sofia, Bulgaria, pp 119–126

Koehn P (2011) Statistical machine translation. Cambridge University Press, Cambridge

Langacker RW (2008) Cognitive grammar: a basic introduction. Oxford University Press, New York

Pinker S (1994) The language instinct. William Morrow and Co., New York

Scott B (1990) Biological neural net for parsing long, complex sentences. Logos Corporation Publication

Scott B (2000) Logos model as a metaphorical biological neural net. Logos Corporation Publication. http://www.mt-archive.info/Logos-2000-Scott

Scott B (2003) Logos model: an historical perspective. Mach Trans 18(1):1–72

Vygotsky L (1934/1986) Thought and language. MIT Press, Cambridge. http://s-f-walker.org.uk/pubsebooks/pdfs/Vygotsky_Thought_and_Language.pdf. Accessed 14 Apr 2016

Chapter 3
Language and Ambiguity: Psycholinguistic Perspectives

Abstract This chapter, based largely on a paper originally written in 1976, deals with the problem of ambiguity as it relates to language acquisition and translation by both mind and machine. We define ambiguity as a linguistic situation capable of more than one interpretation and that obviously has bearing on the accuracy of translation. We enumerate five levels of ambiguity and describe the problem each of these ambiguity levels poses for a translation machine. We note, in contrast, that the mind is able to resolve these ambiguities virtually without thought, and we offer an explanation as to why this is so. We identify several psycholinguistic operations believed to be associated with the acquisition of a second language and that account for the progress of gifted learners, the ambiguities of language notwithstanding. We liken sentence analysis by a translation machine to human language acquisition, and proceed to show how the psycholinguistic factors involved in language acquisition, if simulated in the computer, enable the machine to cope with ambiguities with greater success than might otherwise be possible. Finally, we offer some classic examples of syntactic and semantic ambiguities that illustrate the disambiguating power of these psycholinguistic functions simulated in Logos Model.

3.1 Levels of Ambiguity

THE ACT OF TRANSLATION, WHETHER BY HUMANS OR MACHINE, entails the mapping of sentences of one language into those of another. In practice, this means analysis of a meaningful source string formulated in accordance with source language grammar, and the transfer of this analysis into a semantically equivalent[1] target string in accordance with the grammar of this second language.

---

[1] By equivalence here is meant *literal* translation for publication purposes, i.e., where accurate information transfer is of paramount consideration, the sort of translation we are concerned with. We are not concerned with translation for *gisting* purposes, and least of all with translation for purposes of edification, i.e., where style supersedes information transfer in the order of importance.

© Springer International Publishing AG, part of Springer Nature 2018
B. Scott, *Translation, Brains and the Computer*, Machine Translation:
Technologies and Applications 2, https://doi.org/10.1007/978-3-319-76629-4_3

Among the various manipulations that this transfer entails are the following (illustrated with English to French):

(a) Lexical substitution:

    (i) *typewriter* ➔ *machine à écrire*

(b) Equivalencing of syntax and style, such as:

    (ii) *the blue pencils* ➔ *les crayons bleus*
    (iii) *children are playing here* ➔ *des enfants jouent ici*
    (iv) *the man should be told* ➔ *on doit informer l'homme*

Assuming reasonable competence in both source and target languages, manipulations (ii) through (iv) pose no inherent difficulty for the human translator. Linguistic operations of this sort are ordinarily performed effortlessly, on the fly as it were, normally without any consciousness of difficulty. Later we will consider why this is so in the case of the mind; more immediately we want to examine why the case is so different with the machine, where at times the simplest constructions can stump it. The reason for this resides not so much with the linguistic operations themselves, but rather with ambiguities that are often associated with these operations, ambiguities the machine may find difficult to handle.

We define ambiguity as a linguistic situation capable of more than one interpretation. And such ambiguity may occur at any of five distinct language levels, enumerated below. Clearly, a translation machine cannot be effective unless it can resolve ambiguities occurring at each of these levels. The translator's mind obviously has to deal with them as well.

Briefly, these ambiguity-prone language levels are:

(a) lexical-syntactic, introducing ambiguity having to do with a word's part(s) of speech.
(b) sentential-syntactic, introducing ambiguity having to do with the order, scope, and dependencies of words in a sentence.
(c) lexical-semantic, introducing ambiguity having to do with the meaning(s) of words at the lexical level.
(d) sentential-semantic, introducing ambiguity having to do with the meaning(s) of words at the sentential level.
(e) extra-sentential semantic, introducing ambiguity having to do with words whose meanings depend upon extra-sentential information, such as, e.g., the antecedents of anaphora. (We will not be dealing with (e).)

Each of linguistic levels (a) though (d) is liable to an ambiguity peculiar to that level alone. And, interestingly, ambiguity at any one of these levels is typically resolved by accessing information available at the next higher linguistic level, which information of course may also be ambiguous. We elaborate on these ambiguity levels in what follows.

(aa) lexical-syntactic ambiguity is lexical ambiguity as to part of speech. For example, the word *check* is found in lexical store both as a noun and as a verb. It is impossible to know at this lexical level which part of speech to select. Part-of-speech resolution must refer to the next higher linguistic level, namely, the sentential-syntactic level, where it becomes possible to examine how *check* functions in the sentence. For example, if *check* is preceded by *should*, its part of speech is most likely to be a verb.

(bb) <u>sentential-syntactic ambiguity</u> is ambiguity as to the sentential-syntactic function that a word takes on in a given sentence. A typical ambiguity of this kind relates to the issue of governance. For example, take the syntactic string (1), below (a prepositional phrase, where N represents noun):

(1)   *to N1 of N2 and N3*

It is not clear, at this purely syntactic level, whether $N3$ is governed by the preposition *to* or by the preposition *of* (or possibly by neither preposition). Once again, the matter is resolved only by referring to the next higher linguistic level, viz., the lexical-semantic level, that is, by examining the semantic values for nouns $N1$, $N2$ and $N3$ as retrieved from the lexical-semantic memory store.

We illustrate this with the following instantiations of (1):

(2)(i)   *to citizens of **Rome** and **environs**.*
(2)(ii)   *to **citizens** of Rome and **friends**.*

In (2)(i) the semantic kinship of $N2$ (***Rome***) and $N3$ (***environs***) causes the preposition *of* to govern $N3$ as it does $N2$ (unambiguously). In (2)(ii) the semantic kinship of $N1$ (***citizens***) and $N3$ (***friends***) causes the preposition *to* to govern $N3$ as it does $N1$ (unambiguously).

(cc) <u>Lexical-semantic ambiguity</u> arises when a given lexical entry has more than one semantic meaning within a single part of speech. For example, the transitive verb ***check*** has multiple meanings, two of which, viz., *examine* or *consult*, are illustrated in (3)(i) and (3)(ii) below. Resolution of this ambiguity is accomplished by referring to the next higher linguistic level, namely, sentential-semantic. That is, the particular meaning of ***check*** is understood by examining the sentential semantic environment. The following two sentences will illustrate:

(3)(i)   ***Check** the newspaper **for dates**.*
(3)(ii)   ***Check** the newspaper **for errors**.*

In (3)(i) the meaning of ***check*** as *consult* is determined in this case not by the verb's object but by the sentential semantics of the entire clause. And the preposition *for* likewise derives its meaning from the entire clause. The preposition *for* here has the extralexical meaning of *for information concerning* (and in Vietnamese, for example, is translated as *để biết, in order to know*).

In (3)(ii) the meaning of ***check*** as *examine* is also determined not by the verb's object but by the next linguistic level, namely the semantics of the entire clause.

And in (3)(ii) the preposition *for* now has the entirely different meaning of *for the presence of* (and is translated in Vietnamese as *có*).

(dd) <u>Sentential-semantic ambiguity</u> arises when words of a given sentence require extra-sentential or extra-textual information to be understood in order to translate them properly. Pronouns often pose this problem. For example, where the English *it* refers to an antecedent noun in French that is feminine, the pronoun's feminine gender must be reflected in a French translation. Other examples are ellipses of various kinds. For instance, one sentence might refer to *ears of corn,* where the next sentence might refer to them simply as *these ears*. More difficult are words whose meanings depend upon inference or pragmatic knowledge. Since Logos Model does not have sentence-carry, let alone inference or pragmatic knowledge, we must set aside further discussion of this species of ambiguity.

Given the above, there can be little doubt that ambiguity challenges the power of translation systems in fundamental ways. Clearly, no MT system can properly translate a sentence where parts of speech, dependencies, and meanings remain ambiguous. And therein lies the problem, more or less, with virtually all machine output, and why human post-editing is invariably needed in translations intended for publication. By contrast, problems of this sort hardly ever arise with human translation; human translators may be faulted at times for less than optimal transfers, but ungrammatical and nonsensical translation is virtually unthinkable in human output. Which raises the interesting question we seek to address here, namely, whether there is something that can be reasonably surmised about the psycholinguistic processes of language comprehension and translation that might be codified and then simulated in the machine.

3.2 Language Acquisition and Translation

Noam Chomsky (1957) voiced a germinal question regarding language, the answer to which underlies much of modern linguistic investigation. He asked: what mental process in a child enables the child to utter grammatical sentences he or she has never heard? Put otherwise, what linguistic process takes place in a child's mind that enables the child, after a finite exposure to language, to generate sentences of infinite variety?

The question is relevant to foreign language acquisition as well. We ask: how is it that a student of a foreign language at some point begins to utter sentences in that language that he or she has never heard? Clearly, some linguistic process is involved beyond that of imitation. Has this principle been identified?

In the discussion that follows, we present an analysis of certain linguistic processes that are believed to be involved in the acquisition of a second language. Then, in the section that comes after it, we briefly outline how these psycholinguistic processes have been imitated to good effect in the analysis/acquisition function of Logos Model.

3.2.1 Linguistic Processes Involved in Second Language Acquisition

In learning French, an English-speaking student at some point is taught to express in French the following sort of English sentence:

(4)(i) *John wants Mary to study music.*
(4)(ii) *Jean veut que Marie s'applique à la musique.*

In the next instant when the student attempts to apply what he has just learned to another English sentence similar in structure to (4)(i), such as:

(5)(i) *John asks Mary to study music.*

he is told, in this case, he must use a different French construction:

(5)(ii) *Jean demande à Marie qu'elle s'applique à la musique.*

or possibly:

(5)(iii) *Jean demande à Marie de s'appliquer à la musique.*

Now, suddenly, the student is confronted with a problem: constructions that appear identical in English require different constructions in French. Faced with this ambiguity (by our definition), the typical student hesitates to render such constructions into French until he "knows French better." The question is, what does the student need to learn?

The situation is no easier for the machine. In its initial effort to deal with English sentences (4)(i) and (5)(i), the system "perceives" a common syntactic construction in (6). (N = Noun, V = Verb):

(6) *N1 V1 N2 to V2 N3*

From such a syntactic string, how shall a machine be further programmed to generate now one French construction, now another?

Obviously, it is the verb *V1* that differentiates between (4)(i) where *V1* = *wants,* and (5)(i) where *V1* = *asks.* Certain verbs in French require certain constructions, other verbs other constructions. Are these constructions arbitrary conventions of a given language, or are they, in part at least, a function of something independent of convention (such as the verb's meaning)? And must the student, to master French, study each verb of the French language for the construction it takes, verb-by-verb, or is there some underlying principle the gifted student intuitively grasps and makes use of, so that after only a short time he begins to express himself rather freely in the foreign language? Must the machine, in its turn, be instructed as to the behavior of each verb, or is there a more elegant way to handle the problem of verbs and the constructions they require?

To answer these questions, we need to observe an important property of language having to do with its conceptual basis. First, we note that the English verbs used in (4)(i) and (5)(i), namely, *want* and *ask*, can also take optional (albeit somewhat awkward) English constructions that parallel their French counterpart, in (7) and (8) respectively:

> (7)   *John wants that Mary study music.*
> (8)   *John asks of Mary that she study music.*

From this we might infer that *want* in (7) and *vouloir* (*veut*) in (4)(ii) take parallel constructions, in part at least, because of the common semantic value that these French and English verbs share. A parallel situation also exists with the verb pair *ask* in (8) and *demander* in (5)(ii). This again suggests that syntactic constructions are not merely conventions of a given language, but are shaped, in part at least, by the semantic values of the verbal concept, independent of a given language and its grammatical conventions.

This inference is reinforced by several other observations. One, the verbs in the English constructions (7) and (8), *want* and *ask*, are not interchangeable. This again implies the existence of a connection between a verb's semantic value and the syntactic construction it engenders. Two, when we substitute other verbs whose syntactic behavior does fit the patterns of (7) and (8), we discover an important fact: verbs that behave alike syntactically look alike semantically (generally speaking). For example, the verbs *request, entreat, beg* belong to the same semantic family as *ask* and exhibit the same syntactic behavior as *ask* in (5)(i) and (8). This is generally true of these verbs in both languages.

The conclusion to be drawn is that syntax and semantics are not separate and unrelated properties of language, as the generativist's wall between syntax and semantics implies, but are rather complementary aspects of the same property, designated as a *semantico-syntactic* property. We may think of syntax and semantics vis à vis verbs as the extreme terminals of a semantico-syntactic verb tree, as in Fig. 3.1.[2]

At the semantic extreme of the tree in Fig. 3.1 are the leaves, i.e., all the verbs of a given language, fully individualized. At the syntactic extreme of this tree is the tree trunk, which embraces all verbs in the single syntactic symbol *V*. In between are the branches and sub-branches, which represent different semantico-syntactic subcategories. As we move up the trunk out onto one or another of the branches and sub-branches, we see that these subclasses of verbs are organized according to the syntactic effects each particular group of verbs engenders. But we also find that the verbs in each group all tend to have something in common semantically. This semantic commonality is only very general on the main branches, but as we move

---

[2]This view of syntax and semantics is consonant with that of Langacker and others in the school of construction grammar. See Schmid (1996, 353).

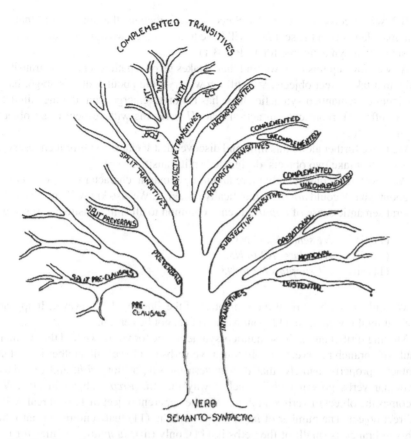

Fig. 3.1 *Verb Tree showing semantico-syntactic subcategories*

out onto sub-branches and sub-sub-branches, both the syntax and the semantics begin to merge. We find that all the verbs of a particular sub-branch are related both with respect to what they mean and how they behave, indicating that the syntactic effects of the subclasses are a function of their semantics.

To illustrate this interconnection between syntax and semantics, let us process a string of words representing a simple sentence (where W = word).

(9)   *W1 W2 W3 W4 W5*

Let us assume each word in (9) is to be found somewhere on a semantico-syntactic tree, and that there is one such tree for all verbs, one for all nouns, and so on. Next, let us assume we climb the semantico-syntactic tree that each word in (9) appears on, starting at the bottom of the tree, at the extreme syntactic end. As we do so, we uncover the primitive syntactic value for each:

(10)   *N1 V N2 Prep N3*

W2, we perceive, is a verb (*V*). Since the verb dictates the relationship that the principal elements in the sentence will have to each other, we immediately focus on the semantico-syntactic tree for *V* (Fig. 3.1).

As we move up this tree, we find that *V* takes us on a path reserved for transitive verbs that take direct objects. We still know very little about *V* at this stage, but a modicum of semantico-syntactic shape has begun to emerge from the meaningless *W2*: in effect, *V* represents an action that *N1* performs with respect to an object, presumably *N2*.

We move further along this limb and discover that *V* enters a sub-branch reserved for verbs that take two objects, designated split transitive verbs.[3]

We now know considerably more about the semantic character of *V*. We know a lot about what *V* could *not* be, semantically speaking. We also know *V* must have the general semantic sense of *impart*, a sense common to all split transitive verbs, e.g.:

(11)(i)   *N1 sends N2 to N3.*
(11)(ii)   *N1 relates N2 to N3.*
(11)(iii)   *N1 supplies N2 to N3.*

We still cannot be sure of the semantics of the *Prep* in (10) however. It appears likely it might be *to*, as in (11), but we as yet cannot be certain.

Moving further along the semantico-syntactic tree for verbs, we find that *V* enters a sub-sub-branch reserved for split transitive verbs that have still another important syntactic property, namely, that they govern the preposition *with*, and that these particular verbs govern *with* in such a way that the *Prep's* object in (10), *N3*, becomes the object of verb *V*, and that *N2*, the apparent object of *V*, is in reality *V's* indirect object. The number of *impart*-type verbs in (11) that venture out onto this sub-sub-branch is small; of the verbs in (11), only (iii), *supplies*, qualifies for this sub-sub-branch. Given *V's* membership on that sub-sub-branch, the probability is fairly high therefore that the *Prep* in (10) is indeed *with*, as in (12):

(12)   *N1 V (supply-type) N2 with N3 (i.e., N3 to N2).*

The position of *V* on the sub-sub branch of our verb tree of course still does not reveal the literal semantics of the verb leaf in (10), or that the *Prep* in (10) does in fact equal *with*. But from the mere accumulation of the verb's apparent syntactic effects, the verb's semantics in (12) has all but emerged. And once we climb the preposition tree to its leaves and discover that *Prep* in (10) is indeed *with*, it becomes clear that the construction of (10) is most likely that as indicated in (12).[4]

---

[3] Ditransitive verbs, in more traditional parlance. We at Logos were prone at times to create our own vocabulary.

[4] Of course *with N3* could also be an adverbial phrase (e.g., *with alacrity*), which would change the interpretation of (10) entirely. However, the use of *with* in (10) for such purposes would confuse

3.2.2   On Learning French

We need now to pick up again with the beginning student of French. Were he to be given an English sentence to translate, like:

(13)   *John provided the students with books.*

the student's first impulse will mostly likely be to render *with* as *avec*, (its principal lexical transfer). The teacher would then have to show the student the correct translation:

(14)   *Jean a fourni des livres aux élèves.*

By way of helping the student appreciate the differences between English and French, the teacher proceeds to illustrate the variety of ways in which the preposition *with* is to be rendered in French:

(15)   *John sees a man with a dog. (with = avec)*
(16)   *John blocks the flow with a valve. (with = au moyen de)*
(17)   *John acquainted his associates with the facts. (with = des)*
(18)   *John does not mix with the students. (with = à)*

However, the teacher does not explain to the student when or why each usage becomes appropriate, except by way of illustration on a sentence-by-sentence, example-by-example basis.

The student must figure out the why as best he can, through the mysterious linguistic process called "learning" a language.

Let us now see what we can fathom about this process in light of the discussion thus far.

If the student is at all gifted, he intuitively grasps that the preposition *with* loses its simple lexical meaning as *avec* in (16) through (18) because the verb in each of these sentences makes a prior claim to the preposition. In (15), on the other hand, *with* can be rendered as *avec* just because the verb in (15) does *not* make a claim to this preposition. Without necessarily formulating it as such in the mind, the student learns to be sensitive to prepositions and to the fact that they might belong, semantico-syntactically speaking, to a verb and as a result possibly take on an unexpected meaning, with differing transfers therefore.

Next, in a largely unconscious way, a mental sorting takes place as to why one verb causes a preposition to function one way, with one meaning and transfer, and

---

reader expectations and therefore would be highly unlikely if not bizarre (e.g., *The school provided students with alacrity*). This circumstance merely illustrates the strength of the claim that this particular group of verbs makes on the object of the preposition *with* as its own object, i.e., how strong the connection is between their semantics and their syntactic effect.

another verb causes it to function another way, with another meaning and transfer. Now, an especially gifted student at this point, usually without realizing it, finds that as he studies the constructions (15) through (18), the changes that the preposition *with* undergoes (or does not undergo) in the French language in each case seems entirely appropriate. He does not articulate it, but the student is aware that something in the nature of the verb seems to call for what happens to the preposition. For example, the verb *block* in (16) calls for explanation as to how, with what instrument, by what means this action is performed. It is difficult to think of the action *to block* apart from a means. When the student encounters this verb, an expectation is unconsciously set up to discover the means. Then when the student encounters the preposition, his mind grasps it as supplying what was deficient in the verb itself. In fact, the meaning of *with* as *by means of* rushes to mind as if it were filling a semantic vacuum. Conversely, in (15) the preposition *with* is taken as a noun complement just because the verb *see* does not create an expectation of means, does not suffer a semantic deficiency (except as to its object, which is true of all transitive verbs), i.e., does not need the preposition to complete its thought.

The situation is the same for (17) and (18). For example, the verb *acquaint* in (17) sets up the expectation as to *about what*. The prepositional phrase introduced by *with* satisfies the *about what* expectation, which in the French is expressed by the prepositional phrase introduced by *de* (e.g., *John a mis ses élèves au courant des faits.*).

Simultaneous with the student's tacit grasp of potential interconnections between verbs and prepositions, the gifted student intuitively grasps another principle: the interconnection between a verb and its prepositional complement holds true in just the same way, not only for this verb but for all other verbs that are semantically like this verb. In short, the student intuits that semantically similar verbs possess the same semantico-syntactic property of needing the particular preposition to complete their semantic intent.

For example, having seen the verb *block* in (16), the student has no trouble recognizing that other verbs such as those in (19) relate to the preposition *with* in the same way:

(19)(i)   *compensate x with y*
(19)(ii)   *cap x with y*
(19)(iii)   *repair x with y*
(19)(iv)   *control x with y*
(19)(v)   *choke x with y*

All these verbs therefore can transfer *with* as *au moyen de*. By the same mental operation, the student recognizes other verbs that make entirely different claims on the preposition *with*. For example:

(20)(i)   *align x with y*
(20)(ii)   *synchronize x with y*
(20)(iii)   *coordinate x with y*

In (20) these verbs generally give *with* the meaning *with respect to*. The gifted student however also realizes that this is not always the case. For example, if the preposition *with* in (20)(i) had as its object an instrument-type noun, as in *align the head with a plumb line*, the student would learn to interpret *with* as *by means of*.[5] There are other potential interpretations for *with* also, of course, depending on its object (e.g., *align x with care*). But unless something in the context compels otherwise, the expectation that the verb *align* sets up in the student's mind will normally cause *with* to be given the meaning *with respect to*, as in *align the head with the body*.

How does the gifted student know these sorts of things? What enables the student to fashion French sentences to which he or she has had no prior exposure? Let us see if we cannot account more formally for the linguistic skills such a student exhibits.

3.3 Psycholinguistic Bases of Language Skills

3.3.1 Analytical Basis

Using verbs as our focal point, we delineate three planes on which linguistic mastery develops. First and most fundamentally, there is the immediate *analytical* knowledge as to the verb's behavior, how it relates to other elements in the sentence, which knowledge the student intuits directly from the semantic nature of the verb itself. That is to say, he grasps the verb's syntactic effects from its semantic character, as something implicit in its semantics. Although the student does not do so consciously, his mind accesses the verb at the point where semantics and syntax intersect, the point that serves as the basis for the verb's coded place on the semantico-syntactic tree. The mind does not articulate these semantico-syntactic codes but there is reason to think, as we shall see, that these codes do indeed articulate what the mind is dealing with in linguistic operations of this sort.

To illustrate this initial plane in linguistic mastery—which we have defined as an unmediated *analytical* knowledge of a verb's syntactic effects gleaned from the semantics of the verb itself—let us observe the linguistic process that occurs when the student encounters a verb like *protect*. This verb announces loud and clear its need for complementation as to what the protection shall be with respect to. The moment the student hears or reads the verb *protect*, an expectation of complementation is implanted in the student's mind. Should the student encounter the sentence in (21):

(21)   *A scarf protects her face X the wind.*

---

[5] Interestingly, it's the semantics of *plumb line* as "instrument" that causes the mind to drop the *with respect to* expectation that *align* had created regarding the preposition *with*, but this shift in interpretation only serves as further illustration of the effect semantics has on syntax.

there would be no hesitation in the student's mind as to both the syntactic function and the semantic import of *X*. *X* is a preposition with the general meaning of *with respect to*.

This characterization of *X*, moreover, will be true regardless of which language (21) might be rendered in, so it is something that is true (and therefore knowable) independently of language conventions of any kind. The student knows the semantico-syntactic function of *X* from an immediate and unmediated *analytical* appreciation of the verb *protect* and what it means.

3.3.2 Empirical Basis

At the same time, however, the student will not know on this basis a single preposition in any given language that actually instantiates *X*. This is an *empirical* kind of knowledge, an acquired knowledge that indeed must be gained from exposure to the conventions of each language. This we term a second plane of language acquisition, the plane on which exposure to usage takes place, along with such activities as memorizing word lists, use of dictionaries, and grammatical exercises of every kind. It is a plane of language acquisition that pedagogy ordinarily treats as the only plane. That it is not the only plane, however, can be inferred from the question to which pedagogy and linguistics have little to answer—namely, what enables the gifted student to very rapidly advance beyond rote learning and mere imitation to begin expressing himself freely in a new language? We answer that the reason is to be found in two distinct psycholinguistic planes of knowledge (besides this *empirical* plane) that underlie the traditional plane of learning by exposure and imitation, the first of which we identified as unmediated *analytical* knowledge.

It seems reasonable to assume that a student's prowess on this first psycholinguistic plane, the *analytical* plane, would greatly reinforce the student's ability to learn the *empirical* aspects of language (the vocabulary and grammatical conventions of any given language). For even though the *empirical* instantiations of *X* are not dictated by the verb, an unmediated *analytical* awareness of the verb's semantico-syntactic claim on *X* will likely help the student to remember its instantiation, even after a single exposure to it.

But it is not this that enables the student to branch out creatively in a language. This final stage of mastery, though it depends on the *analytical* and *empirical* planes, takes place by an act of comprehension on yet another plane.

3.3.3 Analogical Basis

The knowledge developed on this third plane is *analogical* knowledge, knowledge gained through perceiving the proportional similarities between things that differ materially. It is by this *analogical* knowledge that the student's grasp of a language begins to spread like wildfire. For example, the student, having learned what he knows about the verb *protect* and the conventions which serve to instantiate its prepositional complement, when he thereafter encounters a verb like *insulate*, he perceives that in respect of its semantico-syntactic property, *insulate* is very much like *protect*, and that therefore the *analytical* knowledge and the *empirical* conventions which apply to *protect* very likely also apply to *insulate*. This is the *analogical* operation that goes on in the mind of a gifted student. In the next instant, the student is using the verb *insulate* with correct complementation even though he has never had the verb explained to him before.

This then is what accounts for the gifted student's prowess in learning a second language. When he encounters a new verb that he has never seen before, he first tastes its *analytical* properties, so to speak; then he casts about in his mind until he finds an *analogy* for it among those verbs with which he is familiar, and finding one he proceeds to fit the new verb into the *empirical* conventions that apply to the known verb. Without doing so explicitly or consciously, the gifted student is dealing with the semantico-syntactic properties of language that we have been describing. By such stepping-stones he picks his way surefooted among the multiplicity of verbs in a language, using the power of *analogy* to reduce the multiplicity to a smaller, more manageable set of linguistic situations. Having mastered what probably amounts to little more than a few score of these *analogical* patterns, he rapidly expands his command over the whole of the language in all its endless variations, all by the power of *analogy*.

The gifted student thus makes remarkable progress, seemingly able to handle himself in a new language with a swiftness and ease that baffles the less gifted. As a matter of pedagogy, it seems that what the gifted student comes to by virtue of his native intelligence, the less gifted could be taught to see. The semantico-syntactic behavior of words, and the grouping of words on the basis of *analogous* behavior, are aspects of language that the teacher could point out. The student would readily grasp such aids because they conform to linguistic processes natural to the mind.

An indirect sign of these mental processes may be seen in old vaudeville repartees of the sort designed to catch the listener off-guard. Many of these exchanges tend to be socially unacceptable nowadays, but in (22) and (23) we offer a more innocent imitation of one. It begins with the interlocutor asking:

(22)   *Do you usually eat your meal with a beverage?*

to which is given the reply:

(23)   *No, I eat it with a knife and fork.*

Why does the reply inevitably elicit a reaction? The dialogue amuses us because it entails a syntactic pun, having to do with certain expectations that the words *eat* and *with* have set up in our mind, expectations that are being played with in (23). Puns like this depend for their humor on the plausibleness of that syntactic play, and the amusement evoked is a kind of acknowledgment of our own mental operations with language.

What does all of the foregoing discussion mean practically? It means that a student does not have to learn 10,000 verbs and their associated constructions in order to master French. Instead, he learns perhaps 40 or 60 constructions with a representative verb for each, constructions like those implied on the verb tree in Fig. 3.1.[6] Then when the student encounters an unfamiliar verb, he mentally compares the unfamiliar verb to a familiar verb that is like it. Using the verb he knows—whose semantico-syntactic properties he knows—he substitutes in its place the new verb that resembles it and proceeds to express himself in tried and true fashion, as if this verb were one he had already mastered. In a way he has mastered it, by virtue of this *analogical* operation. The student makes errors, to be sure, but through trial and error, he refines his knowledge and his instinct for proceeding in this fashion, learning to detect subtler semantico-syntactic features in the linguistic landscape. Such a student makes rapid progress. Should he study a second foreign language, his skills become sharper still. Indeed, everyone experiences greater ease learning the second and third foreign language. But of what does this increased skill consist if not what we have described?

3.4 Practical Implications for MT

The foregoing suggests that the machine ought to be taught to deal with language in the way the gifted student does, by perceiving words at the point in which the word's semantic properties and syntactic properties intersect. The linguistic data in the system's memory store, therefore, should be encoded according to these properties. The entry for the verbs like *protect, guard, insulate, shield, etc.* should have codes in common that identify their common position on the semantico-syntactic verb tree, and that accounts for their common argument structure, their common valence. These codes would make available to a machine an articulation of both the *analytical* and *analogical* properties of words, properties that the gifted student intuits in a largely unconscious way. And if the *empirical* knowledge that a translation machine must necessarily be fed (vocabulary, conventions of grammar) is represented in semantic-syntactic terms, i.e., in terms that in effect group words *analogically*, then its knowledge base would begin to have the powers of generality that typify a gifted student.

In sum this is the way Logos Model was conceived.

The computer has no mind but it has memory, and an input string can be processed in terms of that memory. Into that memory can be stored linguistic pattern-rules whose patterns are strings of abstract, semantico-syntactic entities (symbolically coded words). When a sentence is input to the machine, the machine regards the string both *analytically* and *analogically*, much in the manner of a gifted

---

[6] Indeed, a teacher of a second language might use such a tree to depict, generically, the semantico-syntactic correspondences between the native language and the language being acquired. In the briefest of times, language students would begin to feel more comfortable with what they are being asked to learn.

student. Practically, in Logos Model, this means that the literal input string is first converted to an abstract semantico-syntactic string via SAL representation. This conversion operation thus mimics the *analytical* operations of the gifted student. Then segments of this SAL input string are progressively matched against stored semantico-syntactic rule-patterns, on a longest and most-semantically-specific match basis. This matching operation thus mimics the *analogical* operation of the gifted student. When a Logos Model match occurs, the action portion of the pattern-rule performs various manipulations, both on the source string itself (creating its quasi parse tree), and (optionally) on a target string equivalent, all in accordance with the *empirical* conventions appropriate to the target language grammar. These operations thus draw upon the *empirical* data that pedagogy is normally all about. In short, the machine has been made to simulate the *analytical* and *analogical* functions of the mind as it operates on the *empirical* knowledge of both source and target languages.

Since these linguistic pattern-rules are based on patterns of abstract (generic) semantico-syntactically encoded entities, it follows that a machine memory adequately stored with a large but finite number of pattern-rules and vocabulary can theoretically deal with virtually infinite varieties of input, doing so in linguistically correct fashion, sensitive to lexical selection and syntactic reordering requisite for good translation. All this is so only theoretically, of course, but the fact that no reason can be adduced why it could not ultimately be so in practice seems not an idle matter. In short, if a truly comprehensive body of generic semantico-syntactic pattern-rules could be assembled and then effectively applied, such that ambiguities at both the syntactic and semantic level are resolved, then one of the main obstacles to consistent, high-quality translation would have been removed.

3.4.1   Semantico-Syntactic Solutions to the Problem of Ambiguity in MT

3.4.1.1   Some Classic Examples

In this section, we discuss two classic, syntactic ambiguity problems and show how the mind, by dealing semantico-syntactically with these ambiguities, is spontaneously able to resolve them. Then we show how this can be made to apply to the machine.

For the first example, we take the ambiguity problem within the noun phrase in (24), posed by Naomi Sager.[7]

   (24)   *Changes in cells produced by digitalis.*

---

[7]Cited in Grishman et al. (1973, 433). Sager led the Linguistic String Parser effort at New York University's Courant Institute until 1995. Her special focus was the treatment of syntactic ambiguity.

Sager asked, how shall a linguistic string parser be instructed to recognize whether *produced by digitalis* complements *changes* or *cells*? Clearly something more than syntax is needed to accomplish this. Sager points to one suggested route: if rules were devised governing permissible word-associations within a subfield of knowledge, it should be possible to determine that *digitalis* can be associated with the production of *changes* but not of *cells*. Yet it seems fairly obvious that trying to capture pragmatic knowledge through literal word associations in order to disambiguate (24), even if remotely feasible in the narrowest of domains, would make disambiguation more problematic than ever.

According to the method we are proposing, it takes no specialized knowledge for a reader to know that the participial phrase *produced by digitalis* modifies the noun *change*. All it takes is a modicum of linguistic sense of the sort we have been describing, and as we shall show below.[8]

To illustrate this, consider the two phrases (25) (and (26), where two different participles have been substituted for *produced* in (23):

(25)   ***changes*** in cells ***effected*** by digitalis.
(26)   changes in ***cells*** ***affected*** by digitalis.

We see at once in (25) that the participle ***effected*** can only have ***changes*** for its referent. There is no ambiguity about this because, *analytically*, the semantico-syntactic behavior of the verb ***effected*** is such that its object must be a noun associated with a verb, like a gerund or process noun. When the mind encounters a verb like ***effected***, it seeks out and expects to find a process noun or gerund somewhere in its vicinity. That requirement is satisfied in (25) by ***changes*** alone.

In (26), by contrast, we see that the participle ***affected***, while it could theoretically complement ***changes***, in fact complements ***cells***. There is little ambiguity about this either. An inexorable law of grammar (at least for lightly inflected languages like English) says that modifiers shall modify the element that is most adjacent to them unless there is a compelling reason to do otherwise. No compelling reason can be found in (26), so by default the referent for ***affected*** is the adjacent noun, ***cells***. Communication would not be effective without such a law.

In contrast to (25) and (26), the noun phrase in (24), with *produced* as the participle, might actually seem to be ambiguous, as Sager claims. After all, both ***cells*** and ***changes*** can be produced. But is this really the case in (24)? We do not believe so. Just as with *effect*, the association of *produce* with *change* seems too strong. The preconscious *analytical* play of the mind in all likelihood will recognize this right off.[9]

To summarize, the phrase in (24) is only ambiguous when considered purely at the syntactic level, as Sager seems to have been doing. And it is unrealistic for a

---

[8] Sager was correct in thinking that word associations hold the key to disambiguation in (22), but only if the associations are between abstract, semantico-syntactic representations of words rather than between literal words.

[9] This was born out by a number of random tests involving linguists applying for jobs at Logos Corporation.

machine process to have to depend on pragmatic, real-world knowledge in order to resolve it. On the other hand, when the phrase is viewed semantico-syntactically, the ambiguity virtually vanishes.[10]

For our second classic example, we take Chomsky's famous sentence (27), which he employed to illustrate ambiguity in language (Chomsky 2006, 45).

(27)   *John **kept** the car **in the garage**.*

There is indeed a two-fold potential for ambiguity here, one having to do with the semantics of the verb, ***kept***, the other having to do with the syntactic function of the prepositional phrase ***in the garage***, i.e., whether this prep phrase modifies *car* or is adverbial to ***kept***. But almost certainly, the human mind would not consider (27) in any way ambiguous, no more than it would have in the earlier example in (24). That is because (27) is processed by the mind *analytically*, i.e., semantico-syntactically. It is clear that Chomsky sees (27) as ambiguous precisely because he views it in purely syntactic terms and believes that is the way the mind initially processes an input sentence. He would not agree with our view that the mind actually processes (27) semantico-syntactically, and consequently would never see it as ambiguous. Like many in the linguistic community, linguists like Chomsky and Sager have viewed syntax and semantics as distinct and separate aspects of language and of how language is processed, both by mind and by machine.

It is true that the meaning of the verb ***kept*** in (27) is ambiguous, at least until the mind (and the machine) encounters the prepositional phrase ***in the garage***. But the encounter with ***in the garage*** clears up the ambiguity; the combination of the verb and the prep phrase resolves both the semantics of ***kept*** and the syntactic function of ***in the garage***. What goes on here is straightforward and hardly arguable. Of the several different senses of the verb ***kept***, one of those senses invites complementation as to where something is being ***kept*** (*held*), and when the mind encounters the prep phrase ***in the garage***, the mind instantly seizes upon it, resolves the ambiguity of the verb, and thus unambiguously grasps the structure and meaning of the sentence. Interestingly, unlike in many of the other examples we have been using, the cognitive movement in (27) is from the verb to the preposition and then back to the verb. And that reciprocal movement disambiguates both the meaning of the verb and the syntactic function of the prep phrase. Chomsky's claim that (27) is ambiguous merely indicates that he does not view language in this semantico-syntactic manner. But apart from some compelling context forcing the contrary, anyone who intends (27) to mean *John kept the car that was in the garage* is simply not communicating. That's because the association between ***keep*** and the prepositional

---

[10] It's true of course that an expression like *changes in cars produced by Ford* suggests that *cars* and not *changes* are what Ford has *produced*. Sager's point is certainly true that pragmatic associations like that between *Ford* and *cars* may (at times) be dispositive in ambiguous situations, but this is not necessarily so. For example, because of the strong semantico-syntactic association between *produced* and *changes*, the formulation of the above expression would more properly be *changes in cars manufactured by Ford*, just to avoid misreading.

phrase *in the garage* is too strong to allow the prepositional phrase to modify *car*. If someone were asked *which car did John keep*? the response would almost inevitably have to be *John kept the one in the garage,* precisely because one instinctively knows that to answer with (27) would thoroughly obfuscate the intent of the reply.

Sentence (28) is another classic example of ambiguity offered by the syntax-first school.

(28)   *John saw Henry walking through the library.*

The ambiguity in (28) has to do with who is walking through the library, *John* or *Henry*. We maintain neither the mind nor the machine would properly see ambiguity here, for the simple reason that a complement always complements the thing nearest to it unless a compelling reason exists to override that basic law of social communication, what we call the law of adjacency.[11] In (28), no compelling reason exists to override that law; anyone uttering a sentence where *walking through the library* complements *John* rather than *Henry* does not want to communicate.[12]

3.5   Psycholinguisitcs in a Machine

In this final section, we briefly illustrate how the psycholinguistic processes we have been describing are made use of in Logos Model. We focus our discussion on the expression in (24).

As we envision the psycholinguistic process, when (24) is input to the student's (or translator's) mind, the mind immediately tries to make sense of these signals. In so doing, the mind is simply reacting to signals, whether visual or auditory. There are prescribed pathways for dealing with the input, of course, but no overarching algorithm needs to get activated to manage the process. So too with the machine as Logos Model conceives it. There is a pipeline (or network) through which the input must pass, and as the input stream passes through the pipeline/network, stored memory reacts to the input stream and does things with it. The key thing to understand is that this process is not driven algorithmically. It is driven by the input stream itself, and by stored data's unmediated reactions to it.

Before getting into that process, let us digress a moment to say something about the intelligence reflected in this stored data, as it may help the reader to better under-

---

[11] A non-technical law, not to be confused with Chomsky's formal law of *subjacency*, although clearly if spelled out technically, adjacency might not look very different. The difference of course has to do with whether the law denotes unique, innate linguistic behavior (Chomsky) or simply an intelligent, grammatical convention, much like the intelligence involved in not pointing to B if you wish to call attention to A.

[12] As with previous examples, it is always possible to force a larger context that might allow such aberrant interpretation of (28), but if one could devise such a context, the exception would merely serve to prove the rule.

stand the connection we have been making between mind and machine in this matter of language acquisition and translation. It concerns the SAL representation of language and our attempt to codify (for the benefit of the machine) the *analytical* and *analogical* intelligence that operates in the gifted student (and translator) as they deal with linguistic signals. SAL is our simulation of that linguistic intelligence, and to that extent functions as a kind of connecting tissue between mind and machine. Accordingly, when the participle in (24), *produced*, is originally entered into the system's lexicon, it is given the SAL code of a preverbal/preprocess verb, letting the machine know what the mind knows *analytically*, namely that the object of this verb could likely be a word or phrase denoting a process of some kind. In like manner, when the noun *changes* is entered into the lexicon, it too receives a semantico-syntactic code, in this case the *superset* code of a process noun.[13]

Recall that the SAL designations for *produced* and *changes* denote not just these individual words but entire subclasses of related words. These SAL codes therefore are also giving the machine the benefit of the mind's *analogical* intelligence, namely that *produced* and *changes* belong to subclasses of verbs and nouns and consequently take on the behavior of these subclasses.

To this of course must still be added learned linguistic convention, i.e., the *empirical* matter that instruction and exposure alone can provide.

In sum, this combination of linguistic intelligence and learned linguistic convention operating in the gifted language student's mind is precisely what Logos Model has sought to emulate in the machine.

Now let's return to the machine and see how it uses this linguistic intelligence, based on the translation of literal string (24):

(24)   *changes in cells produced by digitalis*

Translation Step One
At run time, literal input string (24) gets converted to its equivalent SAL string, shown below as (24)(i). For clarity sake, we have expressed (24)(i) in clear English rather than in coded SAL notation.

Conversion of input phrase (24) to a Semantico-Syntactic (SAL) input string
(24)(i)   *N(PROCESS; pl) Prep(in) N(ANmicro; pl) VAdj(PREPROCESS; past) Prep(by) N(MAchem; sg)*

Note that <u>Translation Step One</u> corresponds to the inherent *analytical* aspect of language acquisition and use, where the semantico-syntactic implication of words is unconsciously registered by virtue of gifted intelligence.

---

[13] For our purposes here we have omitted enumerating SAL's taxonomic *set* and *subset* codes that are also assigned to *changes*.

Translation Step Two
In Translation Step Two, converted input string (24)((i) is matched with a stored pattern (24)(ii) that sufficiently corresponds to it semantico-syntactically. Note that stored pattern-rule (24)(ii) is more abstract than input string (24)(i).

SAL Input String (24)(i) Matches Stored SAL Pattern (24)(ii).
(24)(ii)   *NP(PROCESS) Prep(locative-type) NP(non-process)*
            VAdj(PREPROCESS; past) Prep(by, via, etc.) NP(any agent) →
            (NP(prep NP)) VAdj Prep NP

Note that Translation Step Two corresponds to the *analogical* aspect of language acquisition and use, where input words are associated with members of their semantico-syntactic subclass stored in memory.

The chief intent of pattern-rule (24)(ii) is to effect resolution of the structural ambiguity in (24)(i) regarding which of the two nouns *produced by digitalis* relates to, *changes* or *cells*. The resolution of this structural ambiguity is accomplished via the action portion of pattern-rule (24)(ii) described in Translation Step Three.

Translation Step Three
Once this match is made, the source-action component of stored pattern-rule (24)(ii) is executed. The action here advances the source parse by re-writing input string (24) as the concatenated phrase shown after the arrow → in (24)(ii), effectively posting this intermediate analysis of phrase (24) in the source parse under construction.[14]

Translation Step Four
In Translation Step Four, a target-action component is linked to and executed. This target action component makes notations for the corresponding target string equivalent, preparatory to its eventual generation. Note that Translation Step Four embodies the developer's *empirically* acquired knowledge pertaining to target conventions as these relate to the source pattern at hand.[15]

Commentary
Note that the SAL codes in stored pattern-rule (24)(ii) are more general than those of input (24)(i). This is typical, and well illustrates the power of abstraction and the use of *analogy* in Logos Model.

---

[14] As sentence (24) passes through the *analytical* pipeline, it gets progressively rewritten until (24) in its entirety is reduced to *NP* (with *changes* as its head word).

[15] The target action is not an actual component of the source pattern, but is linked to by the source action. In general, target linking is optional and a source rule whose chief purpose is analytical may not always imply a target action. Activation components for many different target languages can be linked to from a single source pattern-rule, making Logos Model multi-target: one source language analysis, multiple target language generations.

3.5.1 Generate Target Translation[16]

In (24)(iii) we provide the eventual translation of (24) that occurs at the very end of the translation pipeline. In this case the output is in French.

(23)(iii)   ***Changements*** *de cellules* ***produits*** *par la digitaline.*

Commentary

Had Logos Model not resolved the structural ambiguity in (24), the past participle ***produits*** in (24)(iii) would have been incorrectly rendered with the feminine inflection, *produites*, reflecting the feminine gender of the adjacent noun *cells* rather than the masculine gender of ***changes***.[17]

3.5.2 OpenLogos and Logos Model

Logos Model development came to a halt in 2000, and the commercial version of this Model is no longer available, not even for testing. However, the German Research Center for Artificial Intelligence (DFKI) has adapted the commercial version to an open-source variant known as OpenLogos. Apart from DFKI's adaptation, no further development has taken place.[18] Except where noted, all translations in this book were done on an OpenLogos installation at INESC-ID in Lisbon, Portugal.[19]

It is not surprising that current MT systems, benefiting from continuous development, often outclass OpenLogos. The underlying Logos Model has undeniable strengths but it also had its weaknesses at the time of its shutdown, most especially in matters of target-language word selection (i.e., the *empirical* aspect of processing).

---

[16]Notations for target language generation are created in Translation Step Four but generation of the literal translation occurs at the end of the translation process.

[17]The French translation in (24)(iii) is taken from (Scott. 2003, 17) and was produced by a developmental version of Logos Model that never made it into a release prior to Logos Corporation shut down, possibly because the pattern-rule was too broad as written. In any case, (24)(iii) cannot be reproduced on OpenLogos. None of the other MT systems tested handled the gender of the participle in (24) correctly.

[18]The commercial version of Logos Model, however, has been resurrected for use at KIIT University in Odisha, India in connection with its English-Hindi project. This came about as an outgrowth of earlier work with OpenLogos at the International Institute for Information Technology (IIIT) in Hyderabad, India, again in connection with English-Hindi MT.

[19]It should be noted that output from OpenLogos on rare occasions is unable to reproduce output of the final release of the commercial system in 2000. The reason for this output difference is unknown.

Our claims on Logos Model's behalf chiefly concern its underlying computational principles and the semantico-syntactic translation mechanisms based on them. These mechanisms may be especially relevant as data-driven systems attempt more and more to cope with issues of complexity that hamper system improvements.

Despite shortcomings, Logos Model in 2000 was a competent MT system, as the OpenLogos output shown in this book will demonstrate.

In his book on statistical MT, Phillip Koehn (2011, 19) reproduced a French sentence with English translation that was submitted by the University of Edinburgh's SMT system to the 2005 WMT shared task competition. The French test sentence was taken from the European Parliament's Europarl parallel corpus that was used to train this SMT system. Table 3.1 shows the French test sentence together with its English translation by the University of Edinburgh system. What we have done is to add a Logos Model translation of the English SMT output back into French, the idea being that Logos Model's French output can then be compared with the original French sentence. In Table 3.1, the University of Edinburgh's English translation is in Column A, the original French test sentence is in Column B, and Logos Model back-translation is in Column C. Errors are underlined.

Table 3.1 English translation (in Column A) by University of Edinburgh's SMT system of a French test sentence (in Column B) taken from the proceedings of the European parliament. Column C shows Logos Model translation of the English in Column A back into the original French

A	B	C
English output from U. of Edinburgh's SMT translation of the French text in B	Original French text from the European Parliament proceedings	Logos Model translation of the English output in A back into French
We know very well that the current treaties are not enough and that in the future it will be necessary to develop a different and more effective structure for the union, a constitutional structure which clearly indicates what are the responsibilities of the member states and what are the competencies of the union.	Nous savons très bien que les Traités actuels ne suffisent pas et qu'il sera nécessaire à l'avenir de développer une structure plus efficace et différente pour l'Union, une structure plus constitutionnelle qui indique clairement quelles sont les compétences des États membres et quelles sont les compétences de l'Union.	Nous savons très bien que les traités actuels ne sont pas assez et qu'à l'avenir il sera nécessaire de développer une structure différente et plus productive pour l'union, une structure constitutionnelle qui indique clairement ce qui est les responsabilités des _états du membre_ et ce qui est les compétences de l'union.

Commentary

The original French text in Column B poses little difficulty for MT and, not surprisingly, all the systems we have been testing back-translated the text in Column A correctly, including Google GNMT Translate and Bing NMT Translator. Lack of prior exposure to Europarl and to political text generally would account for Logos Model falsely back-translating *member states* as *états du membre* (*states of the member*) rather than as *États membres*.

3.6 Conclusion

We trust that the above discussions and exercises speak well for the psycholinguistic principles we have outlined regarding language acquisition and use both by mind and by machine. In the next chapter, we examine neurolinguistic issues regarding the brain's handling of language. In that connection, we address a particularly critical problem for MT, one we term *cognitive complexity*. We examine why the translator's brain does not suffer from complexity, and explore the positive implications that complexity-free brain processes might have for MT optimization.

References

Chomsky N (1957) Syntactic structures. Mouton, The Hague/Paris

Chomsky N (2006) Language and mind. Cambridge University Press, Cambridge

Grishman R, Sager N, Raze C, Bookchin B (1973) The linguistic string parser. In: Proceedings of the national computer conference, pp 427–434

Koehn P (2011) Statistical machine translation. Cambridge University Press, Cambridge

Schmid P (1996) Clausal constituent shifts: a study in cognitive grammar and machine translation. Ph.D. Dissertation, Georgetown University. UMI Dissertation Services

Scott B (2003) Logos model: an historical perspective. Mach Transl 18(1):1–72

Chapter 4
Language and Complexity: Neurolinguistic Perspectives

Abstract In the previous chapter we dealt with the problem of ambiguity and how simulation of input-driven, psycholinguistic processes enables a semantico-syntactic translation model to deal effectively with ambiguity. In the present chapter we deal with the issue of complexity, focusing in particular on the constraining effect that *cognitive complexity* has on MT development as it attempts to cope with the ambiguities of langauge. We define *cognitive complexity* as the difficulty developers experience in maintaining complex systems. We show how the associative nature of Logos Model's neural-like translation paradigm allows it to deal more effectively with cognitive complexity than is possible with rule-based technology, or indeed any other MT paradigm. We attribute the reasons for this to Logos Model's serendipitous correspondence to findings of neuroscience on the brain's processing of language, citing the brain's evident freedom from complexity in processing language as a motivation for this direction in Logos Model design. We focus on two regions of the brain that are involved with language: (1) the prefrontal temporal cortex designated as the Broca area, commonly connected with rule-based processes, and (2) the hippocampus, a well-defined reticulum in the medial temporal lobe distinguished for its declarative, associative memory processes, and whose connection with language processes has only recently been proposed by neuroscientists. We provide illustrations and examples of how the associative processes of the hippocampus have been simulated in Logos Model, and how Logos Model has benefited from this simulation.

4.1 On Cognitive Complexity

COGNITIVE COMPLEXITY IS THE SPECIAL COMPLEXITY PROBLEM that traditionally afflicts large-scale MT development, especially MT that is being driven by rules of procedural logic.[1] We called this complexity *cognitive* because it concerns

---

[1] Cognitive complexity has only indirect connection with *complexity science* whose interest is in complex systems the behavior of which is not entirely explainable on the basis of system-component interactions. Complexity science may indeed be an issue in MT but the focus here has to do with the *cognitive* difficulty develops experience in maintaining complex systems.

© Springer International Publishing AG, part of Springer Nature 2018
B. Scott, *Translation, Brains and the Computer*, Machine Translation:
Technologies and Applications 2, https://doi.org/10.1007/978-3-319-76629-4_4

developers' ability to manage logic that must grow ever more complex if it is to cope with the intricacies and ambiguities of unconstrained language. This is especially so when it comes to decoding source language strings containing elements whose meanings or syntactic functions are equivocal.

In rule-based systems, resolution of syntactic and semantic ambiguities is dealt with by sequences of procedural logic that test for revealing contextual clues. The problem is that these procedures are based on generalized rules that will always have exceptions, and these exceptions will have their exceptions as well. Given the nature of language, developers of rule-based systems know there is never an end to these ramifications. And therein lies the cognitive problem. As the logic of these procedures become more complicated, the developers' ability to manage the logic inevitably gets challenged. Problems of logic inconsistencies are bound to arise; logic written to resolve one issue not infrequently undoes the resolution of some other issue. At some subsequent stage in development, these procedures are apt to show signs of conceptual incoherence, making further improvements increasingly difficult to implement. The developmental stasis that cognitive complexity thus gives rise to is nicely captured in the saying commonly heard among MT developers in the earlier days of MT: *"Stoop over to pick up one marble and you find you drop two."*

This issue of cognitive complexity is no less critical for developers of SMT (Koehn 2011) and NMT (Koehn and Knowles 2017) both of which systems internally rely upon nonlinear equations the effects of which can be difficult to interpret.

Fortunately, we at Logos were acutely mindful of this complexity issue from the very start of our own development effort. We intuitively understood we had to incorporate protection against complexity in the system we were building, that this was a make-or-break computational issue even more critical to our success than linguistics. Certainly, we would be dropping marbles too, but the marbles we dropped should be due to developers' momentary blindness to potential conflicts, and should generally be relatively easy to correct. And that is more or less the way it turned out. Dropped marbles were not uncommon, but were rarely if ever unmanageable; and most importantly, they were never signs of approaching stasis.

In this and in the chapters that follow, we hope to demonstrate a methodology for MT that literally removes the threat of developmental stasis altogether. Linguists who have struggled with advanced stages of MT development will recognize this as no small claim.

We begin with an example of the sort of complexity that a procedure-based system typically needs to contend with. Consider, for instance, the complexity of logic that would be needed in order to transfer into German the English morpheme *as* in (1) and (2), below. We highlight the different German transfers that are called for in each case.

(1a)   *as of April* ➔ *ab…*
(1b)   *as few as five* ➔ *nur…*
(1c)   *as many as five* ➔ *bis zu…*
(1d)   *as to his …* ➔ *im Bezug auf…*
(1e)   *as long as possible* ➔ *so lange wie…*

(1f) *as long as you insist, I will* ...→ *solange* ...
(1g) *four times as fast* → ... *so*...
(2a) *As you can see, he is sick.* → *Wie*...
(2b) *As he is sick, we cannot ask him to work.* → *Weil*...
(2c) *As he was being given his medicine, he began to choke.* → *Während*...
(2d) *As he began to recover his health, he realized that his wife
had stood by him through difficult times.* → *Als*...

In any English-German dictionary, the first translation given for *as* is *als*. In (1) and (2), however, notice that only one of the eleven transfers for *as* is rendered by *als*. There are in fact eleven different renderings of *as* in the German, depending on the context, which of course is the locus of the problem. A logic-driven process would have considerable difficulty characterizing (in any generalizable way) the varieties of context shown, especially in (2). It is theoretically possible, of course, but it seems it could hardly be done without persistent, backfiring consequences of the "unintended" kind, all of which is the earmark of complexity. By contrast, complexity is rarely a factor in human translation, and a reasonably competent human translator would have no difficulty whatsoever in handling these sentences.

It is instructive to ask why this is so. What is it about human sentence processing that allows the mind and underlying brain to escape complexity effects? Consider for a moment what must be going on in the human brain as it acquires language from early childhood on. Mistakes are made in the early stages and then, in the course of further sociolinguistic exposure, these mistakes simply cease to occur, virtually without conscious effort to correct them. And at no point in this lengthy development process does the normal brain feel overwhelmed by the intricacies of language. The normal brain's seemingly limitless capacity to absorb vocabulary and grammatical convention appears unaffected by complexity issues of any kind, including the kind alluded to above.

The point here is not that the brain does not make effective use of logic in many cognitive acts. That's hardly an issue. The question rather is the role that logic plays in neurolinguistic function, and whether in fact logic-driven procedures play any essential role at all in normal, spontaneous sentence processing. Because of its potential for complexity effects, it seemed to us that cerebral sentence processing could never be accomplished in logic-driven fashion and must be based on some other processing principle.

We thought we had a good idea of what that processing principle might be. It was a very simple notion, hardly original, but one utterly out of step with prevailing opinion. We conjectured that the brain's grasp of an input sentence emerges spontaneously from stored memory associations, and that the brain accomplishes its comprehension in unpredictable, opportunistic ways by virtue of these associations.[2]

---

[2] Palmer (2006). This author reminds us that Chomsky (1957) attacked Skinner's associationist perspectives expressed in the latter's *Verbal Behavior,* and thereby opened the door to a post-behaviorist era of rule-based linguistics.

This meant that human sentence processing is not driven by a detached body of logic embedded somewhere in specialized circuitry and that, upon input of a stream of words, begins to manage the brain's responses. On the contrary, it means that cerebral language processing is essentially driven by the language input stream itself. Cerebral language processing therefore is essentially declarative, at least as a customary matter—associative memory reacting selectively to input signals. What is pertinent here is that the declarative process we were assuming for the brain would make that process immune to logic saturation and all its attending woes. This declarative process was what we sought to imitate in Logos Model. We felt there had to be a way to do this if we were to avoid cognitive complexity and the risk of developmental stasis.

The declarative, associative process we came up with is illustrated in Fig. 4.1, below. As this Figure shows, Logos Model dispensed with rules and instead allows the input stream to interact with an associative memory store rich in patternized, semantico-syntactic knowledge. Graphic limitations unfortunately do not allow us to show SAL representation in Fig. 4.1, but the brain's actual processing of an input string, in our view, is not conducted chiefly at a literal level, as would be the case with data-driven systems like SMT and NMT, but at an increasingly more abstract, semantico-syntactic level. To simulate in Logos Model this assumption about how language is represented in the brain, literal input strings are converted to SAL strings during lexical lookup, at the very beginning of the MT process. The representational homogeneity that this conversion affords between a SAL input stream and the Model's SAL knowledge store is what enables an input sentence to serve as search argument to the store, freeing Logos Model of any need for mediating logic. In effect, input and linguistic store find each other automatically. This, in essence, is how complexity effects are avoided in Logos Model and we conjectured that something roughly analogous to this associative, data-driven process must also be taking place in the brain.

In Fig. 4.1 we see a simplified depiction of Logos Model's analysis of sentence (9), below, focusing here on just the first clause of the sentence. For simplicity sake, we depict Logos Model operating on literal language rather than on words of the SAL representation language. But SAL is what accounts for the efficiency of the method. For example, if (9) had replaced the phrase *kitchen table* with phrases like *the top shelf* or *the floor of the two-car garage*, etc., the same sequence of matches in [2] and [3] would have applied. Now let's look at how this first clause of (9) gets handled.

9)   *John **took** the things **from** the kitchen **table*** and put them away.

Analysis of the first clause of sentence in (9) is incremental, starting at step [1] with the noun phrase *the kitchen **table**.*[3]

---

[3] Processing prior to the sequences shown in Fig. 4.1 would have resolved the morpheme *table* to a noun rather than a verb.

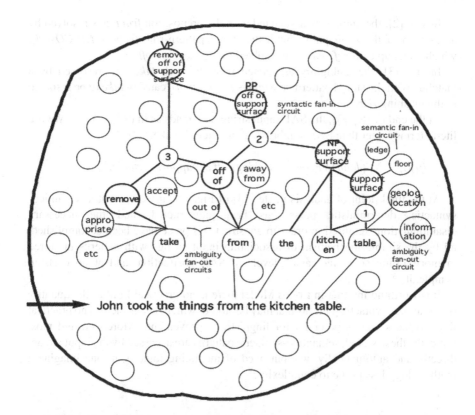

Fig. 4.1 *Sentence analysis by Logos Model, using the brain metaphor.* Blank cells in the Figure represent cells being ignored by the input's search for a match. (This is known both in computer science and in neurophysiology as *content addressable memory*.) Matching sequence begins at [1] and proceeds through [3], with each step dependent upon the results of the preceding match. Note the occurrence of semantic disambiguation of morphemes *took, from* and *table*, simultaneously with the accomplishment of a bottom-up, syntactic parse of the clause

In step [1], the semantic ambiguity of the noun *table* is resolved by its association with *kitchen*. This association is established by a matchup of the words *table* and *kitchen* in a thesaurus-like association table, enabling the pattern-rule to rewrite *the kitchen table* as an *NP* constituent for concrete nouns denoting support surfaces, *NP(COsurf)*.[4]

---

[4] The words *kitchen* and *table* share a common code (307 "eating") in the 4th edition of Cromwell's *Roget Thesaurus*. This shared code constituted a better scoring association between *kitchen* and the correct sense of *table* than was found for any other paired association of these two words. Resolution of common nouns remained experimental at Logos however, and never got to be implemented in the commercial product. See Postscript 4-B for all solutions that were being considered for resolving common noun polysemy.

In step [2], the ambiguity associated with the preposition *from* gets resolved by a matchup of the *from* phrase with the stored pattern-rule *from* + *NP(COsurf)*, which matchup causes *from* to be resolved to the meaning *off of*.

In step [3], the ambiguity associated with the verb *take* gets resolved by a matchup with the stored pattern-rule *take*+ *Prep (off of)*, causing *take* to be resolved to the meaning *remove*.

At the end of step [3], the SAL input string now reads as in (9)(i), below. We use literal terms rather than SAL symbols for simplicity's sake.

(9)(i)   *NP(John) VP(removed things off of support surface)*.[5]

At the final point of analysis in step [3] of Fig. 4.1, it's clear that a semantico-syntactic, deterministic parse has been constructed, and the necessary disambiguations required in order to construct this parse have been accomplished, all by the simple mechanism of associating input strings with patterns in stored memory, doing so at increasing levels of SAL abstraction, and at no costs in complexity.[6]

It is worth noting that in Logos Model there is no practical limit to the quantity of semantico-syntactic patterns that may be stored, which means there is no practical limit to the system's potential for linguistic improvement.[7] Moreover, and most critically, these stored, semantico-syntactic patterns are accessed by the input stream directly and automatically, without need of mediating logic. Can one imagine a methodology less prone to complexity?[8]

4.2   A Role for Semantic Abstraction and Generalization

A further assumption that guided our development concerned the role of abstraction (and generalization) in language processing. Abstraction, we reasoned, was one of the brain's principal means for protecting itself from complexity, for reducing

---

[5] See Postscript 6-B in Chap. 6 for translations of sentence (9) by Google Translate (both SMT and GNMT), by Microsoft's NMT Translator, and by Logos Model.

[6] The absence of semantics in Chomsky's syntax-first theory obliged him to preclude deterministic parsing by the brain. In *Aspects* (Chomsky 1965, 21f) he says that an individual's "internal grammar" unconsciously produces three structural descriptions for the sentence *"I had a book stolen."* One sees here the seeds of complexity being sown in Chomsky's approach to language; one cannot separate syntax and semantics without inviting ambiguities and their attendant complexity effects.

[7] In Logos Model, pattern-rules number in the tens of thousands. Because patterns are content-addressable, memory store size has markedly sub-linear effect on throughput.

[8] David G. Hays, MT pioneer (and originator of the term *computational linguistics*) is known to have identified the application of rules to the input stream as the most troublesome problem confronting MT. His observation was made at a time when MT was driven mostly by algorithms and rules. See Kay and Hays (2000).

unwieldy multiplicities to something more manageable by virtue of that reduction. In effect, abstraction is the means the brain uses to keep things simple. Arguably, an abstraction function seems to account for certain fundamental characteristics of brain physiology. This is suggested by the integrative structure of the brain cell. The prevalence of fan-in circuitry in the brain further suggests a structure designed for abstraction. (See this in Fig. 4.1, and Postscript 4-A for further discussion).

It seems reasonable to assume that the brain's physical provision for abstraction must be connected in some way with the generalization function so fundamental to language acquisition and use. We spoke at length of the role of analogy in Chap. 3, how the capacity for seeing analogies enables learners of a second language to generalize on limited instruction to thereby become fluent.

This role of generalization via analogy seems sufficiently self-evident in language acquisition and use. Below is a simple illustration of the role of generalization via analogy in MT, made possible by the abstraction language SAL, the basis of which rests on analogy.[9]

Suppose we are building an English-Russian translation system, and we are at the point where we need to specify translations for the English preposition *from*. The Russian language renders the English preposition *from* in four different ways, depending on the semantics of the preposition's object. (The different Russian transfers reflect the various senses of *from*, viz., *off of, away from, out of*.) For example, *from a table* takes the preposition *c* (*со стола*); *from a box* takes the preposition *из* (*из коробки*), *from the wall* the preposition *от* (*от стены*); and *from John* the preposition *у* (*у Ивана*).

Let's focus for a moment on the English phrase *from a box*. How might we generalize a single pattern-rule to translate *from a box* so that it would also translate related phrases like *from the tan purse, from my left pocket, from John's coffee cup, from each of the vials*, etc.? One way would be to do as we have done in Logos Model, namely:

a   Encode analogous nouns like *box, crate, socket, pocket, cup, vial,* etc., with a common SAL designation, namely with codes denoting: (a) receptacle-type nouns, (b) nouns that are functional things, (c) concrete nouns. Note that (a) to (c) constitute a SAL taxonomy of subset, set, and superset, respectively.

b   Store a pattern-rule in memory that would look like this:
(7) *from* + *NP(COrecep)*

---

[9] Pinker and Prince (1988) half agree on the role of analogy. They maintain that language use necessarily entails rule-based symbol manipulation, but such rules they say are few in number, supplemented by language patterns based on analogy. Note also Fauconnier (1997, p. 18): "*Analogical mapping is so common that we take it for granted. But it is one of the great mysteries of cognition.*"

This source pattern-rule will link to a target action that transfers the English *from* into the Russian *uз* (with meaning *out of*).[10]

    c   Process a literal input string such as, for example, *from my sister's new purse,* through the stages of analysis until the phrase ultimately gets rewritten as the SAL input string shown in (8):
          (8) *from* + *NP(COrecep)*

    d   At this more advanced stage of source analysis, SAL input string (8) now automatically matches the corresponding, stored pattern-rule in (7), based on their semantico-syntactic similarity. The match in turn causes a target action linked to (7) to transfer the English *from* into the Russian *uз* (*out of*).

The point here is that, because of abstraction, the stored SAL pattern-rule (7) would apply to endless variations of related input strings like, e.g., *from each glass on the table, from all three bags situated by the door,* etc., this because all these literal phrases would eventually get reduced to and represented by the abstract SAL input string pattern in (8). And the match of (8) with the pattern-rule in (7) would automatically occur because, at this level of the parse, input string (8) and stored SAL string (7) are sufficiently similar semantico-syntactically. (In this case of course they happen to be identical.)

The efficiency of this arrangement is obvious: one single, stored pattern-rule handling wide varieties of semantico-syntactically related input strings, which handling moreover gets to be effected automatically, without the need of mediating logic. Moreover, the appropriate pattern-rule is automatically applied only at the point when it should be. And finally, no inappropriate pattern-rule ever gets drawn into the matching process. It is hard to imagine an arrangement more efficient and less liable to complexity effects. Perhaps the most significant aspect of this arrangement is the fact that these pattern-rules can keep growing in number, without that growth in any way diminishing or complicating their individual effectiveness.

Our use of the brain metaphor in Fig. 4.1 is not meant to suggest that brain function was uppermost on our minds in those early days of our development. As a deep background matter, yes, but it wasn't until the late 1980s, almost 20 years after the start of our effort, that we became explicitly aware of actual, serendipitous parallels between the brain and Logos Model.

---

[10]There would have to be a longer pattern-rule to handle *from-to* constructions like *from the crate to the wall,* in which case *from* would be given a different transfer (viz., *om* (*away from*). This longer pattern-rule would preempt the shorter one in (7).

4.3   Connectionism and Brain Simulation

In the mid-1980s, a fascinating new development in cerebral simulation began to emerge in cognitive science. Researchers came on the scene producing interesting, computer-based models of brain function, along with attendant theories about these cognitive processes. This development came to be known as connectionism. It was an exciting discovery for us at Logos when we became aware of this effort. Here were theories and computer models that seemed to substantiate the hunches and intuitions that had been guiding our own work. For the first time we began to envision a rationale for what we were doing by instinct with such positive results.

This connectionist school had been developing in the background for decades, eventually evolving in the 1980s into a kind of computational neuroscience. Connectionism represented an attempt to understand the mind and underlying brain function in ways that radically departed from the classic views then prevailing in cognitive science, views that likened cognition to the algorithmic symbol-manipulations of a computer. Connectionism outright rejected this metaphor, exchanging it with models of neural networks extrapolated from empirically derived, neurophysiological data. As Fig. 4.2 illustrates, there is no role for rules in these models whatsoever. In its repudiation of the so-called classic theory of brain cognition, connectionism was reaffirming the behaviorists' associationist view of brain function, and indirectly confirming what we were doing in Logos Model.

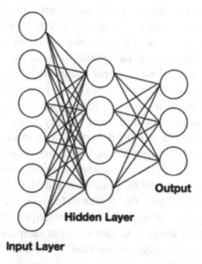

Fig. 4.2 *Early connectionist neural network with one hidden layer.* Interlayer connectivity among units (cells) of the network is universal (never specialized). Units in a layer have non-symbolic, numeric values that together comprise a single vector. In back-propagation models, unit weights are trained through repetitive feedback until an acceptable output is produced for given inputs. Meaning is represented by "spreading activation" across an entire network

Fig. 4.3 *Neuron*. (Image
from NIBS Pie, Ltd)

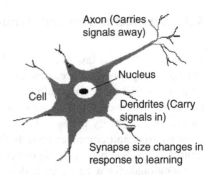

The movement gained considerable attention when researchers Rumelhart and
McClelland (1986) published their theory of Parallel Distributed Processing (PDP),
replete with striking, computer-based models of cerebral processes (Fig. 4.2).

Connectionism gave great encouragement to us at Logos. Here were models of
brain function where cognitive work was accomplished by learned associations
(connections), not by procedural manipulations. The all-sufficient role of connections in these models struck us as a telling reassertion of the role of associative
memory in brain function (Wang et al. 2014), one that would enable us to justify our
own associative methodology (See Postscript 4-C).

Units in these artificial neural nets were sometimes called "neurodes" and were
likened to neurons, with their connections representing synapses. One might regard
these networks as patterned after the anatomy of a single neuron (See Fig. 4.3). By
that analogy, units in the neural net's input layer function as dendrites that pass activation values to units in the hidden layer. (Neural net activation values are numbers
that stand for some feature outside the net.) Units in the hidden layer would then
represent a neuron's body (soma) where the work of the neuron is accomplished. In
these early neural nets, this work entails purely quantitative, algebraic functions that
correlate an input vector to a desired output result. In effect, a hidden layer re-calcu-
lates the activation value of the input vector it has received in accordance with the
connection weights of its own units. (In initial training, these connection weights
will have been set manually, or else automatically learned through a process of
back-propagation.) Hidden layer units then pass on recalculated activation values to
units in the output layer. Following the analogy, units in the output layer might then
be said to represent axonal fibers that convey the accomplishment of the neuron.

One early connectionist model by Rumelhart and McClelland (1986) describes a
neural net with two hidden layers that is able to learn and generate the past tense of
English verbs, both regular and irregular (See Postscript 4-D). This is accomplished
inductively, purely on the basis of numerous input samples, e.g., *place* ➔ *placed*,
sleep ➔ *slept*. No pre-stored rules of any kind are involved. Naturally this got our
attention at Logos. Here was neurolinguistic simulation that appeared to corroborate
our own views of language acquisition and use. Here were models of brain function
that eschewed anything that looked like rules of program logic. Here was a theory
that spelled out (for us at Logos) why the brain's cognitive function (and why
simulations of it) are free of cognitive complexity—for the simple reason that these

processes are driven by input data and feedback, not by pre-stored logic. Connectionist theory and its models were substantiating our conjecture that normal, neurolinguistic function consists of non-procedural responses to linguistic input based entirely on associations that are learned (under human supervision, in the case of Logos Model).

Connectionists admitted their models were never more than *"crude approximations"* of cortical circuits. Units within a neural net layer typically are of one kind only, forward projecting. In PDP models there are none of the lateral connections between units (so-called *local* or *intrinsic* connectivity) that characterize actual cortical circuits.[11] The most radical feature of connectionist nets is that their internal units have no fixed meanings; hidden-layer units are reusable like the receptors of charged couple devices in a digital camera. Moreover, connectionist neural nets represent symbolic meaning strictly by the activation pattern across an entire layer of units; units at the individual level essentially remain meaningless.

And there's nothing in these models comparable to the role of chemical neurotransmitters in interneuronal connectivity, or to the brain's neuromodulation function, a special kind of chemical neuronal output that modulates behavior in a wider population of brain cells. Perhaps as a consequence of its shortcomings, connectionism waned in the decade or so that followed its heyday. More recently, of course, all this has changed. In the past few years, neural net technology has undergone a most profound resurgence with the advent of new models known as "deep neural nets" (Shujie Liu et al. 2014).[12]

Connectionism's effect on neurobiological modeling has nevertheless been lasting. And its widely promulgated thesis that meaning is expressed by *distributed representation* (i.e., by activation across an entire cortical circuit) has likely encouraged a number of neurophysiologists to modify (if not outright abandon) notions of local representation, i.e., representation at the level of a single neuron. (See Postscript 4-E for a discussion of single cell representation.)

To be sure, connectionism has always had its critics among classically oriented cognitive scientists.[13] These critics acknowledge that connectionism is good at making associations and matching up patterns, but argue that higher levels of cognition, like those involved in the processing of language, must necessarily entail something more than word associations. Invariably what these critics are referring to is the need for abstract rules, by which they generally mean rules for syntax. They

---

[11] See image of a canonical cortical circuit in Fig. 4.4.

[12] Deep learning AI centers around the world are combining so-called "deep" neural net technology with statistical technology to produce machine translation (NMT) models of great promise, as the present book seeks to indicate. This new technology however is more motivated by trends in AI and machine learning than by early connectionist concerns for biological verisimilitude. See Chap. 8 for a fuller discussion of this development.

[13] Pinker and Prince (1988) criticize connectionism's weakness *vis à vis* generalization and the absence of any use of analogy in their models.

question whether there is any way apart from rules to account for the assembling of grammatical sentences from conceptual thought. When it comes to sentence generation, their question may be legitimate, but our concern here is with the analysis of a source language sentence, not its generation, and in regard to sentence analysis, an absolute need for rules is certainly questionable.

The present work, while not intended as a defense of connectionism, nevertheless found support there for our conjecture that neurolinguistic processes (sufficient for sentence-level analysis) can be simulated by the application not of rules but of acquired language patterns stored in associative memory. Apart from this common ground, however, Logos Model and connectionism embody significant differences: the numeric patterns in Logos Model represent language symbolically, not literally, and Logos Model's reliance on abstract analogy had no counterpart in connectionism.

4.4   Logos Model As a Neural Network

Figure 4.4, below, depicts Logos Model architecture as a recursive, *symbolic* neural net. Clearly, Fig. 4.4 could not have been drawn before the appearance of connectionism.[14] We reproduce the diagram here because, serendipitously, the associative, rule-free processes of Logos Model depicted in the diagram well illustrates Logos Model's commensurability with more recent deep neural net architecture and function, notwithstanding the computational differences that otherwise separate the two paradigms (Scott 1989, 1990, 2003).[15]

In Fig. 4.4, Logos Model is depicted as a stacked net with six hidden layers, R1–P4. Units in these hidden layers are pattern-rules, organized according to their

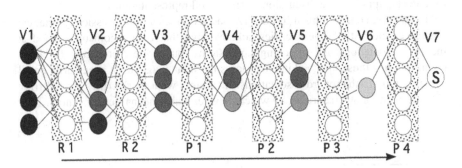

Fig. 4.4 *Logos Model as a hierarchical, symbolic neural net*

---

[14] Figure 4.4, originally drawn for internal use in the mid-1990s, appears in Scott (2000, 2003).

[15] For a fuller depiction of Logos Model connectivity, see Fig. 4.7. See Socher et al. (2011) for description of a *non-symbolic* recursive neural net. It is clear that Logos Model anticipated recursive nets *architecturally*, but hardly so in computational respects (See Chap. 8).

semantico-syntactic pattern as in a dictionary. V1–V7 are variable length input/output layers whose units represent words and phrases of the input sentence. Units in both hidden layers and I/O layers have values expressed in SAL symbology (which happens to be numeric). The weight of hidden layer units affecting matchups is a function both of units' semantico-syntactic specificity and units' pattern length.

Notice how the output of each hidden layer serves as input to the next, and how the progressive reduction in the number of units in the output layers, ending in the symbol S, signifies performance of a bottom-up parse. Changes from dark to light in the shadings of these output units signify progressive semantic disambiguation, mostly with verbs and prepositions.[16]

A hidden layer in Logos Model may contain as many as four thousand units or more,[17] with lateral links (not shown) to an even greater number of local (intrinsic) units that support nested semantic disambiguation functions. Note the all-important fact that matchups (connections) between I/O and hidden layers are never rule-driven, i.e., entail no mediating logic.

Each unit of a hidden layer comprises, as its chief component, a pattern of semantico-syntactic (SAL) elements. Once a potential matchup of input patterns and stored patterns is made, pattern-rule constraints must then be satisfied, e.g., various tests on the input pattern itself, or of neighboring or net-wide conditions that must be true for the pattern-rule to fire. Once the pattern-rule is allowed to fire, certain actions take place. These actions may include any and all of the following: (i) nested matching on a huge body of lateral (local or intrinsic) pattern-rules for purposes of semantic disambiguation; (ii) source-pattern concatenation and rewriting to an output layer (e.g., *DET N* ➔ *NP*), along with incremental parse construction; (iii) communications to its entire hidden layer, and (iv) feedback of some sort of change to the input pattern of its own input layer, calling for a repeat of the original search based on the change of information. Notice how recurrent operations like (iii) and (iv) allow a given pattern-rule to modulate the course of subsequent analysis even within the current layer.

There is also a link (when appropriate) to a target action commensurate with the source action. Target links can be for any number of target languages working off the same source matchup.

Notice in Fig. 4.4 that connectivity between units of input and hidden layers is always specialized, unlike the universal connectivity of connectionist models shown in Fig. 4.2. In effect, units in input and hidden layers automatically connect when their patterns are sufficiently similar to represent the best of all possible matches, i.e., the most semantico-syntactically specific of all potential matches.

---

[16] Logos Model's dealing with common noun polysemy is limited to the use of Subject Matter Codes (SMC) specified at run time. For example, the technical meaning and transfer for the word *bug* would be selected at run time, assuming the lexicon contained an entry for *bug* having the *technology* SMC designation, and that the user specifies this *technology* SMC at run time. In general, this solution has not proved effective inasmuch as the majority of common nouns are not distinguishable by subject matter. See fuller discussion in Postscript 4-B

[17] The function of these hidden layers will be discussed in Chap. 6.

Graphic limitations in Fig. 4.4 only allow depiction of forward-projecting connections. Not shown is Logos Model's use of lateral (local or intrinsic) connections, and recurrent connections that feedback to the input layer (See Fig. 4.7).

As suggested earlier, there were significant differences between these earlier, connectionist neural nets (CNN) and Logos Model (LM). These differences are enumerated in the list of features shown in Table 4.1. Note that Logos Model will be seen to

Table 4.1 Features of neural nets, Logos Model and cortical circuits

Number of hidden (working) layers:
CNN: one to three (later "deep" neural nets typically have many more layers)[a]
LM: six working layers (see Fig. 4.4, above)
CC: six working layers (laminae)[b]
Number of units (cells):
CNN: typically c. 300 or fewer neurodes (deep neural nets may be vastly larger)
LM: c. 25,000 units (pattern-rules) spread over six hidden layers
CC: billions of cells spread over six laminae
Types of units or cells:
CNN: one monolithic type
LM: five types of units (pattern-rules), plus several subtypes (see Fig. 4.7, below)
CC: 12 distinct types, plus numerous subtypes[c]
Types of unit or cell connectivity:
CNN: purely forward-projecting
LM: (a) forward; (b) local (lateral or intrinsic); (c) recurrent
CC: (a) forward; (b) local (lateral or intrinsic); (c) recurrent
Representation:
CNN: meaning represented by spreading activation across entire net
LM: meaning represented by single unit or patterns of such units
CC: meaning represented by single cells or clusters of cells (See discussion in Postscript 4-E)
Architecture:
CNN: monolithic
LM: modular
CC: modular
Fan-in/Fan-out circuitry:
CNN:fan-in only
LM: both
CC: both
Neuromodulation (type of output that modulates an entire cortical region):
CNN: no
LM: yes
CC: yes

[a]See Chap. 8 for discussion of the more recent appearance of deep neural networks
[b]Ramon y Cajal's classical view of cortical lamination envisioned six layers (Crick and Asanuma 1986). Ramon y Cajal (1852–1934) is often spoken of as the father of neuroscience. His landmark studies of brain anatomy are still in use today
[c]Sejnowski (1986). Cells include pyramid, stellate, basket, granular, etc

have closer parallels with cortical circuits (CC). These entirely fortuitous parallels with brain circuits struck us at Logos as a great curiosity when we first became aware of them, causing us to refer to Logos Model as a "*bionet*" (Scott 1990).

These apparent parallels between cortical circuits and Logos Model and what they imply for machine translation will be examined in a moment. But first we need to review briefly the views and conjectures of neuroscientists on how language is processed by the brain. As we will see, there is little consensus on this issue.

4.5   Language Processing in the Brain

Despite many decades of neurological study in schools, clinics and laboratories around the world, much about how the brain comprehends and produces language acts is admittedly still not understood, both functionally and anatomically. And some matters that had been considered settled are now being rethought. For example, in the last quarter of the nineteenth century it was believed that language production is handled by the loosely defined prefrontal temporal area named after Pierre Paul Broca, and that the even more loosely defined parieto-temporal area named after Carl Wernicke handles comprehension. (See Fig. 4.5, below.) These views originated in findings that trauma to these brain areas resulted in language impairment (aphasia). Nowadays these older models of cerebral language processing are steadily

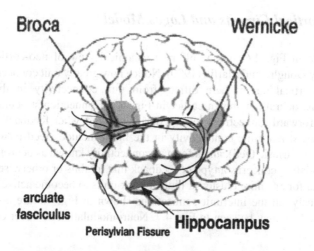

Fig. 4.5 *Language areas of the brain*. Because lesions to the Broca and Wernicke areas have resulted in language impairment (aphasia), these areas have long been associated with language, the former with production, the latter with comprehension. These areas have never been well defined anatomically or functionally. The perisylvian cortex is also now considered an important general language area in the brain. More recently, the highly defined hippocampus reticulum has also been associated with language use and processing. (Image adapted from National Institute of Health publication 97-4257)

being refined by high-tech neuroimaging studies, and a far more complex under-standing of language and the brain is emerging. Associated with language processes now are such areas as the larger perisylvian cortex of the left hemisphere, the basil ganglia and only very recently, the hippocampus, a reticulum within the medial temporal lobe.[18]

Despite progress, no single theory has yet emerged among neuroscientists regarding the brain's handling of language. Are the brain's linguistic processes procedural, driven by neuronal circuits that function like rules, or are they declarative and similarity-based, driven by associations? Is syntax handled separately from semantics, or are these aspects of language interwoven? Is there neurological evidence favoring one view over the other? There is as yet little agreement among neuroscientists on any of these issues.

In what follows we elaborate a bit further on the curious, albeit entirely serendipitous parallels found to exist between Logos Model and cortical circuits. We focus in particular on how units within a circuit or network connect with each other in order to accomplish their work. As we have already suggested, Logos Model connectivity has more in common with actual cortical circuits than with early neural net models. And as we shall go on to show, this commonality is particularly striking in the case of the hippocampus, a uniquely well-defined reticulum in the medial temporal area that has only recently been linked to language processing and to language acquisition in particular.[19]

4.5.1 Cortical Circuits and Logos Model

The graphic in Fig. 4.6, below, offers a canonical view of neo-cortical circuits proposed by Douglas and Martin (1990). Notice how greatly unit connectivity of the canonical cortical circuit here differs from unit connectivity in the standard connectionist neural net shown earlier in Fig. 4.2. Connectionist neural nets only entail feed-forward connectivity (except during training, when feedback occurs.) As Fig. 4.6 shows, real-time connectivity in the brain includes feed-forward, lateral feed (local or intrinsic feed), and a form of connectivity known as neuromodulation. Neuromodulation concerns a type of feedback that inhibits or otherwise modulates the potential for an entire cluster of hidden layer units to become active.

Fortuitously, all the interunit connections shown in Fig. 4.6 are also found in Logos Model, as may be seen in Fig. 4.7. Neuromodulation however could not be illustrated.

---

[18] Kurczek et al. (2013), Duff and Brown-Schmidt (2012, web): *"… we propose the hippocampus as a key contributor to language use and processing.";* Duff and Brown-Schmidt (2017).

[19] In our view, a machine's acquiring of a sentence for translation is akin to human language acquisition. Both have to take in and decode an initially meaningless string of symbols. Note that in machine learning parlance, this acquisition process is called encoding rather than decoding.

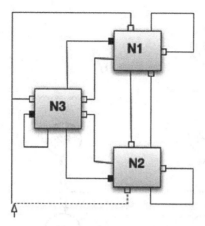

Fig. 4.6 *Canonical view of cortical circuits.* N1, N2 and N3 represent small clusters of neurons. The arrow at bottom left signifies input from some external source. Dark connections between clusters constitute inhibiting synapses. Light connections constitute activating synapses. Although it is not entirely clear in the graphic, all clusters feed forward, laterally, and back on themselves. Note that synapses caused by N3 are all inhibitory. (Graphic adapted from Douglas and Martin (1990))

These interconnections are what allow Logos Model to process language in heuristic ways without incurring complexity problems. In short, input sentences connect with stored pattern-rules in synaptic-like fashion. Output in turn connects with other stored pattern-rules in a process that gets repeated in unpredictable albeit entirely traceable ways until all ambiguities are resolved and optimal abstraction is achieved (i.e., work is complete).

4.5.2   *Hippocampus and Logos Model*

In what follows we discuss a particularly interesting parallel that was found to exist between Logos Model and one of the brain's most recently recognized language areas. This refers to the hippocampus, an unusually well-defined reticulum located within the medial temporal lobe (refer back to Fig. 4.5).

What initially drew us to the hippocampus was its unusual anatomy (See Fig. 4.8.), one that bore an intriguing resemblance to Logos Model architecture depicted in a more traditional pipeline manner in Fig. 4.9. Despite the fact that the hippocampus, at that point in time, had not yet been seen to have any connection with language use and processing, its anatomical parallels with Logos Model, even if superficial, naturally attracted our interest. Compare Fig. 4.8, for example, with the more conventional depiction of Logos Model architecture shown in Fig. 4.9. In the depictions in both Figures, the workflow appears to be accomplished

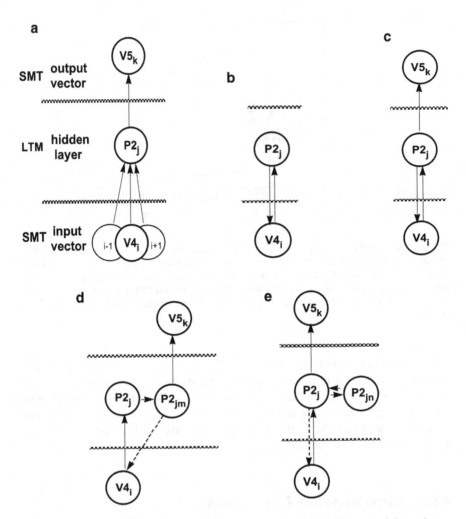

Fig. 4.7 *Varieties of interneuronal connectivity in Logos Model.* (**a**) Upon match by an input-pattern in short-term memory (SMT), hidden layer pattern-rules in long-term memory (LTM) here rewrite input pattern to output vector. (**b**) Here pattern-rules in long-term memory rewrite input pattern back to the input vector or otherwise modulate the entire net. (**c**) Here long-term pattern-rules rewrite to both input and output short-term memory vectors, or modulate the entire net. (**d**) Here pattern-rules conduct nested searches on so-called local or intrinsic pattern-rules which, upon a match, rewrite input to the output vector. They may also modulate the input vector or the entire net. (**e**) These pattern-rules are a variant of those in (**d**)

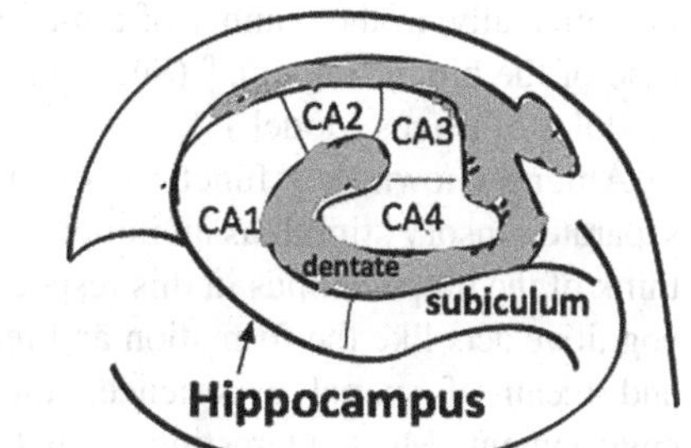

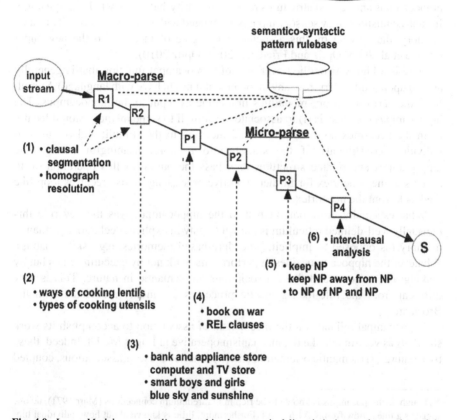

Fig. 4.8 *Quasi-pipeline image of the hippocampus*

Fig. 4.9 *Logos Model as a pipeline*. Graphic shows typical linguistic issues that each module addresses

incrementally, in the manner of a modularized pipeline (rather misleadingly in the case of the hippocampus).[20] (See Chap. 6 for complete elaboration of the pipeline modules of Logos Model.)

Among known, key functions of the hippocampus is the relational binding of separate sensory stimuli as an initial step leading to meaningful cognition. One can think of the hippocampus in this respect as a cognitive assembly area. This includes cognitive acts like the formation and recall of episodic memory, and the formation and recall of spatial experience, allowing rats for example to relate to their environment. Most interesting from the perspective of language is the role the hippocampus and related structures play in similarity-based knowledge acquisition. In such acquisition, new sensory input is associated with stored, semantically related memory, thus giving by this association a degree of meaning to the new input (Henke et al. 2003; Optiz and Friederici 2003; Optiz 2010).

Here is a highly simplified overview of hippocampal function that is generally agreed upon (quite apart from any involvement it might have with language). Stimuli from the various sensory modalities first come as input to the hippocampus. The hippocampus response is (i) to associate the stimuli to some memory stored locally or in the neocortex so as to give initial meaning to the stimuli; and (ii) to bind individual constituents of the stimuli into a more meaningful whole. The hippocampus and related structures then pass the output of this operation on to regions of the neocortex for further cognitive processing. It also receives loop-like feedback from the neocortex.[21]

What especially drew our interest to the hippocampus was the key role this unusually well-defined reticulum is known to play in explicit, declarative, semantic memory (as opposed to implicit, procedure-based memories, e.g., skills, habits). Whatever the hippocampus does, it performs its work not by executing rules but by making associations, and these associations are semantic in nature. This is very different from the rule-like, syntactic processes commonly associated with the Broca area.[22]

Hippocampal reliance on the mechanism of association to accomplish its work struck us as very much like the mechanism operative in Logos Model. Indeed, these two features, (i) semantic orientation and (ii) functional use of associations, coupled

---

[20] Though the hippocampus is known to be rich in intrareticulum connections (Marr 1971), no one suggests a linear flow from CA1 to CA4. Furthermore, little is known about how individual hippocampal modules relate to language use and processing. Wintzer et al. (2014) and Kumaran et al. (2016), among others, find that CA3 is recruited for associative encoding and recall as a general matter. O'Keefe and Dostrovsky (1971) have correlated individual neuron firings in the CA1 module with rats' movements to specific locations. Fanselow and Dong (2010) functionally segregate the hippocampus into a cognitive area (dorsal region) and an affective area (ventral region).

[21] The hippocampal system includes the parahippocampal gyrus, dentate gyrus, entorhinal cortex, and subiculum.

[22] See Postscript 4-F for further discussion. The differences here between the hippocampus and Broca might be gleaned by what is happening in the first versus the second "take" of a troublesome sentence. The first take pertains to ordinary language processes, the double take to puzzle work that typifies much of neuropsychological testing.

with the key role the hippocampus is known to play in cognitive memory, persuaded us right from the start that the hippocampus must surely have something to do with language acquisition and use.[23]

Apart from our interest however, none of the literature in the late 1980s had suggested that the hippocampus had anything to do with language processing per se. Perhaps this delay was due to the following factors: (i) the traditional reliance (before neuroimaging) on brain trauma to identify cerebral language areas like Broca and Wernicke; (ii) the disdain into which associationism had fallen through the influence of early generative grammar and its shift to rule-based processes; and (iii) the fact that there is nothing in the semantically-oriented, similarity-based processes of the hippocampus that suggests unique, language-specific function.

It is true of course that Alzheimer's disease has long been known to affect the hippocampus, and that this disease has always been found to impair a subject's vocabulary recall. But this well-established circumstance notwithstanding, virtually none of the literature suggested the hippocampus had anything to do with the mechanisms of sentence processing. Now this is changing as neuroimaging studies reveal strong hippocampus involvement with language learning and use (Kurczek et al. 2013; Duff and Brown-Schmidt 2012; Duff and Brown-Schmidt 2017), and most notably with second language acquisition.

A recent Swedish study found pronounced hippocampus involvement in an experiment dealing with second language acquisition (Mårtensson et al. 2012). In this study, the brains of language students at the Swedish Armed Forces Interpreter Academy were examined before and after three months of intense, 8-h a day foreign language study. A group of hard-working medical students not involved in any kind of foreign language study were included as a control group. The results of the experiment were quite revealing. The hippocampi of the students at the interpreter school were found to have grown significantly in grey matter as a consequence of second language acquisition. This was especially so in the case of students who found it easiest to acquire the new language. By contrast, none of the related brain structures of the medical students experienced comparable change. Other brain areas that are known to be involved in language (including Broca) also grew as a result of the engagement. The study also found that these various language-related areas developed differently, depending on how proficient the linguist students were and how much effort they needed in order to learn a new language.[24]

---

[23] The present author presciently argued for such a connection in (Scott 1990, 2000). It took almost two decades for the literature to come to the same conclusion (Optiz 2010); Duff, Brown-Schmidt (2012 web): *"We conclude that the relational binding...afforded by the hippocampal declarative memory system positions the hippocampus as a key contributor to language use and processing."* See further discussion of this in Postscript 4-G.

[24] The authors found that the hippocampus became more active in students exhibiting higher proficiency in the foreign language. Students having more difficulty in mastering the language displayed larger gray matter increases in the middle frontal gyrus (general Broca region). This would seem to comport with our impression of Broca as being more analytical in its functioning, virtually the opposite of hippocampal associative binding.

In another study in Germany, 14 healthy young subjects learned a novel vocabulary of 45 concrete nouns via an associative learning principle. In the process, the hippocampi of these students were monitored using event-related functional magnetic resonance imaging (e-fMRI). The study found that successful acquisition of a new vocabulary correlated with marked amplitude changes between the left hippocampus and neocortical regions, and moreover that this correlation was less marked in the case of students less able to acquire and master new vocabulary (Breitenstein et al. 2004).

Even though the hippocampus is becoming recognized as having a key role in the acquisition and use of language, its precise place and function in the cerebral language picture is still far from settled. What seems to have become clear however is that the hippocampus is the first cerebral area to become engaged in language activity, as the language acquisition studies cited above illustrate. But contrariwise, neuroimaging data has also shown that after gaining proficiency, a subject's hippocampus involvement lessens.[25,26]

It is instructive to try and understand this finding because of its bearing on a central topic of our book, namely, the relative roles of the two distinct aspects of language processing—on the one hand the syntactic, rule-driven processes that neuropsychologists generally locate in the neocortical, Broca area, and on the other hand the semantic, declarative processes associated with the hippocampus. Neuropsychologists suggest that areas of the neocortex eventually become dominant once the explicit learning processes of the hippocampus cede dominance to skills consolidated elsewhere in memory.[27] But does this eventual dominance of the neocortex prove that Chomsky and the generativists are correct in their assertions about the priority of syntax? It seems that this is hardly a necessary conclusion. For one thing, other neuronal areas recruited for language, like the perisylvian, the

---

[25] Optiz and Friederici (2003). This and similar studies found reduced hippocampal involvement in *grammaticality* judgments, but do not shed any light on hippocampus involvement in ordinary, everyday language use, a matter exceedingly more difficult to study (See Chap. 5 on this).

[26] Squire and Sola-Morgan (1991, 1380): "*[The hippocampus and related structures], presumably by virtue of their widespread and reciprocal connections with neocortex, are essential for establishing long-term memory for facts and events (declarative memory). The medial temporal lobe memory system [hippocampal area] is needed to bind together the distributed storage sites in neocortex that represent a whole memory. However, the role of the hippocampus system is only temporary. As time passes after learning, memory stored in neocortex may gradually become independent of medial temporal lobe structures.*" Note that the relevance of the foregoing for language is only by implication, and in any case seems outdated.

[27] In neuropsychology, explicit knowledge is knowledge that can be recalled and articulated. Explicit knowledge is also known as declarative knowledge, and is the sort of knowledge dealt with in the hippocampus. Declarative knowledge is characterized as a *knowing that* as opposed to a *knowing how*. Implicit knowledge (the *knowing how* in the neocortex) refers to skills, habits (procedures of an automatic nature) that are largely subconscious, a tacit knowledge that is more or less inarticulable. In *second* language acquisition (L2), one can conjecture that as skills develop, habit may eventually replace the initial, more explicit, declarative role of the hippocampus. The matter is viewed quite differently with *first* language acquisition (L1) however. DeKeyser (2008) holds that children acquire their native languages through implicit, inductive, essentially inarticulable processes right from the start.

parieto-temporal Wernicke area, and even the Broca area, are also known for making semantic associations. Moreover, all of these neocortical areas interact with the hippocampus as well.

Furthermore, even as these neocortex-based language skills develop, neuroimaging data show that the hippocampus still remains active in everyday language processes, even if no longer dominant.[28] Every fresh language string being input to the brain must still undergo a hippocampal binding function, and thus each new input, each new sentence, must undergo a fleeting moment of acquisition, of learning, before being passed on for further cognitive work (McClelland et al. 1995).[29] Such learning, however fleeting, would have to involve the declarative, associative functions of the hippocampus. Certainly this would seem to be especially so in the context of translation where a source language string must first be acquired and then associated with a target language equivalent. As the Swedish study alluded to above suggests, the process in the initial stages of acquiring a second language (both by mind and machine) is not essentially implicit, skill-based and inarticulable, but rather remains declarative and intrinsically explicit, even if later superseded to some extent by honed skills housed in the neocortex.

But what was most interesting to us about the hippocampal reticulum was yet another matter. If the hippocampus, in its handling of language, is performing only general cognitive operations like those described above, and evinces no need of language-specific functionality, this then suggests that the associative processes that typify much of cognition in general could also be a sufficient basis for the cortical handling of language, certainly language as used under ordinary conditions. This is the argument of the cognitive linguistics school which holds that, contrary to generative grammar, language processing cannot be isolated from semantics and the rest of cognition in general (Lakoff 1987; Fillmore et al. 1988; Robinson 2008). In this view, Broca and syntax would become dominant only when a certain level of analysis was called for, as for example in the case of troublesome structural ambiguities that normal declarative, associative processes cannot resolve.[30,31]

---

[28] Recent studies by Verfaellie et al. (2014) and Race et al. (2015) report that even when consolidated elsewhere in the neocortex, semantic memories remain dependent upon the hippocampus for retrieval.

[29] Obviously it takes the higher cognitive regions of the neocortex for the mind to realize that an utterance like *colorless green ideas sleep furiously* is capricious.

[30] A lexical recognition study by Fiebach et al. (2002) found that the Broca area (Brodmann Area 44) is especially activated for low-frequency and pseudowords, whereas high-frequency words activate the middle temporal gyrus (MTG - BA21). The middle temporal gyrus (MTG) is not to be confused with the medial temporal lobe (hippocampus), but studies link MTG to the medial temporal lobe (hippocampus), a link made evident in cases of semantic memory impairment (Chan et al. 2001).

[31] Bonhage et al. (2015). This recent study showed that in a comprehension exercise, the hippocampus, and regions closely linked to it, handled regular sentences and the Broca area handled nonsense sentences.

It may be, of course, that Broca and related regions become activated not only to resolve the puzzles that typify acquisition studies of artificial grammars, but may become active even in ordinary disambiguation tasks of the sort the brain must continually deal with, doing so implicitly (i.e., without articulable awareness).[32] Given that syntactic and semantic ambiguities are to be found everywhere in language, the brain clearly has to somehow deal with them, no less than a translation machine. Take, as a simple example of this (for those who know German), the various roles and meanings that the common morpheme *das* can have, viz., *the, that, who, which* (article, pronoun, relative pronoun). The role and meaning of this ambiguous morpheme have to be resolved every time *das* is heard or read. It is not as simple a matter as one might think. For example, one might expect that the *das* in a string like *das Bier* can only be an article, just like *das* in the first word of (10). But consider the expression in (10):

(10)   *Das Mädchen, das Bier bringt.*

In (10), the second instance of *das* is a relative pronoun with the meaning of *who* (*The girl who brings beer*). No less than in the computer, some area of the brain has to resolve this *das* ambiguity in (10), and the area that does this may very well be Broca-related, with its tacit, analytical processes rather than the more explicit, associative processes of hippocampus.[33]

So it may be that a division of labor exists between association-oriented hippocampus and rule-oriented Broca and related regions.[34] We can speculate that, upon fresh input, the hippocampus would immediately become activated for purposes of assembling meaningful sentences, one after the other, and that Broca would be drawn in whenever some interpretive difficulty is encountered that impedes arrival at meaning, difficulties like ambiguity, embeddings and long-distance dependencies. If that is indeed the case, then all but the simplest, unambiguous sentences in English might well entail this interactive, loop-like division of labor. Indeed, real-time interaction between the hippocampus and the neocortex (including Broca) is now generally recognized,[35] but so far this interaction has not been interpreted. Conceivably, the interpretation offered above just might apply.

---

[32] Glaser et al. (2013) show that IFG areas BA44 and BA45 (Broca area) are recruited when embeddings and long-distance dependencies cause comprehension "*interference*."

[33] The two SMT versions of Google Translate and Microsoft's Bing Translator, not known for parsing, nevertheless both resolved *das* to *who* and thus translate (10) correctly. The subsequent NMT versions of these system (plus Logos Model) also translate (10) correctly. Ironically, the two hybridized, rule-based systems we have been testing, PROMT Translator and SYSTRANet, both misresolve *das* in (10) to the article.

[34] Duff and Brown-Schmidt (2012, 8): "*A compelling approach to addressing these questions is to examine language at the intersection of declarative and non-declarative memory systems and to view the activities of language...as necessitating a division of labor between the memory systems.*" This clearly refers to the declarative hippocampus and procedure-based Broca, respectively.

At any rate, this interaction between binding and analysis, between fan-in concatenation and fan-out analysis is precisely what takes place in Logos Model, as illustrated earlier in Fig. 4.1. Something not too dissimilar might be taking place in the interactions of these separate and distinct regions of the brain. And if that is so, one might ask whether Logos Model, like connectionism three decades ago, might not have something to contribute to neurolinguistic discussion. Logos Model, after all, can rightfully be construed as a highly developed instance of recursive, *symbolic* neural net technology. Neuroscience itself will judge whether there is any theoretical significance to be derived from a model that has shown itself effective in processing language chiefly along hippocampal lines.[35] And most especially a model that, like the brain, is free of complexity effects. Indeed, neuroscientists who argue for a procedurally based approach to cerebral language processing ought to explain how brain performance manages to avoid complexity effects.[37] Apart from Logos Model with its simulation of the brain, no MT system has ever managed to do so.

4.6 MT Performance and Underlying Competence

At the beginning of the present chapter, we presented a set of English sentences in (2) that employed the morpheme *as* in an initial sentence position with various meanings. We observed that the German translations of these various senses of *as* in each case had to be a function of the context that followed. We then suggested that logic-driven systems would find it difficult to specify these contexts in a general way without running into complexity effects of the "unintended" kind. Now, before we conclude the present chapter, it seemed appropriate to examine how all the MT systems we have tested, of whatever methodology, handle the ambiguity of the word

---

[35] Kumaran et al. (2016, web): *"The hippocampus and the neocortex interact...to support interleaved learning... [However] many types of learning are initially hippocampus dependent."*

[36] Duff, Brown-Schmidt (2012, 5): *"These provocative findings regarding the hippocampal contributions to online [language] processing have profound implications for theories of language processing and use...and should encourage increased interest in the relationship between language and declarative memory."*

[37] It is a curious circumstance that complexity effects are so little addressed in neuroscience's discussions of language. A collection of papers entitled *Pattern Perception and Computational Complexity,* edited by W. Tecumseh Fitch et al. (2012), largely focuses on complexity as a characteristic of different grammars, but not as a general, computational difficulty in the handling of language that needs to be accounted for. One particularly interesting paper in this collection by M. H. de Vries et al. (2012), deals with extreme examples of multiple, long-distance and crossed dependencies, and of the memory *"overload"* that they engender, illustrating in the authors' words the *"upper limits of both human sequence learning and natural-language processing"* (p. 2074). But we still want to learn from neuroscientists their views as to why and how our underlying competence for language handles the complexity potential of everyday language use, language use that so challenges the machine and its MT developers but hardly the brain.

as in (2). We duplicate (2a–2d) as (11a–11d), and then show how *as* is translated into German by the enumerated systems. A human translation by a native German translation professional has also been added as a point of reference.

In this exercise, we employ the newer NMT versions of Google Translate and Bing Translator. These data-driven, neural systems, along with Logos Model (LM) and LISA Lab's NMT system, all perform better than PROMT Translate and SYSTRANet, the two hybridized, rule-based systems we have been using. It is impossible to know why this is so, of course, but the poorer performance by the two rule-based systems may possibly illustrate our point that rule-based methodologies invite complexity effects that limit competence and negatively affect output. Other explanations for these errors are also possible, of course. Shortcomings are underlined.

(11a)   *As you can see, he is sick.* → *Wie...*

Human	Google	Bing	PROMT	SYSTRAN	LM	LISA
Wie	*Wie*	*Wie*	*Wie*	*Wie*	*Wie*	*Wie*

Commentary

Note that the German *als* does not convey as many senses as the English *as*.
Unlike *as* for the English, *als* would be incorrect for the German context in (11a).

(11b)   *As he is sick, we cannot ask him to work.* → *Weil...*

Human	Google	Bing	PROMT	SYSTRAN	LM	LISA
Da	*Da*	*Da*	*Wie*	*Da*	*Weil*	*Da*

Commentary

Da means *since*, *Weil* means *because*. Both are correct. *Wie* is entirely incorrect.

(11c)   *As he was being given his medicine, he began to choke.* →
        Während ... (While ...)

Human	Google	Bing	PROMT	SYSTRAN	LM	LISA
Als	*Als*	*Als*	*Wie*	*Da*	*Während*	*Als*

Commentary

Während means *while*. *Als* has multiple senses (including *while*) just like the English *as*, and is probably preferable here. Both *Wie* and *Da* (*since*) are incorrect.

(11d)   *As he began to recover his health, he realized that his wife had stood by him through difficult times.* → *Als*

Human	Google	Bing	PROMT	SYSTRAN	LM	LISA

Als	*Als*	*Als*	*Wie*	*Während*	*Als*	*Als*

Commentary[38]

Wie is incorrect and *Während* (*while*) seems less suitable.

We trust the reader will understand that these exercises are not meant to oppose the performance of one MT system against others. Our concern rather is to explore the upside and downside of the different underlying methodologies. And the only way to do this, in the final analysis, is to look at output. But clearly enough, when it comes to the translation quality of a given sentence, any of these systems at one time or another may be seen to outperform the others. Our interest lies rather in the ultimate performance potential that is offered by underlying technology.

4.7 Conclusion

We have argued throughout this Chapter that the chief factor affecting a system's ultimate potential for high-quality translation lies in its ability, or lack of ability, to cope with complexity. And we sought to explore reasons why, in its handling of language, the human brain seems utterly free from these complexity issues. We examined two regions of the brain known to be responsible for language, one dealing chiefly with rules of syntax (Broca), and the other dealing chiefly with semantic associations (hippocampus). We discussed reasons for believing that the associative processes of the hippocampus appear to be less prone to complexity. We discussed the question of how syntax-related Broca and semantics-related hippocampus interrelate, which in turn asks the more general question of how syntax and semantics interrelate. In the next chapter, we try to answer that question.

Postscripts

Postscript 4-A

> Arguably, an abstraction function seems to account for certain fundamental characteristics of brain physiology. This is suggested by the integrative structure of the brain cell; the prevalence of fan-in circuitry in the brain further suggests a structure designed for abstraction. (See this in Fig. 4.1.)

On the input side, McCormick (1990, 52) believes as many as twelve or more neuro-active (chemical) substances may affect a given neuron. On the output side, Crick and Asanuma (1986, 338) speculate that neurons output only one neurotransmitter. If this

---

[38] See Postscript 4-H for translations of (11d) by these systems as an entire sentence.

many-to-one synaptic picture for neuronal input and output holds true, it would seem to support our view of the neuron as an abstracting device from the biochemical perspective as well as from the more self-evident anatomical viewpoint.

Postscript 4-B

A matchup of the terms [*kitchen table*] in an associative, textual entailment function enables a sequence of SAL pattern-rules to eventually rewrite the string correctly as the abstract SAL constituent *NP(COsurf)* (denoting concrete noun, *support surface*).

This particular operation in step [1] of Fig. 4.1, viz., resolving the ambiguity of the common noun *table*, remained purely experimental at the time development ceased in 2000. The account below describes the various processes in place or under consideration for resolving common noun ambiguities, the most interesting of which never got to be implemented in a release.[39]

1. If the noun in question were entered into the lexicon with a Subject Matter Code (SMC) corresponding to the SMC specified at run time, the term would be considered unambiguous and the SMC-specific entry would be selected. For example, in such cases where SMC = *electrical*, the French transfer for *power* would be *alimentation* rather than the more general default transfer, *pouvoir*. This solution to the noun polysemy problem only works in narrow, domain-specific translations and even then is quite limited in effectiveness, given that many common noun ambiguities are obviously not going to be solved on the basis of domain specificity.

2. In the absence of helpful SMC settings, the meaning of an ambiguous term like *board*, for example, would be attempted by finding words in its immediate neighborhood with similar SAL codes, as for example *chairman* in *board chairman*. Here *chairman* is an animate noun and hence would allow for the animate sense of *board*. But this would not work for *board* in *board room* where neither term shares a common SAL code at any taxonomic level. This solution is too simplistic to be effective, especially with such a coarse-grained semantico-syntactic taxonomy such as SAL.

3. More effective would be to employ the finer-grained, purely semantic taxonomy afforded by a thesaurus. For example, the ambiguous term *front* would be resolved to its military sense in the neighborhood of words like *battle, soldier, attack*, etc. All these terms fall under the thesaurus category for *contention* in the 4th (1977) edition of Cromwell's *Roget Thesaurus* that we digitized for our experiments. Similarly, terms *kitchen* and *table* also have meanings that fall under an identical thesaurus category (307, for *eating*) and hence are readily

---

[39] Clearly, in the decade since Logos closed its doors, the availability of big data and the emergence of deep learning algorithms have made the problem of sense recognition more tractable by orders of magnitude.

resolvable. Unfortunately, opportunity to implement this solution was not given before development had to cease.

4. We also experimented with WordNet.[40] See, for example, the definitions that WordNet provides for *table* and for *kitchen*, illustrated in Postscript Figure 4B.1. As Figure 4B.1 indicates, we were able to resolve *table* to its desired sense on the basis of a single shared term, *meal*, in the WordNet definitions for *table* (as *support surface*) and for *kitchen*. (The Figure shows hand-drawn linkage between the SAL codes for the different senses of these words with their corresponding WordNet definitions.)

Promising as these solutions seem, common noun disambiguation has always been recognized as particularly challenging for NLP. For one, resolution often depends upon extra-sentential clues well beyond the ken of single sentence-based systems.

Interestingly, had a bilingual, big data collection of sentences containing the word *table* been available to us, and had we had in place anything resembling a "bag-of-words" learning model, we would have had a far more effective means for rendering proper translations. But bag-of-word associations (absent a relation to definitions) do not explicate meanings, and in the absence of meanings (e.g., that *table* is a *support surface*), subsequent steps [2] and [3] in Fig. 4.1 would not have been possible.

<u>*Table* as noun is stored in the Logos Model lexicon with three SAL codes</u>

INdata = *Table* qua information (links to WordNet sense 1)
COsurf = *Table* qua support surface (links to WN sense 2 and 3)
PLundif = *Table* qua mesa (links to WordNet sense 4)

WordNet meanings for *table*

1 • <u>S</u>: (n) **table**, <u>tabular array</u> (a set of data arranged in rows and columns) *"see table 1"*
2 • <u>S</u>: (n) **table** (a piece of furniture having a smooth flat top that is usually supported by one or more vertical legs) *"It was a sturdy table"*
3 • <u>S</u>: (n) **table** (a piece of furniture with tableware for a meal laid out on it) *"I reserved a table at my favorite restaurant"*
4 • <u>S</u>: (n) <u>mesa</u>, **table** (flat tableland with steep edges) *"the tribe was relatively safe on the mesa but they had to descend into the valley for water"*

<u>*Kitchen* is stored in the Logos Model lexicon with only one SAL codes</u>

PLencl = *Kitchen* qua enclosed place

WordNet meanings for *kitchen*

• <u>S</u>: (n) **kitchen** (a room equipped for preparing meals)

Postscript Figure 4B.1 *Graphic adapted from a screen shot taken from WordNet 3.1*

---

[40] http://wordnetweb.princeton.edu/perl/webwn

Postscript 4-C

The all-sufficient role in these models of connections alone struck us as an implicit, telling reassertion of the role of associative memory in brain function, one that would enable us to account for our own associative methodology.

Neuroscience recognizes two kinds of associative memory: (a) auto-associative memory where coincidence occurs between one memory (e.g., a newly input pattern of impressions in short-term memory), and a second virtually identical memory (e.g. a previously stored pattern in long-term memory); and (b) hetero-associative memory, where the two memories are more loosely associated (Wang and Morris 2010). In Logos Model, coincidence of an input pattern in short-term memory with a stored pattern in long-term memory may be of either type. In general, patterns in long-term store are often more abstract than the input pattern that coincides with it.

Postscript 4-D

Connectionist theory and its models seemed to substantiate the conjecture we had made that normal neurolinguistic function consists of non-procedural responses to linguistic input based entirely on declarative memory associations.

Rumelhart and McClelland (1986), quoted by Elman (2001: 295ff): "*We have, we believe, provided a distinct alternative to the view that children learn the rules of English past-tense in any explicit sense. We have shown that a reasonable account of the acquisition of past tense can be provided without recourse to the notion of a 'rule' or anything more than a description of the language.*" This is the declarative basis of both connectionism and Logos Model.

Postscript 4-E

And its widely promulgated thesis that meaning is expressed by distributed representation (i.e., by activation across an entire cortical circuit) has likely encouraged a number of neurophysiologists to modify (if not outright abandon) notions of local representation, i.e., representation at the level of a single neuron.

Classical neuroanatomy had traditionally held that individual cells in long-term memory tend to be permanent, non-reusable records of information (Sherrington 1941), spoken of by connectionism as "*local representation*" (Rumelhart and McClelland 1986). Such cells are said to have been "*grandmothered*" for their informational content, a term derived from experiments where a single simian brain cell was found to fire upon the appearance of the monkey's maternal grandmother. This "*single cell doctrine*" has largely given way in recent years to a more "*clustered-cell*" or "*semi-local*" explanation of cognitive function (Thorpe 1995), although the notion of meaning at the level of a single cell is hardly dead.[41] (See study on single cell memory by Sidiropoulou et al. (2009). See also Crick and Asanuma (1986, 368).

Postscript 4-F

> Whatever the hippocampus does, it performs its work not by executing rules but by making associations, and these associations are semantic in nature. This is very different from the rule-like syntactic processes commonly associated with the Broca area.

Associationism as a general, cognitive mechanism has long been established in neuroscience, but its special role in linguistics has largely been disregarded by generative grammarians. Very likely UG's pervasive influence on cognitive and neuroscience explains why most neuroscientists have attributed language processing to the rule-based, procedurally oriented Broca area, and as a consequence failed to see the associative processes of the hippocampus as potential mechanisms for processing language, at least until recent neuroimaging studies began to correct this picture.

Postscript 4-G

> Indeed, these two features, (a) semantic orientation and (b) functional use of associations, coupled with the key role the hippocampus is known to play in cognitive memory, persuaded us right from the start that the hippocampus must surely have something to do with language use.

Authors Duff and Brown-Schmidt (2012) hold that the hippocampus, in its capacity for relational binding, representational flexibility, and online maintenance and integration of multimodal relational representations, is a key contributor to language processing. To test their hypothesis, a small number of participants with bilateral hippocampal damage and severe declarative memory impairment, were compared with four healthy participants for their ability to identify the antecedent of a pronoun in a simple sequence of sentences. The healthy participants had no difficulty performing the exercise correctly. The hippocampus-impaired participants clearly faltered. The authors believe these findings demonstrate that the processing features of the hippocampus are employed in a variety of cognitive domains including language.

---

[41] See observations on single cell memory by Sidiropoulou et al. (2009). See also Crick and Asanuma (1986, 368).

Postscript 4-H

Below are translations of (11d) in Chapter 3 by all the enumerated models we tested. Only the more egregious flaws have been underlined.

(11d)   *As he began to recover his health, he realized that his wife had stood by him through difficult times.*

Human Translation
Als er begann, seine Gesundheit zurückzuerlangen, realisierte er, dass seine Frau ihm durch schwierige Zeiten hinweg beigestanden hatte.

Logos Model
Als er anfing, seine Gesundheit zurückzubekommen, erkannte er, dass seine Frau ihm durch schwere Zeiten beigestanden hatte.

Google Translate (GNMT)
Als er begann, seine Gesundheit zu erholen, erkannte er, dass seine Frau von ihm durch schwierig Zeiten gestanden hatte.

Microsoft Translator (NMT)
Als er begann, seine Gesundheit zurückzugewinnen, erkannte er, dass seine Frau von ihm durch schwierige Zeiten gestanden hatte.

PROMT
Wie er begann, seine Gesundheit wiederzuerlangen, begriff er, dass seine Frau bei ihm im Laufe schwieriger Zeiten gestanden hatte.

SYSTRANet
Während er anfing, seine Gesundheit wieder herzustellen, stellte er fest, dass seine Frau ihn durch schwierige Zeiten bereitgestanden hatte.

LISA's Neural MT
Als er anfing, seine Gesundheit zu erholen, erkannte er, dass seine Frau von ihm durch schwierige Zeiten UNK.

References

Bonhage CE, Mueller JL, Friederici AD, Fiebach CJ (2015) Combined eye tracking and fMRI reveals neural basis of linguistic predictions during sentence comprehension. Cortex 68:33–47

Breitenstein C, Jansen A, Deppe M, Foerster AF, Somme J, Wolbers T, Knecht S (2004) Hippocampus activity differentiates good from poor learners of a novel lexicon. NeuroImage 25(3):958–968. https://doi.org/10.1016/j.neuroimage.2004.12.019. S1053-8119(04)00770-0 [pii]

Chan D, Fox NC, Scahill RI, Crum WR, LWhitwell J, Leschziner G, Rosser AM, Stevens JM, Cipolotti L, Rosser MN (2001) Patterns of temporal lobe atrophy in semantic dementia and Alzheimer's disease. Ann Neurol 49(4):433–442

Chomsky N (1957) Syntactic structures. Mouton, The Hague/Paris

Chomsky N (1965) Aspects of the theory of syntax. MIT Press, Cambridge

Crick F, Asanuma C (1986) Certain aspects of the anatomy and physiology of the cerebral cortex. In: McClelland JL, Rumelhart DE (eds) Distributed parallel processing, vol 2. MIT Press, Cambridge, pp 333–371

de Vries MH, Petersson KM, Geukes S, Zwitserlood P, Christiansen CH (2012) Processing multiple non-adjacent dependencies: evidence from sequence learning. Philos Trans R Soc B 367:2065–2076

DeKeyser R (2008) Chapter 11: Implicit and explicit learning. In: Doughty CJ, Long MH (eds) The handbook of second langauge acquisition. Wiley Online Library. https://doi.org/10.1002/9780470756492.ch11. Accessed 21 July 2016

Douglas R, Martin K (1990) Neocortex. In: Shepherd G (ed) The synapatic organization of the brain, 2nd edn. Oxford University Press, Oxford/New York, pp 389–438

Duff MC, Brown-Schmidt S (2012) The Hippocampus and the flexible use and processing of language. Front Hum Neurosci 6:69. https://doi.org/10.3389/fnhum.2012.00069. Accessed 23 Sept 2016

Duff MC, Brown-Schmidt S (2017) Hippocampal contributions to language use and processing. In: Hannula DE, Duff MC (eds) The hippocampus from cells to systems. Springer, Cham, pp 503–536

Elman J (2001) Connectionism and the acquisition of language. In: Tomasello M, Bates E (eds) Essential readings in language acquisition. Basil Blackwell, Oxford, pp 295–306

Fanselow MS, Dong H-W (2010) Are the dorsal and ventral hippocampus functionally distinct structures? Neuron 65(1):7. https://doi.org/10.1016/j.neuron.2009.11.031. Accessed 9 June 2016

Fauconnier G (1997) Mappings in thought and language. Cambridge University Press, Cambridge

Fiebach CJ, Friederici AD, Müller K, Yves von Cramon D (2002) fMRI evidence for dual routes to the mental lexicon in visual word recognition. J Cogn Neurosci 14(1):11–23

Fillmore C, Kay P, O'Connor C (1988) Regularity and Idiomaticity in grammatical constructions: the case of let alone. Language 64:501–538

Fitch WT, Friederici AD, Hagoort P (2012) Pattern perception and computational complexity: introduction to the special issue. Philos Trans R Soc 367:1925–1932. https://doi.org/10.1098/rstb.2012.0099. Accessed 22 Jan 2016

Glaser YG, Martin RC, Van Dyke JA, Chris Hamilton A, Tan Y (2013) Neural basis of semantic and syntactic interference in sentence comprehension. Brain Lang 126:314–326

Henke K, Treyer V, Nagy ET, Kneifel S, Dursteler M, Nitsch RM, Buck A (2003) Active hippocampus during nonconscious memories. Conscious Cogn 12(1):31–48

Kay M, Hays DG (2000) In: John Hutchins W (ed) Early years in machine translation. John Benjamin Publishing, Amsterdam/Philadelphia Company, pp 165–170

Koehn P (2011) Statistical machine translation. Cambridge University Press, Cambridge

Koehn P, Knowles R (2017) Six challenges for neural machine translation. In: Proceedings of the first workshop on neural machine translation. Vancouver, pp 26–39. http://arXiv:1706.03872v1. Accessed 13 Dec 2017

Kumaran D, Hassabis D, McClelland JL (2016) What learning systems do intelligent agents need? Complementary learning systems theory updated. Trends Cogn Sci 20(7):512. https://doi.org/10.1016/j.tics.2016.05.004. Accessed 12 Jan 2017

Kurczek J, Brown-Schmidt S, Duff M (2013) Hippocampal contributions to language: evidence of referential processing deficits in amnesia. J Exp Psychol Gen 142(4):1346–1354

Lakoff G (1987) Women, fire, and dangerous things: what categories reveal about the mind. CSLI, Chicago

Liu S, Yang N, Li M, Zhou M (2014) A recursive recurrent neural network for statistical machine translation. In: Proceedings of the 52nd annual meeting of the association for computational linguistics. Maryland, Baltimore, pp 1491–1500

Marr D (1971) Simple memory: a theory for archicortex. Philos Trans R Soc B Biol Sci 262:23–81. https://doi.org/10.1098/rstb.1971.0078

Mårtensson J, Eriksson J, Bodammer NC, Lindgren M, Johansson M, Nyberg L, Lövdén M (2012) Growth of language-related brain areas after foreign language learning. NeuroImage 63(1):240–244

McClelland JL, McNaughton BL, O'Reilly RC (1995) Why there are complementary learning systems in the Hippocampus and Neocortex: insights from the successes and failures of connectionist models of learning and memory. Psychol Rev 102(3):419–457

McCormick DA (1990) Membrane properties and neurotransmitter action. In: Shepherd G (ed) The synaptic organization of the brain. Oxford University Press, New York/Oxford, pp 39–78

O'Keefe J, Dostrovsky J (1971) The hippocampus as a spatial map. Preliminary evidence from unit activity in the freely-moving rat. Brain Res 34(1):171–175

Optiz B (2010) Neural binding mechanisms in learning and memory. Neurosci Biobehav Rev 34:1036–1046

Optiz B, Friederici AD (2003) Interactions of the hippocampal system and the prefrontal cortex in learning language-like rules. NeuroImage 19:1730–1737. https://doi.org/10.1016/S1053-8119(03)00170-8. Accessed 25 Jan 2016

Palmer DC (2006) On Chomsky's appraisal of Skinner's verbal behavior: a half-century of misunderstanding. Behav Anal 29(2):253–267

Pinker S, Prince A (1988) On language and connectionism: analysis of a parallel distributed processing model of language acquisition. Cognition 23:73–193

Race E, Keane MM, Verfaellie M (2015) Sharing mental simulations and stories: hippocampal contributions to discourse integration. Cortex 63:271–281

Robinson P (2008) In: Ellis NC (ed) Handbook of cognitive linguistics and second language acquisition. Routledge, New York

Rumelhart DE, McClelland JL (1986) Chapter 18: On learning the past tenses of English verbs. In: Parallel distributed processing: explorations in the microstructure of cognition, vol 2. MIT Press, Cambridge, pp 216–271

Scott B (1989) The logos system. In: Proceedings of MT Summit II, Munich, pp 137–142

Scott B (1990) Biological neural net for parsing long, complex sentences. Logos Corporation Publication. (Available from the author (logos.institute@gmail.com))

Scott B (2000) Logos model as a metaphorical biological neural net. Logos Corporation Publication. http://www.mt-archive.info/Logos-2000-Scott

Scott B (2003) Logos model: an historical perspective. Mach Transl 18(1):1–72

Sejnowski TJ (1986) Chapter 21: Open questions about computation in cerebral cortex. In: Parallel distributed processing, vol II. MIT Press, Cambridge, pp 372–389

Sherrington C (1941) Man on his nature. The Macmillian Company, New York

Sidiropoulou K, Lu FM, Fowler MA, Xiao R, Phillips C, Ozkan ED, Zhu MX (2009) Dopamine modulates an mGluR5-mediated depolarization underlying prefrontal persistent activity. Nat Neurosci 12(2):190–199

Socher R, Lin CC-Y, Ng AY, Manning CD (2011) Parsing natural scenes and natural language with recursive neural networks. In: Proceedings of the 28th international conference on machine learning, Bellevue, pp 129–136. http://ai.stanford.edu/~ang/papers/icml11-ParsingWithRecursiveNeuralNetworks.pdf. Accessed 17 Apr 2016

Squire LR, Sola-Morgan S (1991) The medial temporal lobe memory system. Science 253(5026):1380–1386

Thorpe SJ (1995) Localized versus distributed representation. In: Arbib MA (ed) The handbook of brain theory and neural networks. MIT Press, Cambridge, pp 643–646

Verfaellie MK, Bousquet MK, Keane MM (2014) Medial temporal and neocortical contributions to remote memory for semantic narratives: evidence from amnesia. Neuropsychologia 61:105–112

Wang S-H, Morris RGM (2010) Hippocampal-neocortical interactions in memory formation, consolidation, and reconsolidation. Science 345(6200):1054–1057

Wang JX, Rogers LM, Gross EZ, Ryals AJ, Dokucu ME, Brandstatt KL, Hermiller MS, Voss JL (2014) Targeted enhancement of cortical-hippocampal brain networks and associative memory. Science 345(6200):1054–1057

Wintzer ME, Boehringer R, Polygalov D, McHugh TJ (2014) The hippocampal CA2 ensemble is sensitive to contextual change. J Neurosci 34(8):3056–3066

Chapter 5
Syntax and Semantics: Dichotomy Versus Integration

Abstract This chapter deals in a general way with the linguistically-oriented mechanisms in the brain that enable it to decode an input stream of individual words into unambiguous, meaningful sentences. Do we know what the mechanism is that tells the brain that a string of words like "*He wants an answer*" constitutes an intelligible expression and that a gobbledygook string like "*Answer he an wants*" does not? Is the mechanism behind these judgments initially syntactic or semantic? We examine various views as to which of these mechanisms most accounts for the brain's handling of language, particularly in the case where an input stream of words must then lead to its translation. And we try to understand how it happens that all of this is done in the brain without complexity effects. The intent here is not academic but practical, namely, to try and glean from among the competing views of cerebral language processing something of value for MT itself. Does the brain's way of handling syntax and semantics have something to teach MT? In turn, we consider whether MT modeling itself might not have something to offer neuroscience on its open questions regarding language and the brain.

5.1 Syntax Versus Semantics: Is There a Third, Semantico-Syntactic Perspective?

VIRTUALLY EVERYONE ENGAGED WITH LANGUAGE *QUA* LANGUAGE sees it as comprising just two components: an item-specific lexicon and a generalized grammar consisting of a body of abstract rules for syntax and morphology.[1] That is true regardless of theoretical orientation, whether one is a cognitive linguist like Langacker, a connectionist like Rumelhart, a generativist like Pinker, or a neuropsychologist like Friederici. For all of them, lexicons instantiate the concepts of thought, and grammars provide for the arrangement of these instantiations into

---

[1] We obviously are only speaking of written language here.

© Springer International Publishing AG, part of Springer Nature 2018
B. Scott, *Translation, Brains and the Computer*, Machine Translation: Technologies and Applications 2, https://doi.org/10.1007/978-3-319-76629-4_5

word strings that convey thought into sentences. Put in other terms, lexicon provides the semantics of verbalized thought and grammar its syntax and morphology.[2]

There is scant agreement on much else, however. Yes, everyone agrees that language consists of lexicon (semantics) and grammar (with emphasis on syntax, since Chomsky), but there's no consensus, for example, on what actually accounts for the ordering of lexical elements into grammatical sentences, that is, on how the communicative intent of an agent is encoded and decoded by the brain. Do abstract rules of syntax on their own determine the shape of a sentence, or is lexical semantics a principal determinant? The issue appears to be moot.[3] Nor is there any accord on the even deeper question of which is primary. Is it syntax that makes language what it is, or is it semantics? Theoreticians and researchers are of different minds about all of this.

The generativists, following Chomsky, clearly opt for syntax. For them, the faculty for language *per se* consists essentially in our ability to order our thoughts in principled, organized ways. In effect, syntax is what turns thought into language. And generativists hold that a specialized, biologically innate faculty for syntax must account for this ability and that preconditions how, in individual cultures, lexical items get to be ordered into sentences. The mechanism of this preconditioning has never been described with any specificity, but the generativist school holds that this biological mechanism is exclusively syntactic. In his minimalist program, Chomsky calls this mechanism *"merge,"* which can be taken to mean the putting together of lexical items into progressively larger syntactic units until a grammatical sentence is formed in accordance with the idiosyncratic conventions of a given linguistic culture. The telling point here is that, according to Chomsky, this metacultural merge mechanism operates without reference to the meaning of the constructions that it generates.[4]

Others could not more disagree with this. Cognitive linguists like Langacker (2008) say that language is simply a product of human intelligence. As an aspect of human cognition in general, language can never be broken apart into distinct and unrelated syntactic and semantic components. Cognitive linguists known as *constructionists* see syntax and semantics as forming an inseparable continuum (Goldberg 2003). We at Logos of course have always been of this opinion.[5]

Chomsky's famous sentence, *"colorless green ideas sleep furiously,"* is supposed to illustrate the independence of grammaticality from meaning, syntax from semantics. Chomsky claims the sentence demonstrates that one can have grammatical meaninglessness, i.e., that a syntactic string can be valid grammatically while its

---

[2] In *Aspects of the Theory of Syntax* (1965, p. 162), Chomsky rightly acknowledges that the practice of equating semantics with lexicon *"isn't satisfactory."* The meaning of words in a sentence can be extralexical. For our purposes in this chapter, however, we will keep to this common practice of equating semantics with literal words of the lexicon.

[3] Ullman (2004, p. 233): *"Language depends upon a memorized 'mental lexicon' and a computational 'mental grammar,'"* which latter *"is not available to conscious access"* [i.e., constitutes tacit, implicit knowledge].

[4] Chomsky (1977, p. 138). He expresses skepticism that syntax is ever based on semantics. See Postscript 5-A for a discussion of this point.

[5] Schmid (1996) notes the kinship between Langacker's Cognitive Grammar and the implicit semantico-syntactic grammar of Logos Model.

semantics is devoid of meaning.[6] But does he make his case? One can question whether this sentence really illustrates anything, least of all this thesis about the autonomy of syntax. One can easily argue that his string of paradoxes is perfectly meaningful. Paradoxes after all depend upon meaning in order to be paradoxes. How else could we see it as amusing nonsense? It is true that a totally garbled string like *green furiously ideas colorless sleep* would indeed have no meaning whatsoever, but then the sequence would also not be grammatical; it would not be a sentence, just a string of words. It seems that by "meaning" Chomsky here is referring to pragmatics, not to semantics in the commonly understood sense. To be meaningful in his terms, a sentence like this must comport with human experience in some way, which of course his sentence fails to do. But this pragmatic failure does not make the sentence meaningless. We cannot be amused by semantic nothingness.

One is forced to conclude that Chomsky's sentence in fact demonstrates just the opposite of his intent. It does not seem possible to compose a grammatical sentence in natural language that does not trigger at least some degree of comprehension, however meager, if only a judgment that its meaning is capricious or irrational or pragmatic silliness, as in the present case. And if that is so, syntax and semantics will always entail each other in a valid sentence. The formal, theoretic separation of syntax from semantics by the generativist school strikes us as the biggest *faux pas* in modern linguistics.

Chomsky as we know was the first to seriously study syntax as a separate matter, and to argue not only for its autonomy but for its priority and primacy in language (Chomsky 1977, 69). We noted earlier in the Introduction that the likely motive for this was Chomsky's desire to formulate insightful generalities about language and the way language works, a purpose that syntax readily supports and semantics does not. Whatever one thinks of these views, there is no disagreement that his theories about syntax stimulated and profoundly influenced linguistics for the entire second half of the twentieth century. Chomsky had made the study of grammar universally more interesting than it was under Bloomfield and the structuralists.

Not surprisingly, a great many linguists have adopted the generativist view that syntax is what turns thought into language. And Chomsky's influence extended to brain science as well. Many neuroscientists engaged in the study of language have come to believe that his theories about syntax are correct. The following rather bald pronouncement by one neuroscientist is not untypical:

> ... *syntactic analysis is autonomous and initially not influenced by semantic variables....* *Semantic integration can be influenced by syntactic analysis, but does not contribute to the* *computation of syntactic structure.*[7]

Researchers claim to have found neuroimaging support for Chomsky's syntax theory, particularly in the Broca region of the brain. The evidence for this is derived from experiments involving participants who are shown word strings in an artificial

---

[6] Chomsky (1957, p. 15): "*The notion of 'grammatical' cannot be identified with 'meaningful' or 'significant' in any semantic sense.*"

[7] Hagoort (2015, p. 406). It is hard to imagine MT developers making such a statement.

language and are asked to make grammaticality judgments about them. It is assumed that participants' ability to make these judgments correctly must depend upon their implicit acquisition of rules prescribing how such sentences are to be constructed, in short that they are applying rules of syntax. And the loosely defined Broca area is the brain region found by neuroimaging to be most recruited in performing these exercises.

Interesting as these investigations are, they are all *"theory-guided."* Virtually all are premised upon theoretical assumptions that syntactic rules offer the best explanation for participants' ability to make valid grammaticality judgments (Pulvermüller 2010, 167). And participants' effective performance here is seen as a demonstration of the existence and application of these rules of syntax in and by the brain. But one must note that these studies are based on *artificial* language, not on natural language.[8]

Most tellingly, these studies also presuppose with generative grammar that syntax operates independently of meaning. This seems to be the more critical of their theoretical perspectives. Given this, and the fact that semantics obviously plays no part in artificial language experiments, one must ask how relevant can their findings possibly be on the relationship between syntax and semantics?[9] Indeed, the linguistic relevance of neuroscientific investigations based upon generativist presuppositions can hardly be said to prove anything about the priority and independence of syntax.

As stated, the brain area most recruited by these artificial language exercises is the inferior frontal gyrus (IFG, the general Broca area). In the previous chapter, Broca was seen to be recruited more by the exceptional rather than by the more ordinary demands of language processing, by demands arising from problematic language strings. On these grounds, one would fully expect Broca to become active in exercises involving artificial languages. In contrast, we conjecture that the handling of ordinary linguistic contexts (where semantics is an integral part) is done largely by the declarative, associative processes of the hippocampus and related associative regions of the brain. Nothing in these artificial language studies disproves that conjecture.

A number of recent studies have begun to corroborate this conjecture. For example, an investigation by Bonhage et al. (2015) shows that the hippocampus, along with regions closely linked to it, handles regular sentences, whereas the Broca area (BA44, BA45) handles *"nonsense"* sentences. The substitution of the term

---

[8] Ever since the pioneering work of Reber (1967), many of these neuropsychological studies have involved *artificial* rather than natural languages. This distinction must surely have some bearing on the relevance of these studies to *natural* language processes of the brain.

[9] Bastiaansen and Hagoort (2015) claim that brain frequencies for semantics and syntax judgments were functionally distinguishable during grammaticality testing. But one questions the pertinence of data derived from tests of *artificial* language to our understanding of *natural* language processes.

nonsense for *artificial* here reveals a perspective on the part of these neuroscientists that is clearly no longer generativist.[10]

We shall consider these recent studies in a moment, but first let us examine one of these earlier studies that were guided by generativist theory and see where it takes us.

In 2003, neuropsychologists Optiz and Friederici conducted an investigation into the interactions of the hippocampus and the prefrontal cortex (Broca's area), using functional MRI for data collection. The exercise was specifically designed to demonstrate the learning of syntactic rules during the acquisition of an artificial language. The study's object was to determine the extent to which hippocampus versus Broca becomes engaged during the learning of these rules. Researchers acknowledged that at stake was one of two hypotheses about language acquisition—a rule-based hypothesis connected with the Broca area, and an associative, similarity-based hypothesis associated with the hippocampus.

For the test, they developed an extremely simple artificial language called BROCANTO, consisting of just two determiners, two nouns, two verbs, and two modifiers (one adjective and one adverb). The language was designed to mimic simple NP and VP structures of a natural Subject-Verb-Object (SVO) language. Its eight-word lexicon comprised meaningless letter strings like *trul, pel, aak,* etc. No semantic values were assigned to these BROCANTO strings; they remained meaningless throughout the exercise. In Table 5.1, below, we offer a greatly simplified version of the exercise where single letters have been used in place of BROCANTO words.

Seventeen participants were initially exposed for 70 s to a block of ten grammatical BROCANTO sentences, five to eight words in length. Next they were shown a series of such sentences half of which violated some aspect of the underlying BROCANTO grammar. Each sentence was seen for 7 s. Participants were asked to make grammaticality judgments about each sentence, and were provided right/ wrong feedback to assist in learning. Finally, with a new series of sentences only half of which were grammatical, participants were again asked to make quick grammaticality judgments, this time without feedback. This entire sequence was repeated a number of times.

Participants did well on the test. Over the course of the exercise, participants learned to make correct grammaticality judgments well above chance. The researchers conclude from this that correct judgments strongly infer rule acquisition. The participants, having seen (in our terms) that the medial position of z or y is a pattern that gets repeated in all correct sentences, begin to infer that this pattern likely constitutes a rule in BROCANTO grammar (i.e., that BROCANTO is an *SVO* language). The more this pattern is seen, the stronger the inference grows, until it becomes an unconscious grammatical rule accounting for correct judgments.

The exercise also suggests participants must have inferred that these two words z and y, for example, belong to a common syntactic category, viz., the verb category.

---

[10] One of the authors of this 2015 study is Angela Friederici, who a decade earlier had worked within the generativist framework (Optiz and Friederici 2003). Angela Friederici is neuropsychology director of the Max Planck Institute for Human Cognitive and Brain Science in Leipzig. She has authored or co-authored over 400 papers, at least one including co-author Noam Chomsky.

Table 5.1 *Simplified version of grammaticality exercise*

I	II	III
Initial learning	Learning test	Final test
b m z b n	*b m z b n*	*b n z b m*
b n y b m	*b̲ z̲ m̲ b̲ n̲*	*b̲ n̲ m̲ b̲ z̲*
a n z b m	*a n z b m*	*a n z b m*
b m y b n	*a̲ n̲ m̲ b̲ y̲*	*a̲ n̲ b̲ y̲ m̲*
a n y a m	*a n y a m*	*a m y b n*
a m z b n	*y̲ n̲ a̲ a̲ m̲*	*y̲ m̲ n̲ b̲ a̲*

Letters *a, b* represent two different BROCANTO determiners; *m, n* represent two different nouns; *y, z* represent two different verbs (bolded for the benefit of the reader). (For simplicity sake we have ignored the two modifiers (adjective and adverb).) Sentences are all *SVO* constructions. After a brief introduction, participants are initially exposed to the language in Column I. In Column II, to aid learning, they receive feedback correcting any wrong grammaticality judgments (we have underlined the erroneous patterns). In the final, unaided test in Column III, correctness of grammaticality judgments presumably indicate extent to which rules of BROCANTO grammar have been learned. Note that we have also underlined sentences in the Column III that violate some aspect of BROCANTO grammar

This, the researchers say, illustrates the formation of category abstractions, which abstraction is another aspect of language-rule acquisition.

Regarding this exercise, one must note the extent to which theory-guided presuppositions concerning the primacy of syntax have predetermined the researchers' conclusions. For example, the prefrontal Broca area, a central focus in this study, is held (by well-tested theory) to be specifically involved in the handling of syntax, making Broca of inevitable interest to those who hold that syntax is what makes language what it is. The researchers in this particular study clearly hold to this syntactocentric point of view. That the language developed for this test should be called BROCANTO is indicative of that.[11]

Equally indicative of their generativist, syntax-first orientation is their statement (p. 1731): *"BROCANTO differs from natural language only in that it does not include embedded structures."* To these researchers, BROCANTO differs from natural language only by being simpler. In short, just as in their view of natural language, semantics-free BROCANTO does not require semantics for it to consti-

---

[11] Our purpose in these remarks is not to denigrate this particular study. It was well done by highly respected neuroscientists, and certainly the exercise is interesting.

tute a language. Notice also that BROCANTO differs from natural languages in that words in this artificial languages are never ambiguous, not even syntactically.

From a non-generativist perspective, one wonders how a syntax-only artifice like BROCANTO can possibly claim to simulate natural language. To a non-generativist, BROCANTO consists simply of arbitrary patterns of alpha strings, some frequent, some infrequent, patterns that never rise to the level of language. To do that the patterns would have to mean something. One must argue that studies dealing with syntax-only languages like BROCANTO do not tell us much of anything about learning the rules and conventions of natural language. Such studies seem more like exercises in the solving of puzzles.[12]

Also, the claim of rule formation is little more than an inference. Other explanations can also account for these correct grammaticality judgments, such as probability. A participant may judge an artificial sentence ungrammatical for no other reason than its statistical improbability relative to training experience.[13,14]

Researchers Optiz and Friederici however have no hesitation in proposing that participants *"learned an abstract linguistic grammar system on the basis of rules"* (2003, 1733). They base this conclusion on their theory-guided interpretation of neuroimaging data showing increasing recruitment of Broca during the course of the test.

These authors also report evidence of hippocampal interaction with Broca. Hippocampus involvement was found to occur chiefly during earlier phases of learning, with declining involvement as participants began to acquire the grammar rules. They conclude from this that learning by association, i.e., hippocampal, similarity-based learning, inevitably declines as rule-knowledge grows. They cite similar studies affirming an initial but diminishing role for the hippocampus, and that appear to confirm their view of the ascendancy of rule-based learning. It does not seem to occur to these authors that the reduced involvement of semantically oriented hippocampus might have other causes, namely that BROCANTO has no semantics.

In their view, declarative, similarity-based learning by the hippocampus is *"superficial"* and invariably *"item-specific,"* a kind of learning that *"cannot explain*

---

[12] The researchers acknowledge that the participants, who were all native German speakers, may have made correct judgments about BROCANTO simply by virtue of unconscious influence from their native language. Brief German sentences in the present tense are very similar syntactically to the *SVO* sentences of BROCANTO. If that influence should really be the case, then of the two hypotheses about learning postulated by the authors, a rule-based hypothesis and an associative, similarity-based hypothesis, their study would actually seem to demonstrate the latter.

[13] Connectionists McClelland and Patterson (2002) contend that rules of grammar do not have neuronal counterparts in the brain, and that the mechanism for stringing words into sentences is probability. See also Kempen and Harbusch (2003).

[14] Neuropsychologist Pulvermüller (2010) acknowledges that what tests like these prove must remain inconclusive (p. 170): *"... it is difficult to decide whether the brain response to an ungrammatical string reflects its syntactic features or rather the conditional probability with which words follow each other. As every ungrammatical string is usually also a very rarely occurring item, it is also possible that the degree of expectedness – or string probability – is reflected."*

the acquisition of abstract, or rule-based knowledge of more complex artificial paradigms" (p. 1731). These researchers however do acknowledge that others (e.g., Shanks 1995) maintain a contrary position, that similarity-based associations can indeed provide sufficient grounds for accomplishing what rules are supposedly needed for. A secondary purpose of the 2003 Optiz-Friederici study was to try and help settle this debate, settling it in favor of rules.

Optiz and Friederici are hardly alone in their assertions concerning the dominant role they ascribe to Broca and to rules of syntax in language acquisition and processing. A number of other neuropsychological studies around this time, working within the same linguistic framework, assert similar findings. For example, one study claims to have fMRI readings that "*provide insight into the neuronal underpinnings of 'Universal* [i.e., syntax-first] *Grammar'.*" This allows its authors to conclude that the Broca area is the "*neuronal counterpart of UG*" (Musso et al. 2003).

As we shall see in the discussion that follows, newer findings by neuropsychologists in the past decade are rendering less and less tenable these earlier views of how syntax and semantics relate, especially in light of increasing recognition of the hippocampus and its declarative role in language processing (Duff and Brown-Schmidt 2012). (See Postscript 5-B).

5.2 Recent Views of the Cerebral Process

Recent neuroimaging-based studies in the past decade have begun to reveal a considerably more nuanced picture of the cortical language process. For one, brain areas hitherto not particularly known to be recruited for language are increasingly being recognized, areas such as the subcortical basal ganglia, the premotor cortex, and the middle temporal gyrus (see Postscript 4-C). And the sharp division between syntax in the Broca area and semantics in the hippocampus is giving way to a better understanding of their interaction, a recognition being arrived at even by the authors of the 2003 project described above.[15]

For example, in a subsequent study by Optiz and Friederici (2007), while confirming that complex violations involving long-distance dependencies and embeddings (called "*hierarchical dependencies*") are handled by the Broca area, these researchers now propose that the hippocampus responds to "*violations of local dependencies*" (Optiz and Friederci 2007). In effect, the semantically-oriented hippocampus is now also seen to be making simple grammaticality judgments, i.e., judgments about syntax. This is clearly a new development.

---

[15] Grodzinsky and Friederici (2006), Optiz and Friederci (2007), Bonhage et al. (2015), which includes Friederici as co-author; Optiz and Hofmann 2015, 77): "*... results indicate that rule- and similarity-based mechanisms concur during AGL [artificial grammar learning].*" In Mueller et al. (2009, web), co-author Friederici now subscribes to the finding that "*present results support learning theories that assume a statistical learning mechanism rather than a rule-based extraction mechanism as an initial acquisition stage.*"

A study by Hauser et al. (2012), and that includes Optiz as a co-author, again takes up the question of the two types of knowledge—rule-based versus association-based—and which of them best accounts for human ability to make grammaticality judgments.[16] The object, again, is to investigate the interplay of these two knowledge types and the neuronal correlates that they recruit when engaged in grammaticality judgments. The study employs the BROCANTO artificial language, but with the difference that participants now are instructed in the underlying rules beforehand.

This 2012 study is still in the generativist spirit of the original 2003 BROCANTO study, but nevertheless offers some telling new insights. For one, they found that the two forms of knowledge—rule-based and similarity-based—operate in parallel and compete in processing efficiency. For another, they found that participants differ individually in their use of the two types of knowledge, a finding that documents a subjective factor in cerebral language processes.[17]

Not unexpectedly, individuals who rely on similarity are seen to recruit the hippocampus, whereas participants who rely on rules are seen to activate the left prefrontal areas (Broca) and the premotor cortex. In the case of similarity-prone participants, neuroimaging data show that after initial recruitment of the hippocampus, an activation shift occurs to the frontal area and premotor cortex. These theory-guided researchers still interpret this shift to mean that the word-specific combinations formed in the hippocampus are subsequently fed to areas believed to generate a syntactic grasp of these combinations. Syntactic knowledge, they still propose, is what enables correct grammaticality judgments.[18] The assumption is still that the hippocampus is not capable of generating the kind of abstract knowledge requisite for grammaticality judgments because it is *"item-specific,"* too *"superficial"* therefore.[19]

A 2013 natural language study at the University of Iowa offers a considerably more robust view of the hippocampus (Kurczek et al. 2013). The investigation shows that impairments to the hippocampus disrupt an individual's ability to relate pronouns to their antecedents, thus suggesting a distinctly grammatical, non-trivial

---

[16] Hauser et al. (2012, web): Researchers found that *"Increasing [sentence] complexity was linked to increasing activity in the left inferior pars opercularis [Brodmann Area 44 in the Broca region] whilst ungrammaticality items evoked increased activity in the left operculum [in the broader Broca area.]"*

[17] One wishes the researchers had attempted to correlate the type of knowledge participants preferred with an individual's inherent language skills, e.g., that the more gifted participants might naturally rely more on similarity, etc., a circumstance we suggested in Chap. 3 and found documentation for in Chap. 4 (Mårtensson et al. 2012).

[18] Hauser et al. (2012, web): *".... rule and similarity knowledge work in parallel and compete in processing-efficiency, leading to an initial superiority of similarity-based classification, and a subsequent dominance of rule-based processes, once a critical amount of abstract knowledge of adjacent dependencies was acquired."*

[19] It is interesting that researchers of studies like these generally *"propose"* rather than *find* the conclusions they draw, a tacit acknowledgment that the empirical evidence they've uncovered still has to be interpreted. Moreover, in all this, one must not lose sight of the fact that BROCANTO is a semantics-free, ambiguity-free, *artificial* language. Its explanatory value for the brain's *natural* language processes may legitimately be questioned.

syntactic role for this semantics-oriented reticulum. The researchers specifically propose that the hippocampus cannot be seen as just specialized for certain kinds of declarative, item-specific memory.

The natural language comprehension exercise by Bonhage et al. (2015), noted earlier, claims an even fuller role for the hippocampus. The exercise shows that the hippocampus, along with allied associative areas, was found to handle regular sentences, and that the Broca area (BA44, BA45) handled *"meaningless jabberwocky sentences."*[20] Interestingly, this 2015 study has as one of its co-authors Angela Friederici of the 2003 BROCANTO study described earlier. This 2015 study would appear to indicate the growing extent to which the declarative, similarity-based mechanism of the hippocampus is becoming recognized in all aspects of language processing, including abstract syntactic handling of non-problematic sentences.

Recent exercises are also showing the converse of these findings, viz., that similarity-based functions are found to recruit syntactic, rule-oriented Broca as well (Glaser et al. 2013).[21] And evidence for the interconnectedness of semantics and syntax continues to grow. A paper by Duff and Brown-Schmidt (2012, web) describes the integrated nature of the brain's language processes. Interestingly, what these researchers say about the integration of syntax and semantics in the brain would pertain no less to the process of a translation machine. To wit:

> Because the meaning of many words is unclear until later in the sentence, language is processed incrementally and multiple sources of information must be generated, integrated, and maintained in real-time to create meaning.

These authors then go on to say:

> This work points to rapid, bi-directional communication between multiple levels of representation. In healthy adults, this would include ... syntax, semantics, pragmatics and phonology, along with social and contextual knowledge.

Virtually everything in these remarks about incremental processes and integrated levels of multiple sources of representation, specifically syntax and semantics, can be said of a translation system like Logos Model.

5.3   Syntax and Semantics: How Do They Relate?

In the preceding section, we documented the tendency among language-oriented neuropsychologists to work within the generative, syntax-first viewpoint, the view that holds that syntax is autonomous and that syntax alone is what turns conceptual

---

[20] The study's methodology entailed fMRI tracking of anticipatory eye movements as participants read the various kinds of sentences. A study by Rouder and Ratcliff (2006) that compared rule-based theories and similarity-based (exemplar-based) theories found that individuals use rules when new items are confusable or problematic in some way, and use exemplars when they are distinct.

[21] Optiz and Hofmann 2015, 77): *"... results indicate that rule- and similarity-based mechanisms concur during AGL [artificial grammar learning]."*

thought into language. Their studies invited us to assume that the shape of natural language sentences is legislated by rules of syntax independently of semantics, using as evidence studies involving semantics-free, artificial languages.

We then documented more recent findings that entail significant challenges to the generativist, syntax-first perspective (Friederici and Weissenborn 2007). The newer data indicate close interaction between semantics and syntax, and in particular between the hippocampal area with its semantic, similarity-based mechanism, and Broca and allied areas with their mechanism for abstract rules of syntax. And most tellingly, in the current and preceding chapters we documented findings that in these interactions, the associative, semantic operations of the hippocampus have been found to occur first, and that the syntax-related operations of Broca and allied areas occur secondarily, in response to processing obstacles met by the hippocampus such as in sentences entailing long-distance dependencies or ambiguities of some kind.

Perhaps the most immediate evidence that sentences are decoded semantically ahead of syntax can be seen in the way one is often able to complete the partial utterances of others. Indirect evidence for this may be found in various hippocampal studies (unrelated to language) showing that the hippocampus not only decodes but also predicts stimuli (e.g., Chadwick et al. 2012). A recent study of rodent travel by Bendor and Spiers (2016) bearing the title, "Does the Hippocampus map out the future?" demonstrates the ability of the hippocampus to anticipate the direction of rodent travel. These and other studies show that the hippocampus completes partial stimuli based on similarity associations with stored patterns.[22] Relating this to language input, the findings indirectly support semantics-first processing by the hippocampus against the syntax-first views of the generativists.

A study by neuroscientists at Peking University in 2010 more directly supports this rebuff to the functional primacy of syntax (Zhang et al. 2010). They examine whether the syntactic organization of a sentence must in fact precede semantic processing in order for sentences to be formed and thereby for comprehension to occur. The study's amusing title, "Semantics does not need a processing license from syntax in reading Chinese," indicates the object of the exercise: to adduce evidence opposing the generativist view that syntactic violations block semantic integration.

The investigation involved electroencephalogram (EEG) measurements of event-related potentials (ERP) taken during the reading of Chinese sentences. Sixteen Mandarin-speaking students, rigged with an EEG cap and seated before a screen in a darkened room, are briefly shown a series of sentence combinations consisting of a correct sentence and a variety of syntactic and semantic violations of that sentence, English versions of which are shown below.

(a) Syntactic violation: *The girl bought a _very_ skirt and gloves.*

---

[22] E.g., Nakazawa et al. (2002, web): *"The ability to retrieve complete memories on the basis of incomplete sets of cues, is a crucial function of biological memory systems. The extensive recurrent connectivity of the CA3 area of hippocampus has led to suggestions that it might provide this function."* Kumaran et al. (2016, web): *"Pattern completion: recurrent connections from the active CA3 neurons onto other active CA3 neurons are strengthened during the experience, such that if a subset of the same neurons later becomes active, the rest of the pattern will be reactivated."*

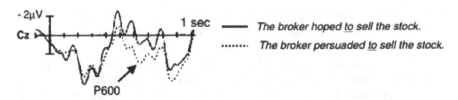

Fig. 5.1 *P600 response to sentence with syntactic violation.* Such readings help locate the neural substrate for syntax in the prefrontal (Broca) area. (Figure from Osterhout and Holcomb (1992) in Kuperberg (2007, 25))

(b) Semantic violation: *The girl <u>ate</u> a skirt and gloves.*
(c) Combined violations: *The girl <u>ate</u> a <u>very</u> skirt and gloves.*

Researchers measured the negative ERP responses (N400) that are known to be elicited for semantic violations, and the positive ERP responses (P600) that are associated with syntactic violations, recorded both in terms of time and amplitude.[23]

Results indicated that while participants correctly reacted to syntactic violations, these violations did not impede sentence comprehension (i.e., no N400 semantic violation responses occurred despite syntactic violations). Researchers conclude that no evidence could be found of a functional primacy of syntactic over semantic processes in sentence comprehension.[24]

Figure 5.1 shows the P600 amplitudes elicited upon reading a sentence with pronounced syntactic violation.

The authors refer to other studies supporting their challenge, among them one by Kuperberg (2007) who proposes that the semantic combination (associations) of words and semantic–thematic relationships, driven not by syntax but by lexical semantic memory, can reasonably account for constructions that lead to comprehension.[25]

Generativists might respond to this challenge by pointing out that their syntax-first theory pertains to sentence generation, not sentence comprehension. And that indeed may be so, and have possible bearing on the matter. But this explanation does not alter the fact that the generativist-based studies we have referred to all

---

[23] N400 is a negative-going event-related potential (ERP) that peaks at around 400 ms after the onset of a content word. It was discovered by Friederici in 1980 when negative N400 amplitudes were found to be elicited by semantically incongruous words, e.g., *He spread the warm bread with socks.* P600 is a positive ERP response elicited by syntactic ambiguities or by violations in agreement or word order (Kuperberg 2007, 24f).

[24] Yaxu Zhang et al. (2010, 765). Researchers conclude: "... *we found that semantic interpretation proceeded despite the impossibility of a well-formed syntactic analysis.*"

[25] Kuperberg (2007) argues that syntax-related P600 responses can also be trigged by semantic factors such as verb-argument violations and violations in associative semantic relationships, therefore raising doubt to the attribution of P600 to syntactic violations alone. According to Kuperberg, P600 responses to both syntactic and semantic factors suggest that normal language comprehension proceeds dynamically along two complementary streams, one semantic and memory-based, the other syntactic and rule-based, neither of which are purely one or the other. Moreover, the two streams compete, which he says helps explain individual differences in mode of comprehension.

pertain not to generation but to grammar acquisition. As we saw, their operative assumption has been that a sentence (and therefore presumably its meaning) may be considered acquired if and only if it is shown to be grammatical. It seems these generativist-based acquisition and comprehension studies have little to do with actual sentence generation.[26]

The following is a little experiment of our own to see whether the claim that the Peking researchers and others make for the brain can also be said of any MT system, namely that syntactic violations do not impede semantic comprehension. We present a sentence in (3) with a pronounced syntactic violation (one that is somewhat more ambiguous and therefore possibly more confounding). In our exercise, the measure of sentence comprehension will be the quality of its target translation, as shown in (3) (i) for Logos Model, in (3)(ii) for five of the MT systems we have been testing, and in (3)(iii) and (iv) for two neural MT system. Comprehension errors are underlined.

(3)   *The weather bureaus all **reports** that the winter will be mild.*

Translation by Logos Model
(3)(i)   *Les services de temps **signalent** tous que l'hiver sera doux.*

Translations (with minor variations) by Google SMT Translate, Bing SMT and NMT Translator, PROMT Translator and SYSTRANet
(3)(ii)   *Les bureaux météorologiques tous **les rapports** que l'hiver sera doux.*

Translation by Google GNMT translate
(3) (iii)   *Les bureaux météorologiques **signalent** tous que l'hiver sera doux.*

Translation by LISA Lab NMT
(3)(iv)   *Les bureau météorologiques **indiquent** que l'hiver sera doux.*

Commentary
Interestingly, only systems with neural net architecture, viz., Logos Model in (3)(i), Google's GNMT Translate in (3)(iii), and LISA Lab NMT in (3)(iv), properly treat *reports* in (3) as a verb in the French translation, and moreover get *reports* to agree in number with its plural subject. This may be said to simulate a case of semantic comprehension overcoming a seriously violated syntactic construction, semantic comprehension sufficient for translation purposes. The other MT systems (including Bing NMT Translator) misresolve *reports* to a plural noun, indicating miscomprehension. Notice that all of these systems handle the French transfer for the noun phrase *weather bureaus* more aptly than Logos Model. This can be attributed to the empirically-derived basis for the lexicons of these other systems. As previously observed, inaptness of transfer is a not uncommon weakness of Logos Model in domains the system has not been prepared to handle.

---

[26]Chomsky (2000, 69) himself envisions generative grammar as a means for mapping input preparatory to its interpretation. (See Postscript 5-D).

On this matter of syntax and semantics and how they relate, the simple analogy of *Donner und Blitzen* may be instructive. We experience thunder and lightning as separate and distinct matters, but everyone understands that, while distinct, they are inseparable aspects of a single phenomenon. The same may be said about semantics and syntax in natural language. Put as simply as possible, they go together and can only be seen as separate if observed at a distance (see Postscript 5-E for an illustration of this). No one appreciates this interconnectedness of syntax and semantics better than MT developers who spend their days pulling sentences apart to render their equivalence appropriately in another language.

Academic linguists of course also look at language analytically, but not nearly as relentlessly at MT developers. And academic interest in a sentence has more commonly been for its syntax, less often for its semantics, and rarely for purposes of translation. Noam Chomsky once provided direct evidence of this latter circumstance in his own case. In one of his earlier writings he admitted that he had been working in linguistics for some time before he became aware that the particle *to* in infinitive constructions could have entirely different meanings, as in sentences like (4) and (5) (our examples, not his).

(4)   *John asked him **to** fix the problem.*
(5)   *John hired him **to** fix the problem.*

By contrast, virtually all MT developers involving English source will tell you that the differences the particle *to* may have in translation is one of the very first matters they were obliged to deal with in building their system. This is attested to by the correct translations below of (4) and (5) by all MT systems we have been testing, without exception.

<u>Translations of (4) and (5) by all MT systems tested</u>

(4)(i)   *John lui a demandé **de** résoudre le problème.*
(4)(ii)   *John bat ihn, das Problem **zu** lösen*
(5)(i)   *John l'a embauché **pour** résoudre le problème.*
(5)(ii)   *John stellte ihn ein, **um** das Problem zu lösen.*

No one appreciates better than MT developers how form and function, syntax and semantics interrelate. Instead of looking at language either syntactically or semantically, Logos developers felt obliged to consider both at the same time, dealing with language *in medias res* so to speak, at a midpoint between the two extremes. In dealing with language semantico-syntactically, we at Logos were able to employ linguistic generalities more productively than is possible just with syntax alone.

The fact is we did not know how to look at linguistic patterns in any other way.[27] And the underlying preoccupation of this book is whether the brain might not be

---

[27] Pothos (2007) argues that semantic patterns rather than syntactic rules form the deeper basis of linguistic learning, and he connects these patterns with hippocampal exemplars. We contend that these exemplar-patterns are semantico-syntactic, allowing them to function at an abstract level

doing likewise, that it might actually work with language abstractly in this same integrated, semantico-syntactic fashion. Our view of this, though arrived at independently, was hardly original. There is a school of metalinguistic thought, construction grammar, which understands that the mental processing of language necessarily entails the integration of syntax and semantics. What was perhaps original about our efforts at Logos was to flesh out this integration with a workable, taxonomic semantico-syntactic language called SAL, a second-order abstraction language. SAL enabled our hypotheses about integrated mental processes to be simulated in the computer, and in so doing to satisfy the machine's need for generality in language processing in a way that included semantics.[28] And, we should add, by making semantics available at every stage of the process, SAL helped to all but eradicate complexity effects in MT.

5.4 Conclusion

We conclude this examination of syntax versus semantics with a brief review of construction grammar (Hoffman and Trousdale 2013), a loosely defined perspective on language that is supportive of Logos Model. Construction grammar began to emerge in the last decades of the previous century largely in reaction to generative theory. Construction grammar is an umbrella term for variously held views that language consists of inseparable pairings of *"form and function."*[29] It was begun largely by George Lakoff (1987) and Charles Fillmore (Fillmore et al. 1988) and may be thought of as a conceptual sibling to the Cognitive Grammar of Ronald Langacker (1991, 2008) with which Logos Model has much in common (Schmid 1996).

Among the main tenets of construction grammar is the notion that our knowledge of language consists of stored constructions (Goldberg 2003), of patterns of paired form and function, and that these constructions are learned by general cognitive processes that receive input from language exposure and that then generalize upon it.[30] Furthermore, the network of these constructions represents the basis of our knowledge of any given language.[31]

---

semantically as well as syntactically. We argue that semantico-syntactic abstraction accounts for the brain's effectiveness and efficiency in the use and processing of language, an effectiveness Logos Model feebly attempts to simulate.

[28] See Part Two for a full presentation of SAL on the open parts of speech.

[29] The term "function" in construction grammar denotes meaning or semantic intent.

[30] Note how this combination of *exposure* together with *cognitive processes* seems to comport with the *empirical, analytical* and *analogical* operations ascribed to language acquisition in Chap. 3. Relative to this, see Postscript 5-F for a construction grammarian's discussion of a child's acquisition of language through an initial exposure to patterns of language and a subsequent mechanism of generalization upon these patterns.

[31] Note how this comports with Logos Model, where the store of pattern-rules constitutes Logos Model's working knowledge of a given source language. See Postscript 5-G for further discussion.

Finally, construction grammar holds that these constructions, these linguistic patterns, are represented by a continuum that may range anywhere between the lexicon-syntax extremes. In sum, the construction grammar perspective does not allow language to be divided up into "core" grammar and a largely secondary "periphery" of lexicon, offering instead an integrative view of lexicon and grammar. This fully comports with the semantico-syntactic representation in Logos Model, where grammar and lexicon are integrated in abstract patterns of paired form and meaning.[32,33]

In the next chapter, Chap. 6, we elaborate on the design, process and performance of Logos Model.

Postscripts

Postscript 5-A

> The telling point here is that, according to Chomsky, this metacultural merge mechanism operates without reference to the meaning of the constructions that it generates.

Chomsky is not saying that language is innately structural in some *predetermined* way, only that structure is language's essential characteristic. One wants to ask, however, whether this claim to structure is special to language, as opposed to thought in general. Certainly thought as well as language entails order. Coherence whether in thought or language would be impossible without some ordering principle. Syntax is simply that ordering principle as applied to language. Chomsky however holds that syntax is an ordering principle that exists independently of meaning, without reference to the semantics of what is being ordered. That position seems questionable at best.

One wants to ask whether the structure of a sentence, its syntax, has any reason to exist apart from its content, apart from the semantics of what is being structured. Surely, one can isolate structure as a special topic of investigation, but to assert that the structure has a separate and autonomous existence, that the relationship (syntax) between concepts has an existence apart from the concepts (semantics) being

---

[32] There is little similarity between SAL and Fillmore's subsequently developed Frame Semantics that has now become a part of construction grammar. Just the opposite was the case with Fillmore's earlier work with Case Grammar, where similarities clearly exist between it and SAL. SAL however evolved inductively from issues relating to sentence analysis in MT, independently of Case Grammar. Moreover, Case Grammar's syntactic subdivisions never came to be developed into a full-blown, second-order language anywhere near resembling the semantico-syntactic elaborations of SAL.

[33] The neurolinguist Pulvermüller (2010, 2013)) holds that the tendency of most grammatical frameworks to list syntactic rules and lexicon as separate components is not neurologically founded. In Pulvermüller 2010, 28) he attempts to *"define mechanisms … that may help to neurologically underpin the tight link between syntax and semantics postulated in the context of Cognitive and Construction Grammar."*

related, seems truly mystifying, like saying A and B are in a structural relationship without being A and B. The very notion of a structural relationship has to presuppose the existence of the things that are being related, and in language those things are *concepts* represented by words and phrases.

Chomsky not only separates syntax from semantics but insists that syntax comes first. But how order can be separated from things being ordered is indeed puzzling. It would be far more natural to assume that the two are interdependent and inseparable, that the very notion of order arises out of the relationships concepts assume in a proposition, i.e., because the concepts engender order. Certainly, you can speak of order as a separate and distinct notion, but you cannot speak of orderings without considering the actual things being ordered. It takes little reflection to see that the things being ordered surely must have some say on how they are ordered; in short, that the semantic intent of a sentence has something to do with its word order. Sentence word order can hardly be independent of its semantic intent.

Postscript 5-B

> ... newer findings in the past decade are rendering these somewhat earlier views less and less tenable, especially in light of increasing recognition of the hippocampus and its declarative role in language processing.

The following quote from Bonhage et al. (2015, web) implies that, short of instruction (instructional feedback), the learning of a second language is essentially based on hippocampal-like, associative mechanisms. This would seem to comport with our argument regarding the efficiency of an *analogical* mechanism in second language acquisition, as laid out in Chap. 3, the point being that this *analogical* mechanism is what enables the student to exploit the instruction-free exposure he or she may have experienced.

> *A recent study on L2 learning compared native and non-native speakers after brief exposure to correct Italian sentences without any feedback (Mueller et al. 2009). From the diverging pattern of brain responses between native and non-native speakers, it can be inferred that non-native speakers did not acquire an abstract representation of the underlying syntactic rules after mere exposure to simple Italian sentences, suggesting that feedback is necessary for the acquisition of a grammatical rule set.*

Postscript 5-C

> Recent neuroimaging-based studies in the past decade or so have begun to reveal a considerably more nuanced picture of the cortical language process. Brain areas hitherto not especially known to be involved with language are increasingly being recognized.

Pulvermüller (2010) lists various anatomical areas associated with semantic processing, itemized below. He points out that there is no single hub for semantic processing in the brain. Note that the broadly defined Broca area, included in this list, is also involved with meaning.

(i) Inferior frontal cortex (iFC): the anterior part of Broca's area and adjacent tissue in left IFC (Brodmann areas, BA44, 45, and 47).

(ii) Superior temporal cortex (STC): Wernicke's area, the classic posterior language area in and adjacent to the superior temporal gyrus and sulcus.

(iii) Inferior parietal cortex (iPC): angular and adjacent supramarginal gyrus in iPC provides another candidate region for a semantic hub.

(iv) Inferior and middle temporal cortex (m/iTC): a general semantic binding site between words and their meaning. (Note that the interaction between the inferior and middle temporal cortex and the medial temporal cortex (MTC – hippocampus area) is not well established, but their semantic functions clearly overlap.)

(v) Anterior temporal cortex (aTC): semantic dementia (SD), a severe and specific semantic deficit, is characterized by severe lesions of both temporal poles (TPs); some neuroimaging results also point to a role of TPs in semantic processing.

Postscript 5-D

> As we saw, [the] operative assumption [of generativist-inspired brain studies] has been that a sentence (and therefore presumably its meaning) may be considered acquired if and only if it is shown to be grammatical. In short, these generativist-based acquisition and comprehension studies have nothing to do with generation.

There's a certain irony in this with regard to MT. In the decades before the turn of the century, MT models based on generativist theory sought to analyze/acquire/decode sentences by applying rules of sentence generation. In effect, a sentence would be considered acquired if and only if the sentence was found to be generatable by stored rules of grammar. If the sentence could be generated, it could be considered acquired. A second irony may be noted here in passing. In *Aspects*, Chomsky (1965) stated that *"the problem for one concerned with operational procedures is to develop tests that give the correct result."* None of the earlier MT models predicated on syntax-first principles had ever risen anywhere near the level of an effective, working system, i.e., had ever given *"the correct result."*

Postscript 5-E

> The same may be said about semantics and syntax in natural language. Put as simply as possible, they go together and can only be seen as separate if viewed from a distance.

Notice how impossible it is to separate the roles of semantics and syntax in resolving the meanings of the verb *put* and the two instances of the preposition *on* in (a).

(a)   *John **put** his report **on** the election **on** the table.*

In order to resolve the meanings of the words *put* and *on* in the above sentence (and *table* as well), the interaction of both their semantics and syntactic relations must be grasped. In effect, the sentence must be processed semantico-syntactically. For example, the semantics of the verb *put* (as *place*) is established by the preposition *on* in its second syntactic instance, not *on* its first instance. And what keeps the first instance of *on* away from *put's* potential syntactic claim to it is the semantics of this *on's* object, *election*. One does not put (place) a *report* on an *election*. (Also, note that *report* determines the semantics of this first instance of *on* as *about*). And the second syntactic instance of *on* (now because of *put's* legitimate claim to it) influences the meaning of its object, *table* (as *support surface* rather than as *information*). In short, one can hardly deal with either the syntax or the semantics of this sentence as independent matters. One must deal with it semantico-syntactically.

Note in the sentences below how dependent the translations of the preposition *on* are on the implied SAL codes of its object, and how proper translation depends upon a semantico-syntactic pattern-rule in SEMTAB. In (b'), for example, a pattern-rule that too narrowly constrained the SAL designation of the preposition's object failed to cause the first instance of *on* to be rendered correctly as *über* (*about*) in the German. In (c'), by contrast, that same pattern-rule in SEMTAB did what it was meant to do.

<u>Translations by Logos Model</u>
(b)   *His book **on** the war lay **on** the table.*
(b')   *Sein Buch **auf** dem Krieg lag **auf** dem Tisch.*
(c)   *His report on the war lay on the table.*
(c')   *Sein Bericht **über** den Krieg lag **auf** dem Tisch.*

It is interesting to speculate whether in fact the brain might not have semantico-syntactic-like patterns in its memory as well, enabling it to do exactly what these pattern-rules in SEMTAB achieve for an MT system. We speculate that the exemplar patterns employed by the hippocampus in its work of binding and detection of local dependencies suggest a functioning not unlike that of SEMTAB with its semantico-syntactic pattern-rules.

Postscript 5-F

Among the main tenets of construction theory is the notion that our knowledge of language consists of stored constructions, of patterns of paired form and function, and that these constructions are learned by general cognitive processes that receive input from language exposure and that then generalize upon it.

A paper by the developmental psycholinguist Michael Tomasello (2001) presents an interesting, usage-based model of language acquisition, one exemplified by children as they begin to acquire their first language. Much of what the author proposes seems to comport with the data-driven, pattern-based processes reflected in Logos Model.[34]

First, the child acquires and stores utterances [meaningful patterns] rather than just words in the child's early exposure to language. Utterances, patterns of words rather than individual words, become the primary linguistic unit of the child's early memory. The child hears these utterances and attempts to imitate them. These utterances are *"item-based"* and as such are contextually constrained.

Next, the child learns to extend these item-based utterances to newer contexts that differ from the context in which they were originally learned. Tomasello says the child does this by treating an original utterance as a *"template"* or *"schema"* wherein individual items get replaced with new items that make the original utterance appropriate to newer contexts. In effect, specific items in the originally learned schema have become *"slots"* that can be filled with other items. For example, when a mother asks of her child, *want X?* the child might reply *want Y*.

The child is treating X as a slot fillable with new items, but these new items of course cannot be so different as to violate constraints otherwise imposed by the original utterance. Y cannot be semantically dissimilar to X; if X is *milk*, Y is not likely to be *daddy* in the same exchange. In short, the semantics of Y is constrained by the semantics of the X slot, and it is a significant aspect of the language facility that the child intuitively operates within this constraint.

So now we see that the child's emerging language faculty includes an ability not only to learn by imitation but also to semantically generalize on what it has learned, making the learning appropriate to newer contexts. The above example is rather trivial, but the principle is not. As the child's linguistic facility matures, concrete *"items"* in the original pattern come to function abstractly as *"types,"* allowing the original pattern to be used creatively (p. 67). Tomesello implies that language could not be acquired and used apart from this generalizing power of semantic abstraction, and we of course agree.

Tomesello's proposal for the development of linguistic competence based on abstract patterns of form and meaning is clearly akin to Logos Model and the

---

[34] Tomasello is a co-director of the Max Planck Institute for Evolutionary Anthropology in Leipzig, Germany. His usage-based, psycholinguistic studies fall within the general constructionist framework of cognitive linguists.

abstract, semantico-syntactic patterns serving as the basis of Logos Model competence. Refer back to Fig. 4.1 of Chap. 4 for a depiction of this.

Postscript 5-G

Constructionist theory holds that these constructions, these linguistic patterns, are represented by a continuum that may range anywhere between the lexicon-syntax extremes. In sum, the constructionist perspective does not allow language to be divided up into *"core"* grammar and a largely secondary *"periphery"* of lexicon, an integrative view that fully comports with semantico-syntactic representation in Logos Model, where grammar and lexicon are integrated in abstract patterns of paired form and meaning.

In 2008, at a conference in Barcelona on the evolution of language,[35] two conceptual papers were delivered on the topic of linguistic expressions and how they get to be interpreted by the receiver. Both papers were written in an avowed construction grammar framework, one dealing with the semantic end of the semantico-syntactic continuum, the other paper dealing more with the syntax.

The semantics paper, "Constraint-based compositional semantics," by Wouter Van den Broeck (2008), focuses on the processes by which a language agent comes to interpret the meaning of verbal expressions. To illustrate how the meaning of an expression gets assigned (or as we would say, decoded), the author offers several simple examples, one of which is the simple noun phrase: *the red ball.*

Van den Broeck suggests that a language agent decodes the meaning of such an expression by deconstructing the composition into its separate semantic *"building blocks."* With *ball*, for example, the language agent effects an association of this as yet unassimilated term with the stored conceptual *"exemplar"* to which the literal string *ball* corresponds. In effect, this operation applies a similarity constraint that excludes all dissimilar conceptual prototypes such as, e.g., *box*. This interpretation of *ball* is initially effected at an abstract, purely conceptual level. Its *"grounded"* meaning in the given expression has yet to be gleaned.

The fuller meaning of the noun *ball* in the noun phrase is arrived at via the constraint provided by the adjective *red*, such that the combination now effectively *"grounds"* the semantics of *ball* unmistakably as *round physical object colored red*, a grounding that eliminates other possible but erroneous referents of the term such as, e.g., *baseball.*

The example of *red ball* seems trivial but Van den Broeck argues that the grounding of expressions of whatever complexity are all similarly handled by some process of constraint satisfaction.[36] Constraint satisfaction is accomplished in various ways according to the particular situation posed by each of the expression's building

---

[35] 7th International Conference on the Evolution of Language.

[36] The adjective modifier *red* constrains the semantics of the noun *ball* much the way the adjectival noun *kitchen* constrains the semantics of the noun *table* in Fig. 4.1 of Chap. 4.

blocks. With "*richer*" expressions, Van den Broeck notes that the grounding process must be prepared to deal with a veritable explosion of possible interpretations.[37]

Van den Broeck characterizes this semantic grounding process as a form of "*learning*." The author suggests that, computationally, a language agent accomplishes this learning by any (and potentially all) of the following familiar methods, depending on the requirement posed by the particular context: (i) employment of something like discrimination networks; (ii) use of probability estimations; and/or (iii) application of neural net processes. Which method used depends on the individual agent who "*constructs and maintains his own repertoire of concepts*".

Van den Broeck's three learning methods reflect kinship with the *analytical*, *empirical* and *analogical* methods that a translation machine (and quite possibly the brain) employs in processing linguistic input, as we have proposed. The parallels here are quite close in fact.[38]

From our perspective, Van den Broeck's most interesting observation, by impli-cation, is that these constraint-based processes can be thought of as applications of second order semantics. Second order semantics is a form of logic that, among other things, allows predicates in logical expressions to themselves have predicates, and that allows semantic sets to themselves have sets. The latter in particular has distinct bearing on our employment of SAL as a second order language.[39] Van den Broeck's piece does not explicitly argue for second–order semantic sets, certainly not as we have been doing in this book, but one can clearly infer support for second-order sets from his work.[40]

Van den Broeck dos not attempt to link these psycholinguistic processes to underlying neural substrates, but the role he assigns to constraint satisfaction has clear parallels with the similarity-based processes of the hippocampus (Pothos 2007). In the hippocampus, newly input words undergo decoding by being associated with a stored item functioning as *exemplar* to semantically related terms. This binding of unknown input strings with stored exemplars may be said to represent a

---

[37] None of the particular computational approaches the author suggests for keeping this explosion "*in check*" seem relevant to Logos Model, or to what we have postulated for the brain. One indication of this is that neither the brain nor Logos Model seems troubled in the least by threats of combinatorial explosion. Some other mechanism is obviously at work in the brain (and Logos Model), quite different from those the author speaks of. But in other respects Van den Broeck makes interesting observations that bear on our discussion.

[38] To remind the reader, the methods discussed in earlier chapters are, in the order Van den Broeck places them: (i) the *analytical*, procedure-driven methods of rule-based MT; (ii) the *empirical*, probabilistic, data-driven methods of statistical MT; (iii) the *analogical, symbolic* net-like approach of Logos Model. The methods of course are not mutually exclusive. (The statistically-rooted neural-net approach of NMT would appear to fall between (ii) and (iii).)

[39] If we think of the concept *chair* as the set of all particular *chairs*, then the SAL concept *support surface* may be seen as the *set of sets* that share this common property (sets such as *shelf, floor, seat,* etc.).

[40] The NLP advantage manifested by Logos Model stems precisely from its ability to process semantics at an abstract level. Note, for example, in the depiction of Logos Model in Fig. 4.1 in Chap. 4, the role that second-order semantics plays in interpreting the ambiguous terms *from* and *take,* allowing these words to be semantically "grounded," preparatory to their translation.

cognitive process whereby, in the author's terms, concepts get partially grounded. And though the hippocampus' exemplars may be literal items, they appear to function abstractly as archetypical semantic categories, much like the *"prototypes"* to which Van den Broeck alludes, and seemingly not unlike the second-order semantic categories illustrated by SAL words.[41]

The second paper of interest at this conference on the evolution of language is by Joris Bleys (2008) and is entitled "Expressing Second Order Semantics and the Emergence of Recursion." Like Van den Broeck, Bleys also works within the framework of construction grammar and its form-meaning pairings. His interest in the evolution of language concerns how a communication system could emerge that entails these properties of recursion and second order semantics. Bleys' specific focus here is of no interest to our purposes, but his general postulates about language, and in particular about the process whereby hearers decode uttered sentences, are clearly in line with our basic intuitions, and seem worth reviewing.

This author states that *"the meaning of a sentence is a semantic constraint network that the speaker wants the hearer to resolve to achieve the communication goal of the speaker."* And he divides this semantic constraint network into three layers: (i) the words themselves (lexical semantics); (ii) the words' syntactic form and structure; and (iii) the contextual whole, which whole may be greater than the sum of layers (i) and (ii). To illustrate (iii), he offers the simple expression *very big* as an example of a construction that is more than the mere conjunction of its parts, i.e., where the modifier *very* constrains the meaning of the adjective *big*.

Bleys' account of how the hearer decodes a sentence *qua* semantic network is by now, hopefully, not unfamiliar. He suggests an interpretive process that begins with (i) the association of the sentence's as yet unassimilated words with stored, previously learned semantic prototypes, such that, by virtue of the association, provisional meaning is given to the words. The process then proceeds to (ii) a syntactic grasp of word form and sentence structure conducted under the constraints of the semantics of (i); and finally the process ends by (iii) resolving any context-level constraints so as to meaningfully ground in understanding both individual words and the sentence as a whole.

What is of particular moment in this account is the role that semantics plays in the decoding of a sentence, a role played right from the start. In Bleys' account, literal words of an input sentence get associated with semantics immediately in step (i), cited above, i.e., at the outset of analysis, just as in Logos Model. And in step (ii), the decoding of word forms and sentence structure is also conducted under the constraints of the semantics of (i), again as in Logos Model. And finally, in step (iii), the meaning of the sentence depends upon detecting and satisfying contextual constraints among the form-meaning pairs as a function of the sentence as a whole.

---

[41] Note in this connection the observation by Pothos (2007, 228): *"An influential tradition in categorization assumes that category exemplars are stored, and the potential membership of new instances to a category is determined through a process of (whole) exemplar similarity."* Of course, what exactly is meant by similarity is another matter. Most commonly, similarity pertains to the overlapping of features (Daltrozzo and Conway 2014).

Stored, previously learned pattern
functioning now as a prototype

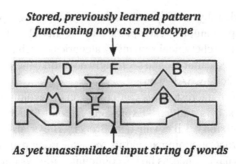

As yet unassimilated input string of words

Postscript Figure 5G-1 *Similarity-based binding of an unassimilated symbolic string with a stored, previously learned, prototypical pattern of symbols.* The process described here is perfectly consistent with that of Logos Model and with what is now generally understood about the hippocampus and its dealings with language input. Note the complete absence of mediation by rule logic. (Adapted from Bleys 2008)

A perfect example of (iii) in Logos Model may be seen in sentence (3)(i) from Chap. 3: *check the newspaper for dates*, where the meanings of the verb *check* and the preposition *for* are constrained by the entire context, just as these same words are constrained by the entire context in (3)(ii), with entirely different meanings for the verb *check* and the preposition *for*: *check the newspaper for errors*.[42]

One also sees in the semantics-syntax interaction in (i) and (ii) clear parallels with the interactions of the semantics-oriented hippocampus and the syntax-oriented Broca area.[43] Moreover, the author clearly agrees with recent neuroscience (and the intuitions instantiated in Logos Model) that, in the processing of language, syntactic operations do not occur independently of semantics.

Bleys' paper focuses chiefly on the structural end of the semantico-syntactic continuum. His object is to account for the emergence of recursion in the evolution of language, by which he means a language agent's re-use of previously learned "*rules*" in the decoding of a new utterance. Interestingly, what Bleys refers to are not rules as commonly understood but rather patterns functioning as rules, not unlike in Logos Model. This becomes evident in Bleys' graphic in Postscript Figure 5G-1.

Postscript Figure 5G-1 depicts a string of unassimilated words and their association with (binding to) a stored, previously learned pattern functioning as an exemplar or prototype. The matchup imparts the meaning of the stored pattern to the input string, thus cognitively grounding it, in part at least. The binding of ungrounded patterns with a stored, previously learned pattern shown in Figure 5G-1 is virtually

---

[42] In the first instance, *check* has the meaning of *consult*, in the second instance the meaning of *examine*. The sense of the preposition *for* differs in each instance also. See discussion in the early part of Chap. 3.

[43] The intricate, cognition-related interactions of the hippocampus and the prefrontal cortex (including the Broca area) now seems fully established in the literature, as reflected, e.g., in Jadhav et al. (2016): *"Interactions between the hippocampus and the prefrontal cortex (PFC) are critical for learning and memory."*

identical with the associative, neural net-like architecture of Logos Model. In both instances, the binding of new data with stored data is effected by the simple mechanism of similarity-based association.

The association mechanism depicted in Postscript Figure 5G-1 mimics the associative mechanism known to characterize the hippocampus, where new input is cognitively assimilated on the basis of similarity with stored exemplars, unmediated by procedural logic. What Logos Model has done is to make explicit an assumption that cerebral sentence-decoding entails the matching-up of patterns not at the level of literal words but at the level of second-order semantics.

References

Bastiaansen M, Hagoort P (2015) Frequency-based segregation of syntactic and semantic unification during online sentence level language comprehension. J Cogn Neurosci 27(11):2095–2107

Bendor D, Spiers HJ (2016) Does the hippocampus map out the future? Trends Cogn Sci 20(3):167–169

Bleys J (2008) Expressing second order semantics and the emergence of recursion. In: Smith ADM, Smith K, Ferrer-i-Cancho R (eds) Proceedings of the 7th international conference on the evolution of language. World Scientific Publishing Co, Ltd., Singapore, pp 34–41

Bonhage CE, Mueller JL, Friederici AD, Fiebach CJ (2015) Combined eye tracking and fMRI reveals neural basis of linguistic predictions during sentence comprehension. Cortex 68:33–47. https://www.ncbi.nlm.nih.gov/pubmed/26003489

Chadwick MJ, Bonnici HM, Maguire EA (2012) Decoding information in the human hippocampus: a user's guide. Neuropsychologia 50(13):3107–3121. Paris: Elsevier

Chomsky N (1957) Syntactic structures. Mouton, The Hague/Paris

Chomsky N (1965) Aspects of the theory of syntax. MIT Press, Cambridge

Chomsky N (1977) Essays on form and interpretation. Elsevier North-Holland, New York/Amsterdam

Chomsky N (2000) New horizons in the study of language and mind. Cambridge University Press, Cambridge

Daltrozzo J, Conway CM (2014) Neurocognitive mechanisms of statistical-sequential learning: what do event-related potentials tell us? Front Hum Neurosci 8:437. http://journal.frontiersin.org/article/10.3389/fnhum.2014.00437/full. Accessed 7 Nov 2016

Duff MC, Brown-Schmidt S (2012) The hippocampus and the flexible use and processing of language. Front Hum Neurosci 6:69. https://doi.org/10.3389/fnhum.2012.00069. Accessed 23 September 2016

Fillmore C, Kay P, O'Connor C (1988) Regularity and idiomaticity in grammatical constructions: the case of let alone. Language 64:501–538

Friederici AD, Weissenborn J (2007) Mapping sentence form onto meaning: the syntax-semantic interface. Brain Res 1146:50–58. https://doi.org/10.1016/j.brainres.2006.08.038. Accessed 2 Mar 2016

Glaser YG, Martin RC, Van Dyke JA, Chris Hamilton A, Tan Y (2013) Neural basis of semantic and syntactic interference in sentence comprehension. Brain Lang 126:314–326

Goldberg AE (2003) Constructions: a new theoretical approach to language. Trends Cogn Sci 7(5):219–224

Grodzinsky Y, Friederici AD (2006) Neuroimaging of syntax and syntactic processing. Curr Opin Neurobiol 16(2):240–246

Hagoort P (2015) The binding problem for language, and its consequences for the neurocognition of comprehension. In: Gibson EA, Pearlmutter NJ (eds) The processing and acquisition of reference. A Bedford Book/MIT Press, London, pp 403–436

Hauser M, Hofmann J, Optiz B (2012) Rule and similarity in grammar: their interplay and individual differences in the brain. NeuroImage 60:2019–2026. http://epubs.surrey.ac.uk/737179/1/Hauser.2012.NI.AGL_rule_similarity.final%20Revision.pdf

Hoffman T, Trousdale G (eds) (2013) The Oxford handbook of construction grammar. Oxford University Press, Oxford

Jadhav S, Rothschild G, Roumis D, Frank L (2016) Coordinataed excitation and inhibition of prefrontal ensembles during awake hippocampal sharp-wave ripple events. Neuron 90(1):113–127

Kempen G, Harbusch K (2003) An artificial opposition between grammaticality and frequency: comment on Bornkessel, Schlesewsky, and Friederici (2002). Cognition 90(2):205–210

Kumaran D, Hassabis D, McClelland JL (2016) What learning systems do intelligent agents need? Complementary learning systems theory updated. Trends Cogn Sci 20(7):512. https://doi.org/10.1016/j.tics.2016.05.004. Accessed 12 Jan 2017

Kuperberg GR (2007) Neural mechanisms of language comprehension: challenges to syntax. Brain Res 1146:23–49. https://www.ncbi.nlm.nih.gov/pubmed/17400197. Accessed 7 Nov 2016

Kurczek J, Brown-Schmidt S, Duff M (2013) Hippocampal contributions to language: evidence of referential processing deficits in amnesia. J Exp Psychol Gen 142(4):1346–1354

Lakoff G (1987) Women, fire, and dangerous things: what categories reveal about the mind. CSLI, Chicago

Langacker R (1991) Foundations of cognitive grammar, 2 vols. Stanford University Press, Stanford

Langacker R (2008) Cognitive grammar: a basic introduction. Oxford University Press, New York

Mårtensson J, Eriksson J, Bodammer NC, Lindgren M, Johansson M, Nyberg L, Lövdén M (2012) Growth of language-related brain areas after foreign language learning. Neuro Image 63(1):240–244

McClelland JL, Patterson K (2002) Rules or connections in past-tense inflections: what does the evidence rule out? Trends Cogn Sci 6(11):465–472

Mueller JL, Oberecker R, Friederici A (2009) Syntactic learning by mere exposure– An ERP study in adult learners. BNC Neurosc 10:89. https://doi.org/10.1186/1471-2202-10-89

Musso M, Moro A, Glauche V, Rijntjes M, Reichenbach J, Büchel C, Weiller C (2003) Broca's area and the language instinct. Nat Neurosci 6:774–781

Nakazawa K, Quirk MC, Chitwood RA, Watanabe M, Yeckel MF, Sun LD, Kato A, Carr CA, Johnston D, Wilson MA, Tonegawa S (2002) Requirement for hippocampal CA3 NMDA receptors in associative memory recall. Science 297(5579):211–218. https://doi.org/10.1126/science.1071795

Optiz B, Friederci AD (2007) Neural basis of processing sequential and hierarchical syntactic structures. Hum Brain Mapp 28(7):585–592

Optiz B, Friederici AD (2003) Interactions of the hippocampal system and the prefrontal cortex in learning language-like rules. NeuroImage 19:1730–1737. https://doi.org/10.1016/S1053-8119(03)00170-8. Accessed 25 Jan 2016

Optiz B, Hofmann J (2015) Concurrence of rule- and similarity-based mechanisms in artificial grammar learning. Cogn Psychol 77:77–99

Osterhout L, Holcomb PJ (1992) Event-related brain potentials elicited by syntactic anomaly. J Mem Lang 31(6):785–896

Pothos EM (2007) Theories of artificial grammar learning. Psychol Bull 133:227–244

Pulvermüller F (2010) Brain embodiment of syntax and grammar: discrete combinatorial mechanisms spelt out in neuronal circuits. Brain Lang 112(3):167–179

Pulvermüller F (2013) How neurons make meaning: brain mechanisms for embodied and abstract-symbolic semantics. Trends Cogn Sci 17(9):458–470. http://www.sciencedirect.com/science/article/pii/S1364661313001228. Accessed 13 Dec 2015

Reber AS (1967) Implicit learning of artificial grammars. J Verbal Learn Verbal Behav 6(6):855–863

Rouder JN, Ratcliff R (2006) Comparing exemplar- and rule-based theories of categorization. Curr Dir Psychol Sci 15(1):9–13. Hoboken: Wiley-Blackwell

Schmid P (1996) Clausal constituent shifts: a study in cognitive grammar and machine translation. Ph.D. dissertation, Georgetown University. UMI Dissertation Services

Shanks DR (1995) The psychology of associative learning. Cambridge University Press, Cambridge

Tomasello M (2001) First steps toward a usage-based theory of language acquisition. Cogn Linguist 11(1–2):61–82. https://doi.org/10.1515/cogl.2001.012

Ullman MT (2004) Contributions of memory circuits to language: the declarative/procedural model. Cognition 92:231–270

Van den Broeck W (2008) Constraint based compositional semantics. In: Smith ADM, Smith K, Ferrer-i-Cancho R (eds) Proceedings of the 7th international conference on the evolution of language. World Scientific Publishing Co, Ltd., Singapore, pp 338–345

Zhang Y, Yu J, Boland JE (2010) Semantics does not need a processing license from syntax in reading Chinese. J Exp Psychol Learn Mem Cogn 36(3):765–781. https://doi.org/10.1037/a0019254

Chapter 6
Logos Model: Design and Performance

Abstract In this Chapter we describe Logos Model in terms of five fundamental decisions that determined its design: (i) how linguistic knowledge is to be represented; (ii) how that linguistic knowledge is to be stored; (iii) how stored linguistic knowledge is to be applied to the input stream; (iv) how target sentences are to be generated from source analysis; (v) how complexity effects are to be dealt with. We illustrate the implementation of these design factors with translations in a variety of linguistic contexts. Translations by Logos Model are in French and/or German. Translations are also provided by other MT systems for comparative purposes. Finally, we give an example of a translation that exemplifies capabilities that are unique to an MT system like Logos Model, and we give an account of how this particular translation is accomplished.

6.1   The Translation Problem

TO TAKE A SOURCE LANGUAGE SENTENCE AND RENDER IT with any success into an equivalent sentence of another language, the translation agent has to have acquired an abundance of knowledge about the words and grammars of both languages. But to effect this translation, the agent must also have another kind of knowledge, knowledge that perceives how to move from one language to the other, what is equivalent and what is not, e.g., knowledge that enables one to known what to do about the fact (to cite a simple example) that the German counterpart of the plural English noun *eyeglasses* is not plural but singular (*Brille*).[1]

The example may seem trivial, but consider the following. Both English and German can say *many eyeglasses* (*vielen Brillen*), but only German can say *eine*

---

[1] The example of a plural noun in English taking a singular noun in German may seem inconsequential, but it illustrates the potential for confusion that may arise in source and target for terms that look alike but have significant differences (*faux amis*). For example, the French verb *ignorer* looks very much like the English verb *ignore,* but its French meaning is entirely different.

© Springer International Publishing AG, part of Springer Nature 2018

B. Scott, *Translation, Brains and the Computer*, Machine Translation:
Technologies and Applications 2, https://doi.org/10.1007/978-3-319-76629-4_6

Brille (one eyeglasses). The term for *eyeglasses* in German is singular, whereas in English it is plural and requires a plural verb. Its English pluralism notwithstanding, the term normally denotes a singular object (*my eyeglasses are …*), but because the English term happens to be plural, it can also denote a plural object (*All my eyeglasses are …*). This morphological ambiguity explains why, when we translate a simple sentence like that in (1) where **eyeglasses** calls for a singular noun in German, three of the systems we tested variously mistranslate the sentence. Output is shown below in (1)(i) and (1)(ii). Errors with respect to number are underlined.

> (1)   *My **eyeglasses** are dirty.*

> Translation by Google SMT Translate
> (1)(i)   *Meine **Brille** <u>sind</u> verschmutzt.*

> Translation by Bing SMT & NMT Translator
> (1)(ii)   *Meine **<u>Brillen</u>** <u>sind</u> verschmutzt.*

> Translation by SYSTRANet
> (1)(iii)   *Meine **<u>Brillen</u>** <u>sind</u> schmutzig.*

Three MT systems translated the number issues correctly:

> Translation by Google GNMT Translate, PROMT, Logos Model
> (1)(v)   *Meine **Brille** ist schmutzig.*

But then two of these same systems stumble when translating the simple noun phrase in (2).

> (2)   *Three **eyeglasses**.*

> Translations by PROMT and Logos Model Translator
> (2)(i)   *Drei **<u>Brille</u>**.*

Commentary

The plural of **Brille** should be **Brillen** in (2)(i). The exercise reminds us how even simple matters can confound a machine that has not been adequately instructed. As we have shown repeatedly in earlier chapters, the words and structures of a source sentence can be equivocal in many different ways, which is why translation is seldom an entirely straightforward matter.

It is interesting that when the human mind encounters an ambiguous word like *eyeglasses* in some text, it knows its denotation virtually at once. The mind knows this because it sees *eyeglasses* in a context whose structure and meaning it has been assimilating all along. Any potential difficult in translation is resolved by the neuro-psychological operations that constitute the brain's linguistic intelligence. If the machine is to do the same, it too has to be in possession of some semblance of these smarts. And as we have been saying, therein lies the dilemma for MT. The machine can certainly be taught, but the more intelligence the machine is given, the more there arises the problem of complexity, principally complexity as it relates to the difficulties developers experience in maintaining an ever-growing store of intelligence. We have called it *cognitive* complexity and it is bound to become an issue as developers keep seeking to improve the quality of system output. We know of no better explanation for the limitations that persist in MT despite its decades of development.

Foreseeing this risk of complexity in the development of Logos Model, as we mentioned earlier, our approach became defensive from the very outset. We understood that what was needed was a principled computational approach, one that would effectively minimize complexity effects, and we deduced what those principles might be from assumptions about human sentence processing.

We very briefly review these assumptions below:

i. The human sentence processor essentially comprises a lexicon of words and phrases at several levels of semantic abstraction, together with a huge collection of semantico-syntactic language patterns, all stored in associative memory. Sentence comprehension is effected by this linguistic memory store reacting to input strings, and then to sequences of synapse-like connections with other memory circuits as comprehension needs dictate. In essence, the input sentence itself drives the process, not some controlling decision logic. The input sentence itself is the algorithm controlling the translation procedure. Moreover, the entire process is conducted in unpredictable, opportunistic fashion, differing from individual to individual.

ii. Syntactic and semantic aspects of language are integrated (as in a representational continuum).

iii. Language is largely processed at the level of second-order abstractions (e.g., Norway, Chile, Japan → countries). Abstraction is assumed to be the principal means used by the brain to reduce complexity, illustrating nature's law of least effort.

iv. Linguistic memory is content-addressable. This is understood to explain one of the reasons why an ever-increasing knowledge store does not have complexity effects in human sentence processing.

6.1.1   Five Fundamental Design Decisions

Translating this hypothesized mental model into an MT model entailed decisions regarding five fundamental design questions:

1. How do you represent natural language internally to the computer?
2. How do you store that knowledge?

3. How do you apply stored knowledge to the input stream?
4. How do you effect target generation?
5. How do you cope with complexity?

We discuss each of the above in what follows.[2]

6.2　How Do You Represent Natural Language?

Our intention was to build a deterministic parser (where a single parse of the source sentence is produced, preparatory to translation). To produce a single parse right away rather than a set of candidate parses that subsequently have to be pruned to the single parse, one had to integrate semantics and syntax so that both would be available to decisions at every stage of source sentence analysis. What kind of representation language would allow for this?

There were two known ways to accomplish that integration. One could devise a list of semantic primitives and apply them to part-of-speech instantiations (lexicon) as appropriate, or one could develop a semantic taxonomy to which natural language words are mapped. We chose the latter option.

The taxonomy we developed was semantico-syntactic rather than purely semantic. We were generally looking for the semantic aspects of words that had syntactic implications. As previously stated, we dubbed the language SAL (for Semantico-syntactic Abstraction Language). In Fig. 6.1, we present the taxonomy for the SAL noun category *Place*. A full SAL taxonomy for all four open classes is given in Part Two of this book.

As will be evident from the graphic, SAL is an abstraction language organized into supersets, sets, and subsets. There are ten supersets for nouns: *Concrete, Mass, Abstract, Deverbal, Animate, Aspective, Information, Measure, Place* (Fig. 6.1), and *Time*. SAL is intended to look and function like natural language at a more abstract level, such that any NL string could be readily expressed by an equivalent SAL string. The SAL language consists of approximately 1000 elements for all parts of speech combined. SAL nouns and SAL verbs each comprise roughly 100 of these elements. In effect, SAL allows processing at levels roughly two orders of magnitude richer than pure syntax and two orders of magnitude leaner than NL.

SAL has been developed only for English and German.

---

[2] In the following sections, we compare Logos Model translations with output from various other MT systems. See Postscript 6-B of this chapter for a collection of these comparisons.

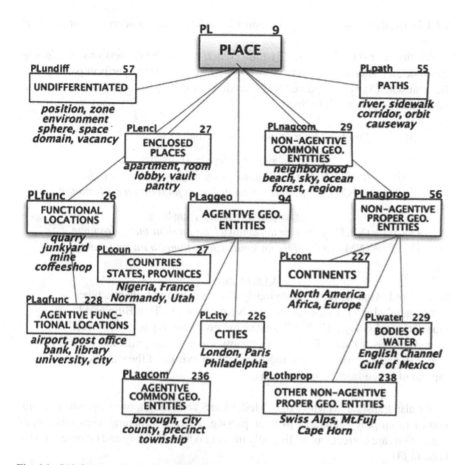

Fig. 6.1 *SAL Superset for the Noun* Place. Note the role of agentiveness. Agentiveness can have a bearing on resolution of noun/verb homographs in English. For example, because *beach* is non-agentive, the string *the beach plans,* would bias analysis away from *plans* as a possible verb, unlike the string *the city plans* … In the expression *from the pantry*, the SAL code for *pantry* as *enclosed space* allows the sense of the preposition *from* to be resolved as *out of*. SAL differentiation here between countries and cities supports needs of targets like French, e.g., *in N(PLcity)* ➔ *à N(PLcity),* as in *à Paris*; *in N(PLcoun)* ➔ *en N(PLcoun),* as in *en France*

6.2.1   Effectiveness of SAL for Deterministic Parsing

As observed earlier, deterministic parsing where a single parse result is desired is not possible on the basis of syntax alone. Semantics is often needed in order to resolve ambiguities, including ambiguities relating to structure. To demonstrate this, we show how the ambiguous construction in (3), below, is handled (or not handled) in various MT systems, several of which employ semantic parsing, several of which do not.

We focus on the ambiguity inherent in the syntactic string *N1 or N2 N3* in sentences (3). The ambiguity here relates to whether *N3* is modified by the string *N1 or N2* or just by *N2* alone. We see that in (3) the string *N1 or N2* does indeed modify

N3. Clearly, the parse must rely on semantics to know which interpretation of (3) is correct.

We first translate sentence (3) into French by the SMT versions of Google Translate and Microsoft Translator, two systems not known to perform parsing. We then translate (3) by the updated NMT version of these systems. Structural errors in the French output are underlined.

(3)   *I prefer a **ham or cheese** sandwich.*

Translation by Google Translate

(3)(i)   (SMT) *Je préfère <u>un **jambon ou du fromage** sandwich</u>.*
(3)(ib)   (GNMT) *Je préfère un sandwich au **jambon ou au fromage**.*

Translation by Bing Translator

(3)(iia)   (SMT) *Je préfère un sandwich au **jambon ou __ fromage**.*
(3)(iib)   (NMT) *Je préfère un sandwich au **jambon ou au fromage**.*

Commentary

In (3), words **ham** and **cheese** obviously share a common semantic type, detection of which is essential for a proper parse of (3). That Bing NMT Translator and Google GNMT Translate are now able to parse (3) correctly strongly suggests the availability of semantics to a not insignificant degree in these neural systems, most probably by virtue of the statistical capture of usage from bi-lingual texts.

We also translate (3) with Logos Model and SYSTRANet, two linguistic systems known to employ semantics in their parsing. From a structural viewpoint, both translations are correct, but stylistically they are inferior to Bing and Google translations of (3).

Translation by Logos Model

(3)(iii)   *Je préfère un sandwich de jambon ou de fromage.*

Translation by SYSTRANet

(3)(iv)   *Je préfère un sandwich à jambon ou à fromage.*

Commentary

Note that on purely stylistic grounds, the SYSTRANet translation in (3)(iv), *un sandwich à jambon ou à fromage*, is to be preferred over Logos Model.

We also translated (3) into German, shown in (3)(v), below. Only Logos Model translation is displayed. Output is correct.

Translation by Logos Model

(3)(v)   *Ich ziehe eine Schinken- oder Käsestulle vor.*

6.3   How Do You Store Linguistic Knowledge?

6.3.1   General Remarks

Traditionally, linguistic knowledge is stored in two principal places: lexicon and rule base. Normally, the lexicon would be the principal repository of linguistic detail, and it is here that whatever semantic information a system will have tends to reside. Lexicons thus tend to be information-rich, and because they are by nature indexable, lexicons can grow to virtually any size with negligible impact on throughput. But because lexical entries are word-specific, the lack of generality in lexically-driven operations can be considered a drawback. Another drawback concerns the cost and difficulty users may experience in building and maintaining information-rich lexicons.[3]

Rule bases, by contrast, are largely confined to syntactic information where generality is assured. Because of their abstractness, syntactic rules can also be relatively few in number, considered a sought-after virtue with respect to throughput issues. But there are drawbacks here as well, chief among which are the large parse forests that parsing with syntax-only rules entails, requiring subsequent heuristic pruning to a single parse.

As we shall show below, the knowledge store in Logos Model differs rather radically from this traditional arrangement.

6.3.2   Logos Model Lexicon

The Logos Model lexicon has notably lean informational content, considering that the lexicon must support semantic processing and the distant goal of high-quality MT. Lexical information for a given entry is confined to the following:

(i)   SAL classification for the part of speech (POS code plus a triplet of SAL codes for semantic superset/set/subset). When updating the lexicon, these codes can be assigned automatically by an expert system, as an option to the user. Coding accuracy by this method is suboptimal however, and interactive means are available to assist users in assigning and reviewing codes, an action that was recommended.

(ii) Alternative parts of speech and transfers for verb and process noun entries to allow for their conversion to each other (*connect* < — > *connection*). This is also true for the class of adjectives that are convertible to adverbs and vice

---

[3] Historically, some otherwise effective systems have been known to founder largely on these grounds (e.g., TAUM Aviation (Juola 1989)).

versa (*quick* < — > *quickly*). These alternative parts of speech and transfers are assigned semi-automatically upon users' update of the lexicon.

(iii) Codes denoting an entry's morphological class and properties. Morphological data (including stems) are automatically assigned upon users' update of the lexicon.

(iv) Optional domain codes (Subject Matter Codes) and user ID's that have been assigned to entries by users. Users specify these codes to guide lexical selection at run time.

(v) Pointers to target transfers (for any number of target languages).

Informational leanness in the lexicon was motivated by the need to keep lexical work as simple and user-friendly as possible. The lexicon was also designed to be developer-friendly. For example, except for SAL coding which is source-oriented, there is no distinction between source and target entries in the lexicon: the same entry serves both source and target purposes. This is also true of morphology tables.

The lexicon of the commercial Logos Model was stored in a relational database (Oracle) and ran under Microsoft Windows OS. The OpenLogos lexicon is stored in PostgreSQL, running under Linux.

6.3.3   The Pattern-Rule Database

Pattern-rule databases in Logos Model are indexed on their SAL pattern and are accessed by the SAL input stream much in the way one would access a dictionary. This is how Logos Model simulates the content addressable memory feature characteristic of the human brain. The pattern-rules are restricted in function, limited in scope, and number in the many thousands. See Fig. 6.2, for their distribution in tables over Logos Model architecture.[4] Note that these pattern-rules are also stored in a relational database.

Pattern-rules have three parts, with an optional link to a target-action component. These are:

(i) the SAL pattern comprising as many as ten elements, up to three of which may be constrained Kleene stars. Each SAL element in the pattern is characterized by a triplet code for (a) Word Class, (b) Type, and (c) Form.

---

[4]As stated in earlier chapters, it is misleading to speak of Logos Model as a rule-based translation system (RBMT). Logos Model is data-driven and pattern-based. What especially differentiates Logos Model from rule-based models concerns the manner in which matching is accomplished. We remind the reader that in Logos Model, pattern-rules are ordered purely on their SAL pattern, and matching is effected by the input stream functioning like a search argument against stored pattern-rules, not unlike in dictionary lookup. No metarule, discrimination network, or decision logic of any kind is involved in effecting these matches.

Logos Model as an Incremental Pipeline Analyzer-Generator

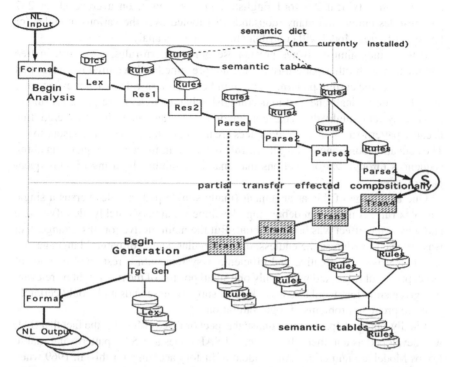

Fig. 6.2 *Pipeline Architecture of Logos Model.* NL text enters at the top where formatting is analyzed and stripped out, and sentence boundaries identified. For each sentence, NL string is converted to a SAL string via lexical substitution. This SAL string then passes down the pipeline and interacts with stored SAL pattern-rules that effect a single, bottom-up parse. The Res1 and Res2 modules perform a macro-parse of the sentence. The next four parsing modules perform a micro-parse, with links to target modules to effect quasi tree-to-tree equivalencing. In this micro-parse, (i) Parse1/Tran1 analyzes and transfers simple NPs; (ii) Parse2/Tran2 does the same for compound NP's, NP complementation, and embedded, absolute constructions within a clause; (iii) Parse3/Tran3 treats intra-clausal structures, e.g., predicate/argument analysis; (iv) Parse4/Tran4 deals with inter-clausal issues. Nested access to semantics-oriented pattern-rules in the Semantic Tables (SEMTAB) may be initiated by any pattern-rule at any stage of analysis or generation

(ii) a constraint component specifying conditions that must be satisfied for the pattern-rule to fire.

(iii) link to a source activation component of the pattern-rule that, among other things, may rewrite an input pattern as a more abstract constituent, and then add that constituent to the source parse.

(iv) optional link to target-activation component, for any number of target languages.

The activation component of pattern-rules is extremely limited in what it is allowed to do. This restriction accounts for the large number of pattern-rules. To illustrate: in a typical 25-word English source sentence, on average about 257 pattern-rules among the many thousands distributed over the various modules (or layers) of Logos Model will contribute to a sentence's analysis.

Pattern-rules almost always presuppose other pattern-rules, and work in free conjunction with other pattern-rules that are presumed to have fired before or that will fire after the current pattern. Thus a number of pattern-rules, each presupposing the other, are typically needed to accomplish what a single, more powerful rule in another system might do. This conjunction of pattern-rules is considered free because pattern-rule matching sequences are not regulated by any supervisory logic. The activation component of a pattern-rule itself can influence subsequent matching sequences through various actions that enable or inhibit the firing of subsequent pattern-rules.

One advantage of this arrangement (many simple pattern-rules versus a single complex rule) is that when debugging, developers can very quickly identify where and why some effect was brought about. But the main motive for this arrangement was the need to address the endless, often irregular details of natural language in a way that was both effective and efficient. A system with a restricted number of large, powerful rules, and where only one small portion of the rule might be relevant in a given situation, would be less likely to support these ends and would certainly be more prone to problems of logic saturation.

Finally, and perhaps the most unusual aspect of Logos Model is the fact that SAL was developed as a numeric language. All SAL codes and SAL patterns internal to Logos Model are numerical. An accident of history accounts for this. In 1969 when work first began on Logos Model, the only programming language available to the developers was Fortran, hence the employment of numbers.[5] Later, when this arrangement might have been changed, the advantages of numeric representation encouraged us to retain the practice.[6]

This use of numbers may seem contrary to good linguistic practice, but consider the efficiency it affords. For example, take an English word like "*techniques*." The developer only has to write five numbers in order to characterize this term as (i) a noun that is (ii) a member of the 'abstract' superset, (iii) the 'verbal abstract' set; and (iv) the 'method/procedure' subset, and one that has (v) plural morphology; in short, the Class/Type/Form triplet, which in the case of *techniques* is: 1 733 2. Here 1 denotes noun Word Class; 733 denotes SAL Type ('method/procedure' subset, which inherits the 'verbal abstract' set code and the 'general abstract' superset code); and 2 in the Form field signifies plural morphology. In mnemonics (used exclusively for documentation), *techniques* and related terms would be rendered N(ABmeth; pl).

---

[5] Logos Model software is now written in C.

[6] See Part II Postscript for discussion about the use of numbers and its advantages. Also notice the numbers in Fig. 6.1.

6.4   How Do You Apply Stored Knowledge to the Input Stream?

In Logos Model, linguistic knowledge gets applied to the input stream in ways that differ quite radically from traditional, rule-based systems. Traditionally, a set of rules would be applied to the input stream via a metarule or discrimination network, in the expectation that one of the rules will be found relevant. In this many-to-one arrangement—many rules seeking a relevant match on a single input situation—throughput considerations require that the "many" be kept to a minimum. Furthermore, the language used for rules and for input stream are heterogeneous, with the consequence that the connection between stored knowledge and input stream could never be automatic, and must always remain an art therefore.

In Logos Model, the practice is just the opposite. Logos Model allows the matching initiative to come from the input stream, not the knowledge base. Matching therefore is one-to-many—a single input situation seeking a relevant match in a body of pattern-rules, like in dictionary lookup. This difference is hardly trivial, as hopefully the following will make clear.

This one-to-many arrangement is made possible by three factors:

(i)   first, and most basically, the representational scheme of input stream and knowledge base is homogeneous, by virtue of both being based on patterns represented in SAL;

(ii) second, because of (i), this SAL pattern base is indexable, very much like a dictionary, albeit one where SAL words are numeric;

(iii) third, because of (i) and (ii), the SAL input stream is able to serve as search argument to the SAL knowledge base.

The effect of this is that the one-to-many matching arrangement often as not becomes virtually one-to-one; a SAL input pattern finds its most relevant pattern-rule directly and always automatically. A second crucial advantage is that the size of the knowledge base can be arbitrarily large, without significant impact on throughput.

A third advantage has to do with the cognitive complexity issue. Allow us to illustrate. Let's say that a particular input phenomenon has been incorrectly handled by some pattern-rule, or perhaps not handled at all. System diagnostics tell the developer virtually at a glance what pattern-rules were matched by this input. The developer determines either that the problem can be addressed by modifying the matched-upon pattern-rule, or that it will require an entirely new pattern-rule (or sequence of such pattern-rules). In the latter case, the developer does not have to ponder where to place this new rule to insure that it gets matched: the new pattern-rule automatically finds its proper place in the knowledge store. And the developer can be certain that the new pattern-rule, assuming it is more specific, will be automatically matched upon in the next test run. If larger testing reveals that the new pattern-rule has had some unintended effects elsewhere in the test corpus, he or she goes back and repeats the procedure, refining the new pattern-rule as necessary. This cycle of trial and error occurs quite often in the course of normal development, but

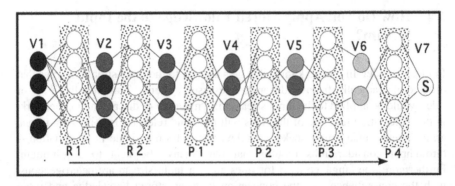

Fig. 6.3 *Logos Model Pipeline as a Cascaded, Six-stage Network.* Figure aptly illustrates how the SAL input stream (V1-V7) interfaces with SAL pattern-rules in stored memory (R1-P4) to create a deterministic, bottom-up sentence parse, ending in S. Each cell in input vectors V1-V7 represents a single SAL constituent (in higher input layers, cells represent concatenated constituents). Cells in hidden layers R1-P4 represent a pattern of one or more SAL elements. Each of these stored patterns links to an activation component called a rule, and these rule components may optionally link to commensurate target actions. Hidden layers (R1-P4) may each contain as many as four or five thousand pattern-rules, with no limit on growth. In operation, input vectors serve as search arguments to SAL pattern-rules stored in hidden layers that are indexed like a dictionary, an arrangement that accounts for Logos Model's ability to access a linguistic knowledge store that is virtually unlimited

always in a straightforward, manageable way. What's important is that at no point in this process has cognitive complexity become a factor inhibiting progress.

The architecture that allows for these advantages was illustrated earlier by Fig. 4.4 in Chap. 4 and is repeated above as Fig. 6.3. The Figure shows how the input stream that passes through the pipeline in Fig. 6.2 interacts with the memory store, using the image of a neural net. As previously indicated, Logos Model shares aspects of both architecture and functionality with neural nets (elaborated in Chap. 8).

In the sections that follow, we offer translations that illustrate the linguistic functions particular to each of the modules/hidden layers in Logos Model's pipeline/ network architecture depicted in Figs. 6.2 and 6.3.

6.4.1   Modules RES1 and RES2 (R1 and R2)

6.4.1.1   Homograph Resolution

Pattern-rules in RES1 and RES2 deal exclusively with resolution of syntactic ambiguities in the input sentence. Two kinds of ambiguity are focused on: (i) part of speech, and (ii) clause types and clause boundaries. We deal first with the part-of-speech resolution problem.

In (4) we have an artificially contrived sentence that shows the word *"building"* in a variety of syntactic roles, the idea of (4) being to maximally challenge the part-of-speech resolution powers of the RES modules. As may be seen from the French and German translations in (4)(i) and (4)(ii) respectively, the pattern-rules in RES correctly resolve the syntax of *building* in each case.

(4)   *In building the building we are building on this building site,
          the costs are building up.*

Translations by Logos Model

(4)(i)   *En construisant le bâtiment que nous construisons sur ce chantier,
          les coûts s'accumulent.*

(4)(ii) *Beim Bau des Gebäudes, das wir auf diese Baustelle bauen,
          entstehen die Kosten.*

Commentary

Note how the correct structural parse of (4) depends upon correct part-of-speech resolution of *building*. Also note how the various instances of *building* are translated in (4)(i) and (4)(ii) with different transfers in all but one instance. These semantic transfers are not the work of RES but of target actions linked to by pattern-rules in the PARSE modules, in conjunction with pattern-rules matched upon in the Semantic Table (SEMTAB).[7]

6.4.1.2   Garden Path Resolution

In sentences (5) and (6) we illustrate RES handling of the classic "garden-path" part-of-speech problem illustrated by the ambiguous word *run*.

(5)   *The horses **run** by the barn.*
(6)   *The horses **run** by the barn are tired.*

As translations in (5)(i) and (6)(i) indicate, pattern-rules in RES correctly resolve the syntactic role of the ambiguous word *run* in (5) and (6). Pattern-rules in RES modules resolve problems like this by a look-ahead function that is invoked by the rule potion of a pattern-rule whenever ambiguous words like *run* are matched upon, the object being to determine whether *run* is or is not a main verb. In the case of (5), this look-ahead function does not find a main verb to the right of *run*, and therefore allows *run* to be resolved to a main verb. In (6), by contrast, a main verb (*are*) is found to the right, allowing *run* to be resolved correctly to a past participle.

---

[7] Microsoft's Bing NMT Translator and Google GNMT Translate both translated (4) correctly with respect to parts of speech, but Google Translate failed to recognize the relative clause, and Bing mistranslated *costs are building up* in the German as *bauendie Kostenauf*.

Translations by Logos Model

(5)(i)   *Les chevaux **courent** par la grange.*

(6)(i)   *Les chevaux **dirigés** par la grange sont fatigués.*

Commentary

Note that the transfer of the past participle ***run*** as ***dirigés*** is the work of
SEMTAB later in the pipeline. Logos Model's initial, lexical transfer for the
participle is *couru*. Except for Google GNMT Translate and Bing NMT
Translator, the other MT systems tested all had problems with the syntax
of ***run*** either in (5) or (6).

6.4.1.3   Clausal Ambiguity Resolution

In (7) and (8) we address the second task of RES, namely, resolution of clause types
and clause boundaries. Note that both (7) and (8) look exactly alike from a purely
syntactic perspective. Resolution of the clausal structures in (7) must therefore
depend upon semantico-syntactic clues, which in (7) are provided by the generic
SAL code for the verb ***gave***, which sets up expectation for an indirect object.

(7)   ` `*John **gave** the car he repaired **to his brother**.*

(8)   *John repaired the car he **gave to his brother**.*

Translations by Logos Model

(7)(i)   *John **gab seinem Bruder** das Auto, das er reparierte.*

(8)(i)   *John reparierte das Auto, das er seinem Bruder gab.*

Commentary

All the other MT models we tested misresolved the structure of (7), uniformly
treating ***to his brother*** incorrectly as part of the relative clause *he repaired*.

6.4.2   Module PARSE1

6.4.2.1   Simple Noun Phrases

Pattern-rules in PARSE1 deal with simple constituents, most of which are noun
phrases. Simple noun phrases are concatenated and re-written as NP.

Odd embeddings within a noun phrase, as illustrated in (9) and (10), can complicate simple noun phrases and at times may not be properly handled by Logos Model. We see an example of this in (10)(i) where source analysis breaks down.

Translations by Logos Model

(9)   *There was a broken (or cracked) glass*
(9)(i)   *Il y avait un verre cassé (ou fêlé).*
(10)   *There was a broken (or slightly cracked) glass.*
(10)(i)   *Il y avait <u>cassé (ou fêlé un peu) un verre</u>.*

Note in (10)(ii) that Google GNMT Translate, Bing NMT Translator, and SYSTRANet are all able to translate (10) correctly.

(10)(ii) *Il y avait un verre cassé (ou légèrement fissuré).*

6.4.2.2   Complex Noun Phrases

Conventionally complex NP structures like (11) are normally handled acceptably by Logos Model, as seen in (11)(i).

(11)   *The very obstreperous, angry young man was asked to leave.*
(11)(i)   *On a demandé au jeune homme très bruyant et furieux de partir.*

Commentary

Notice that Logos Model's translation of (11) transforms the English passive construction into active voice in the French. Translations by the other systems we have been testing are all correct, but retain the passive construction of the English.

6.4.2.3   Adjective Scoping

Proper scoping of adjectives within the compound noun phrases in (12) and (13) depends entirely upon semantics.

(12)   *Blue sky and sunshine.*
(13)   *Smart boys and girls.*

Translation by Logos Model

(12(i)   *Ciel bleu et soleil.*
(13)(i)   *Garçons et filles intelligents.*

All the other systems tested also translated (12) and (13) with correct adjectival scoping. In (12), this could be because *blue sky* may have been lexicalized. Translations of (13) by Google GNMT Translate and Bing NMT Translator were stylistically superior: *Des garçons et des filles intelligents.*

6.4.2.4 Auxiliary Verb Phrases

Pattern-rules in PARSE1 also concatenate and rewrite auxiliary verb phrases like that shown in (14), with German output in (14)(i).

Translation by Logos Model

(14)   *He ought to have gone home.*
(14)(i)   *Er hätte nach Hause gehen sollen.*

6.4.3   Module PARSE2

Pattern-rules in PARSE2 are concerned with the complementation of noun phrases by prepositional phrases and relative clauses. In the translations immediately below, we treat the case of prepositional phrase complementation first.

6.4.3.1 Prepositional Phrase Complementation

Case One

Pattern-rules in PARSE2 examine the semantics of a prepositional phrase to determine whether its relationship to other constituents might affect its meaning and translation. This is illustrated in the translation of (15) and (16) in (15)(i) and (16)(i).

(15)   *A book **about** graveyards.*
(16)   *Flowers **about** graveyards.*

Translations by Logos Model

(15)(i)   *Ein Buch **über** Friedhöfe.*
(16)(i)   *Blumen **um** Friedhöfe.*

Commentary

All the other MT systems we tested translated ***about*** as ***über*** in both (15) and (16), indicating shortcomings in semantics.

Case Two

In (17) and (18), we see that the semantics of the preposition *about* has
to be recognized even when the clue to its meaning lies in another clause.

(17)   *The book he wrote **about** graveyards was interesting.*

(18)   *The flowers he placed **about** graveyards were lovely.*

Translations by Logos Model

(17)(i)   *Das Buch, das er **über** Friedhöfe schrieb, war interessant.*

(18)(i)   *Die Blumen, die er **um** Friedhöfe stellte, waren schön.*

Commentary

Apart from Logos Model, all other MT systems continue to translate *about* as
über, giving (18)(i) the incorrect sense that *lovely flowers* were being *placed
over* (*über*) rather than *placed **around*** (*um*) *graveyards*.

6.4.3.2   Relative Clause Complementation

Case One

Relative clauses can pose problems affecting agreement. For example, in (19),
below, the relative clause does not complement the noun immediately to
its left as might be expected, but rather an earlier noun. The German translation
for the relative pronoun *that* must reflect the gender of the antecedent
noun *attraction* as it does in (18)(i).

(19)   *He has an **attraction** to money **that** cannot be controlled.*

Translation by Logos Model

(19)(i)   *Er hat eine **Anziehungskraft** zu Geld, **die** nicht
gesteuert werden kann.*

Commentary

All the other MT systems tested translate the relative pronoun
that in (19) as *das* rather than *die*, having parsed the relative clause as
complementary to the neuter-gender noun *Geld* (*money*) rather than to
the feminine *Anziehungskraft* (*attraction*).

Case Two

In (20), we have a sentence with an artificially long relative clause inserted
between the subject and the verb. The sentence was constructed to
challenge the system's ability to reflect the gender of the French
subject (*maison*) in the verb phrase of the main clause in (20), given the
lengthy material inserted between subject and verb phrases. The sentence also
challenges the system's ability to reflect appropriate gender
within the relative clause itself. French translation by Logos Model is
in (20)(i), followed by translations from other systems.
Only errors in gender agreement are underlined.

(20)   ***The house*** *we are building and that John **designed** in his earlier*
            days as a young student while he was still in school
            is very large.

Translation by Logos Model

(20)(i)   ***La maison*** *que nous construisons et que John a **conçue** dans*
            ses plus premiers jours comme un jeune élève pendant qu'il
            *était encore dans l'école **est très grande**.*

Translation by Google GNMT Translate

(20)(ii)   ***La maison*** *que nous construisons et que John a **conçue** dans*
            ses premiers jours en tant que jeune étudiant, alors qu'il était
            *encore à l'école **est très grande**.*

Translation by Bing NMT Translator

(20)(iii)   ***La maison*** *que nous construisons et que John a **<u>conçu</u>** en*
            ses jours plus tôt comme un jeune étudiant alors qu'il était
            *encore à l'école **est très grande**.*

Translation by PROMT Translator

(20)(iv)   ***La maison*** *que nous construisons et que John a **<u>conçu</u>** à ses*
            jours plus premiers comme un jeune étudiant pendant qu'il était
            *toujours dans l'école **est très grande**.*

Translation by SYSTRANet

(20)(v)   ***La maison*** *que nous construisons et <u>ce</u> John___ **conçu***
            en ses jours plus tôt en tant que jeune étudiant tandis qu'il était
            *toujours à l'école **est très <u>grand</u>**.*

Commentary

Google GNMT Translate's rendition in (20)(ii) now improves an earlier
SMT mistranslation of (20) (shown in Endnote 6-B of this chapter).
Note the translation failures of all but Google GNMT Translate and Logos
Model to reflect the feminine gender of ***maison*** in the translation
of ***designed*** in the relative clause (***conçue*** rather than ***<u>conçu</u>***).

Case Three

In (21) and (22) we see how pattern-rules in PARSE2 differentiate between the
word ***that*** as a relative pronoun in (21) and as a subordinating conjunction in (22).
Errors in the output of the enumerated systems are underlined.

(21)   *The hope **that** he had was strong.*
(22)   *The hope **that** he would win the race was strong.*

Translation by Logos Model

(21)(i)   *Die Hoffnung, **die** er hatte, war stark.*
(22)(i)   *Die Hoffnung, **dass** er das Rennen gewinnen würde, war stark.*

Translation by Google Translate

(21)(iia)   (SMT) *Die Hoffnung, **dass** er ___ war stark.*

(21)(iib)   (GNMT) *Die Hoffnung, **dass** er stark war.*

(22)(iia)   (SMT) *Die Hoffnung, **dass** er das Rennen <u>zu gewinnen</u> war stark.*

(22)(iib)   (GNMT) *Die Hoffnung, **dass** er das Rennen gewinnen würde, war stark.*

Translation by Bing Translator

(21)(iiia)   (SMT) *Die Hoffnung, **die** er hatte, war stark.*

(21)(iiib)   (NMT) *Die Hoffnung, **dass** er stark war.*

(22)(iiia)   (SMT & NMT) *Die Hoffnung, **dass** er das Rennen gewinnen würde, war stark.*

Translation by PROMT Translator

(21)(iv)   *Die Hoffnung, **dass** er hatte, war stark.*

(22)(iv)   *Die Hoffnung, **dass** er die <u>Rasse</u> gewinnen würde, war stark.*

Translation by SYSTRANet

(21)(v)   *Die Hoffnung, **dass** er hatte, war stark.*

(22)(v)   *Die Hoffnung, **dass** er das Rennen gewinnen würde, war stark.*

Commentary

Only Bing SMT Translator and Logos Model translate (21) correctly.
All but Google SMT Translate translate the construction in (22) correctly.

6.4.4   Module PARSE3

Pattern-rules in PARSE3 are concerned with clauses as a whole, particularly with verbs and their argument structure. Pattern-rules in the Semantic Table (SEMTAB) play an important support role in effecting transfers for verbs appropriate to the context, as translations of sentences (23) and (24) illustrate.[8]

Case One

(23)   *Please **let me know** the result.*

(24)   *Please **let me have** the book.*

Translations by Logos Model

(23)(i)   ***Lassen Sie mich** bitte das Ergebnis **wissen**.*

(24)(i)   ***Erlauben Sie mir** bitte, das Buch zu **haben**.*

---

[8] See Postscript 6-A for this Chapter for further illustration of semantic resolutions by SEMTAB. Note that SEMTAB pattern-rules entail deep-structure patterns, which means that a single, deep structure SEMTAB pattern-rule will handle a variety of different surface structures for a given verbal concept, such as process noun, verbal adjective, as well of course as the verb itself, in all its conjugations.

Translations by Google GNMT Translate
(24)(ii)   *Bitte lassen Sie mich das Ergebnis wissen.*
(24)(ii)   *Bitte lass mich das Buch haben.*

Translations by Microsoft NMT Translate
(23)(iii) *Bitte lassen Sie mich wissen , das Ergebnis.*
(24)(iii) *Bitte lassen Sie mich das Buch ____.*

Translations by PROMT Translator
(23)(iv)   *Teilen Sie mir bitte das Ergebnis mit. (Please share with me
           the results.)*
(24)(iv)   *Lassen Sie mich bitte das Buch haben.*

Commentary

In (24)(i), Logos Model translates *let* as *erlauben* (*allow*, *permit*).
PROMT's translation of *let me know* in (23)(iv) is particularly felicitous.

Case Two

Sentence (25) and its translation in (25)(i) further illustrate SEMTAB's ability
to deal with context-dependent meanings of a verb. Note the variety
of transfers for *kept/keep* effected in (25)(i) by SEMTAB, in stark
contrast to the output of the other two systems, both of which transfer
kept (keep) as *hielt (halten)* regardless of the context. In this instance,
unless a verb has been omitted, translation errors are *not* underlined in (25).

(25)   *John kept the old car. John kept driving the old car. John kept
           the new car in the garage. He did not try to keep his children
           from driving the old car. He told them to keep the old car
           away from the new car in the garage.*

Logos Model Translation
(25)(i)   *John behielt das alte Auto. John fuhr das alte Auto weiter.
           John bewahrte das neue Auto in der Garage auf. Er versuchte
           nicht, zu verhindern, dass seine Kinder das alte Auto fuhren.
           Er wies sie an, das alte Auto vom neuen Auto in der
           Garage fernzuhalten.*

Translation byGoogle Translate
(25)(iia) (SMT) *John hielt den alten Autos. John hielt den Antrieb
           des alten Autos. John hielt das neue Auto in der Garage.
           Er versuchte nicht, seine Kinder von der Fahrt der alten Auto
           zu halten. Er sagte ihnen, das alte Auto vom neuen Auto in der
           Garage zu halten.*
(25)(iib) (GNMT) *John hielt das alte Auto. John fuhr weiter
           mit dem alten Auto. John hielt das neue Auto in der Garage.
           Er hat nicht versucht, seine Kinder davon abzuhalten, das
           alte Auto zu fahren. Er sagte ihnen, das alte
           Auto von dem neuen Auto in der Garage zu behalten.*

Translation by Bing NMT Translator

(25)(iii)   *John **hielt** das alte Auto. John fuhr das alte Auto* ___. *John*
*   **hielt** das neue Auto in der Garage. Er versuchte nicht,*
*   seine Kinder davon zu **halten**, das alte Auto zu fahren.*
*   Er erzählte ihnen, das alte Auto vom neuen Auto in der*
*   Garage **fernzuhalten**.*

Translation by SYSTRANet

(25)(iii)   *John **hielt** das alte Auto. John **hielt**, das alte Auto zu fahren.*
*   John **hielt** den Neuwagen in der Garage. Er versuchte nicht,*
*   seine Kinder vom Fahren des alten Autos zu **halten**. Er bat sie,*
*   das alte Auto weg von dem Neuwagen in der Garage zu **halten**.*

Commentary

Notice how Logos Model translates **kept** with five different German verbs,
reflecting sensitivity to context that is afforded by abstract pattern-rules in
SEMTAB. Translations by the other systems, in various instances,
improperly or infelecitously render **kept** (**keep**) with a single German verb,
hielt (**halten**).

Case Three

One of the functions of SEMTAB pattern-rules is to link noncontiguous
verb particles with their verb, as in (27), below. Of all the systems tested,
only Logos Model and PROMT handled (27) correctly in (27)(i).

(26)   *He **lived down** his bad reputation.*
(27)   *He **lived** his bad reputation **down**.*

Translations by Logos Model and PROMT

(26)(i)   *Il **a fait oublier** sa mauvaise réputation.*
(27)(i)   *Il **a fait oublier** sa mauvaise réputation.*

Translations by Google GNMT Translate and Bing NMT Translator

(26)(ii)   *Il **a <u>vécu</u>** sa mauvaise réputation.*
(27)(ii)   *Il **a <u>vécu</u>** sa mauvaise réputation.*

Translations by SYSTRANet

(26)(iii) *Il **a <u>vécu</u> en bas** sa mauvaise réputation.*
(27)(iii) *Il **a <u>vécu</u>** sa mauvaise réputation **<u>vers le bas</u>.***

Commentary

Of all the systems tested, Logos Model and PROMT both translate (26)
and (27) acceptably. The other systems uniformly fail to recognize
the verbal construct **lived down**. SYSTRANet rendered **lived** in
its intransitive sense (**lived toward the bottom**).

Case Four

In (28) and (29), SEMTAB must distinguish different senses of the intransitive verb **go on**, based on the difference in verb subjects. Errors are underlined.

(28)   *If the light **goes on**, be sure to turn it off.*
(29)   *The conflagration **may go on** for many days before they put it out.*

Translation by Logos Model

(28)(i)   *Si la lumière **s'allume**, soyez sûr de l'éteindre.*
(29)(i)   *La conflagration **peut continuer** pendant beaucoup de jours avant qu'ils ne l'aient éteint.*

Translation by SYSTRANet

(28)(ii)   *Si la lumière **s'allume**, soyez sûr de l'arrêter.*
(29)(ii)   *La conflagration **peut continuer** pendant beaucoup de jours avant qu'ils l'éteignent.*

Translation by Google GNMT Translate

(28)(iii)   *Si la lumière **s'allume**, assurez-vous de l'éteindre.*
(29)(iii)   *L'incendie **peut durer** plusieurs jours avant de l'éteindre.*

Translation by Bing NMT Translator

(28)(iv)   *Si la lumière **continue**, assurez-vous de l'éteindre.*
(29)(iv)   *La conflagration **peut continuer** pendant plusieurs jours avant qu'ils ne l'exposent.*

Commentary

All translations but those by Bing NMT Translate correctly distinguish between the two senses of **go/goes on** in (28) and (29).

Case Five

In (30) we show a chain of nouns. In (30)(i), we see that a PARSE3 pattern-rule has recognized the noun chain as *NP* and has linked to a target action that effects proper French convention regarding repetition of possessive adjectives and prepositions before each noun in a compound *NP*.

(30)   *My father gave **his** house, car and boat jointly **to** his sons and daughters.*

Translation by Logos Model

(30)(i)   *Mon père a donné **sa** maison, **sa** voiture et **son** bateau en commun **à** ses fils et **à** ses filles.*

Commentary

Google GNMT Translate and Bing NMT Translator also observe the proper French convention seen in (30)(i) regarding noun chains. Linguistically based SYSTRANet and PROMT Translator fail to observe this convention. (These other translations are unshown.)

6.4.5   Module PARSE4

Pattern-rules in PARSE4 are concerned with final clausal and interclausal issues, preparatory to target generation.

Case One

In (31) we deal with an example of clause chaining.

> (31)   *The power must be off when putting the cover on, taking it off, or adjusting it.*

Translation by Logos Model

> (31)(i)   *Le <u>pouvoir</u> doit être coupé **en** mettant la couverture, **en** la retirant ou **en** l'ajustant.*

Translation by Google Translate

> (31)(iia)   (SMT) *La <u>puissance</u> doit être désactivé lorsque vous mettez le couvercle <u>sur, il décolle, ou ajuster.</u>*

> (31)(iib)   (GNMT) *L'alimentation doit être désactivée lorsque vous mettez le capot, l'enlevez ou l'ajustez.*

Translation by Bing Translator

> (31)(iiia)   (SMT) *L'alimentation doit être éteinte quand <u>mettre le couvercle sur, enlever ou ajustant</u>.*

> (31)(iiib)   (NMT) *L'alimentation doit être éteinte lorsque vous mettez le couvercle, l'<u>enlever</u> ou le <u>régler.</u>*

Translation by PROMT Translator

> (31)(iv)   *Le <u>pouvoir</u> doit être débranché **en** mettant la couverture, **en** l'enlevant, ou **en** <u>le</u> réglant.*

Translation by SYSTRANet

> (31)(v)   *Le <u>pouvoir</u> doit être <u>outre de</u> **en** mettant la couverture dessus, **en** l'enlevant, ou **en** l'ajustant.*

Commentary

Notice that the two SMT systems in (31)(iia) and 31(iiia) were unable to handle the non-contiguous verbal constructs *putting ... on* and *taking ... off*. Logos Model's transfer for *power* (*pouvoir*) in (31)(i) denotes a non-technical sense, a mistranslation resulting from the default, non-technical setting of the Subject Matter Code employed at run time, affecting lexical selection for *power*.

Case Two

Another concern of PARSE4 is verb mood and tense handling, both intraclausally and interclausally. First, we look at the intraclausal case in (32) where the subjective mood is called for.

> (32) **Unless he receives** instructions to the contrary, he is going to go home.

Translation by Logos Model, PROMT Translator and SYSTRANet

(32)(i)   *À moins qu'il ne reçoive les instructions au contraire,*
            il va aller à la maison.

Translation by Google GNMT Translate

(32)(ii)   *Sauf s'il reçoit des instructions au contraire, il va*
            rentrer à la maison.

Translation by Bing NMT Translator

(32)(iib)   *Sauf s'il reçoit des instructions au contraire, il va rentrer*
            chez lui.

Commentary

Only the linguistically based systems, Logos Model, PROMT, and SYSTRANet
translate (32) with constructions that place the verb *receives* in the subjunctive
mood. The alternative translations by Google and Bing however are acceptable.

In (33) and (34) we see an instance of interclasual tense handling.

(33)   *They **do not want** him to succeed.*
(34)   *They **did not want** him to succeed.*

Translation by Logos Model, Google GNMT Translate and PROMT Translator

(33)(i)   *Sie **wollen nicht**, dass er Erfolg **hat**.*
(34)(i)   *Sie **wollten nicht**, dass er Erfolg **hatte**.*

Commentary

In (34), only Logos Model, Google GNMT Translate and PROMT
Translator reflect the past tense of the first clause in handling the infinitive
clause *to succeed.*

Case Three

Pattern-rules in PARSE4 also attempt to handle intrasentential
pronoun resolution, exemplified successfully in (35), unsuccessfully
in the more complex (36).

(35) *We buy **a house** that catches our fancy and then resell **it** as soon*
*as **it** begins to weary us.*

Translation by Logos Model

(35)(i)   *Nous achetons **une maison** qui attrape notre fantaisie*
            *et ensuite **la** revendons dès qu' **elle** commence à nous lasser.*

Translation by Google GNMT Translate

(35)(ii)   *Nous achetons **une maison** qui attrape notre fantaisie,*
            *puis reventez-**la** dès qu 'elle commence à nous fatiguer.*

Translation by Bing NMT Translator

(35)(iii)   *Nous achetons **une maison** qui attrape notre fantaisie,*
            *puis ___revendons dès qu' **elle** commence à nous fatiguer.*

Translation by SYSTRANet

(35)(iv)   *Nous achetons **une maison** qui attrape notre fantaisie et*
        *puis **la** revendons dès qu' **elle** commencera <u>à se lasser nous</u>.*

Translation by PROMT Translator

(35)(v)   *Nous achetons **une maison** qui frappe notre imagination*
        *et ___ **le** <u>revendre</u> ensuite aussitôt qu' **il** commence à nous lasser.*

Commentary

Only PROMT Translator fails to reflect the feminine gender of the
French noun **maison** when translating the pronouns of (35), although
all of the translations, apart from Logos Model, experience difficulties
of one kind or another in translating (35).

Pronoun resolution remains one of Logos Model's least developed aspects of
PARSE4 analysis, as sentence (36) and its French translation in (36)(i) reveal.
Errors are underlined.

(36)   *John occupied his **house** even before he finished building **it**.*

Translation by Logos Model

(36)(i)   *John a occupé <u>dans</u> sa **maison** même avant qu'il n'ait fini*
        de <u>le</u> construire.

Translation by Google GNMT Translate

(36)(ii)   *John occupait sa **maison** avant même qu'il ne finisse*
        sa construction.

Translation by Bing NMT Translate

(36)(iii)   *John a occupé sa **maison** avant même qu'il n'ait fini*
        *de **la** construire.*

Commentary

Bing NMT Translate correctly captures the pronoun gender in (36)(iii).
Google GNMT neatly finesses the pronoun **it** in its translation
of the dependent clause.

Case Four
Stylistic Transformations

To a limited degree, Logos Model attempts to support the requirements of
preferable target style, as illustrated in (37) and (38) with examples of passive
to active voice transformations.

(37)   *The situation **was alluded to** by my friend in his letter.*

Translation by Logos Model

(37)(i)   *Mon ami **a fait allusion à** la situation dans sa lettre.*
(38)   *The situation **was alluded** to in their letter.*

Translation by Logos Model

(38)(i)   *On **a fait allusion à** la situation dans leur lettre.*

In the French translation of (39) in (39)(i), below, we see another instance of a passive voice construction being made active. Note also, in particular, how the English ellipsis in (39) *"and their information input to the system"* is unelided and made explicit in both the French in (39)(i) and the German in (39)(ii). Note as well the "subjectless passive" treatment of the German in the first clause in (39)(ii).[9] These translations illustrate the limited but real extent to which target linguists working with Logos Model have been able to sidestep the so-called *"structure preserving"* tendencies inherent in MT (Somers 1992/3).

(39)　　　　*Other forms of storage media, such as magnetic cards and computer tape, **can also be accessed** through optional devices, **and their information input to the system**.*

Translations by Logos Model

(39)(i)　　　*On peut également accéder à d'autres formes du support d'information, comme les cartes magnétiques et la bande pour ordinateur, par des appareils facultatifs **et on peut introduire leur information dans le système**.*

(39)(ii)　　*Auf andere Speichermedienarten, wie magnetische Karten und Magnetband **kann auch** durch beliebige Geräte **zugegriffen werden und ihre Informationen können in das System eingegeben werden**.*

Translation by Goggle GNMT Translate

(39)(iii)　*Andere Arten von Speichermedien, wie Magnetkarten und Computer-Band, **können** auch über optionale Geräte ___ ___ und **ihre Informationen in das System eingegeben werden**.*

Translation by Bing NMT Translator

(39)(iv)　*Andere Speichermedien, wie magnetische Karten und Computer-Band, **können** auch über optionale Geräte ___ ___ und **Ihre Informationen Input in das System zugegriffen werden**.*

Commentary

In the Logos Model translation for French in (39)(i), the passive form of the verbs *accessed* and *input* in (39) are rendered in the active voice. It is not a translation flaw, obviously, that the two NMT systems tested have retained the passive voice in their French translations of (39), which are both correct (unshown). It is a curious circumstance however that both of these NMT systems have dropped the passive verb *be accessed* in their German output for (39), as evidenced in (39)(iii) and (39)(iv).

---

[9] Subjectless passives in German require that the main clause subject *not* be the agent of the passive verb, and that the clause's passive verb construction entail the auxiliary *werden*. Both conditions were tested for and satisfied by the target action component responsible for the translation in (39)(ii).

In the section on complexity further below, we briefly illustrate the steps by which (39) was analyzed and translated by Logos Model.

6.5   How Do You Effect Target Generation?

In the foregoing account of Logos Model we have focused almost exclusively on source analysis, reflecting our belief that the decoding of source text is the more fundamental and more difficult aspect of linguistically-oriented MT. Whenever Logos developers responsible for target work were asked what was most needed to improve translation quality, more often than not the answer had to do with improving source analysis.[10] But target work itself is far from trivial and obviously poses its own set of challenges.

6.5.1   Target Components

Target actions in Logos Model (see Fig. 6.2) are triggered by source pattern-rules that optionally link to target actions whenever this seems appropriate. As source analysis moves down through the system and forms nodes on the source parse, these target actions form equivalent nodes on the equivalent target parse. Notations associated with each node are added to guide its treatment in the eventual generation of the target sentence. The scope of these target actions in each instance is restricted to the pattern being dealt with by the source pattern-rule to which the target actions are linked. Nevertheless, within that limitation, target components have a great deal of freedom, as the French and German translations of (39) above illustrate.

In the final generation phase of MT, the module designated "Tgt Gen" (see Fig. 6.2) generates a literal target string from the target parse and applies inflections in accordance with associated notations.

6.6   How Do You Cope with Complexity?

We have argued in this book that, for all the obvious importance of linguistics, it is the computational approach that will ultimately determine how good an MT system can become—the approach regarding (i) how the language input stream and the linguistic knowledge that must deal with it are represented computationally; (ii)

---

[10]Deficiencies in source analysis chiefly concerned shortcomings in ambiguity resolution, particularly ambiguities having to do with part of speech. For data-driven SMT on the other hand, target generation poses the chief difficulty, particularly with respect to proper target word order and morphological agreement among chunks of text. The reason for this is manifold, but the deepest reason is that SMT is phrase-based and not sentence-based.

how this linguistic knowledge is stored in memory; and (iii), how this memory store gets applied to the input stream. All of these factors have pronounced bearing on the one issue that, in our view, most limits a system's potential, namely (iv) complexity. We contend, in effect, that complexity (iv) is taken care of by answering (i), (ii) and (iii) with the approach we describe and illustrate throughout this book.

6.6.1   A Final Illustration

In Figs. 6.4 and 6.5, we illustrate the input-driven, complexity-avoiding process of Logos Model, using for our purpose sentence (39) from the previous section, reproduced below for the reader's convenience.

> (39)   *Other forms of storage media, such as magnetic cards and*
> *computer tape,* ***can also be accessed*** *through optional devices,*
> ***and their information input to the system.***

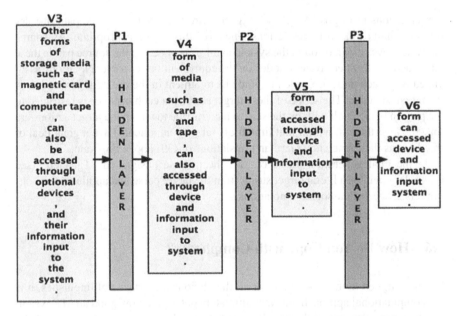

Fig. 6.4 *Input-driven analysis of source sentence (39) as it processes through Logos Model.* Graphic shows literal language rather than SAL codes. V3–V6 are input/output vectors where each cell stands for a NL element. Only headwords of concatenated constituents are shown (rather than its SAL notation). For example, *device* in V6 stands for the prepositional phrase *through optional devices*). P1–P3 are hidden layers, each containing several thousands of stored pattern-rules. Constituents in input vectors match associated stored pattern-rules directly and automatically. The activation portion of the pattern-rule rewrites input and outputs it as a progressively more abstract constituent, in the manner of a bottom-up parse. Stored pattern-rules also link to target actions that create an equivalent target structure

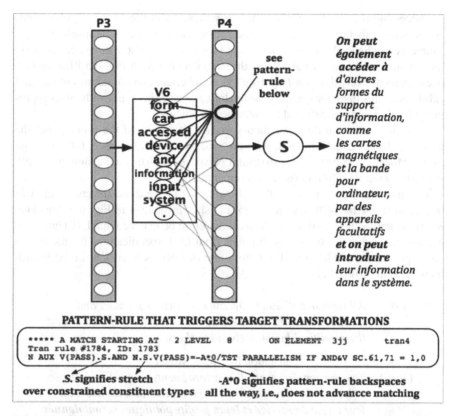

Fig. 6.5 *P4 Pattern-rule that initiates translation.* Graphic shows just the comment line of an 8-level pattern-rule in P4 that allows target linguists to effect radical transformations in the target translation. Target actions linked to this pattern-rule test for the existence (or non-existence) of certain features recorded by source and/or target actions in previous layers, and which now guide the target actions associated with this 8-level pattern-rule. Actual target transformations are made not by this 8-level pattern-rule, but by subsequent matches in P4 as each constituent is subsequently handled individually by source rules and associated target actions, all in accord with signals communicated to them by the 8-level pattern-rule

To make Figs. 6.4 and 6.5 easier to follow, we use the headwords of concatenated constituents rather than show the more fully descriptive SAL representation for these constituents.

Figure 6.4 exemplifies the design feature that most frees Logos Model from complexity effects, in effect showing how the input stream and stored linguistic knowledge connect with each other.

In Fig. 6.5 we depict the final analysis stage of sentence (39) and show the resultant target output sentence. As stated earlier, the PARSE4 module is concerned chiefly with interclausal relations, in effect, allowing target linguists to deal with the sentence as a whole, at its most abstract, semantico-syntactic representation, doing so fairly easily therefore.

Processing the input sentence in the way depicted in Figs. 6.4 and 6.5 enables target actions to fashion target sentences that are semantically equivalent to the source yet stylistically appropriate to the target. This can sometimes entail fairly radical structural transformations, as the output sentence in Fig. 6.5 illustrates. It does not seem likely that *non-linguistic* MT could effect transformations of the kind exhibited in this Figure, especially the uneliding of an ellipsis, not without an appropriate level of comprehnsion of the sentence as a whole.

To further illustrate the semantico-syntactic sensitivity of the process and the power it affords target linguists, we now process another sentence, (40), through Logos Model. Note that from a structural perspective, (40) is quite similar to (39), but (40) is entirely different from (39) semantically.

Our purpose here is to show the following: (i) because the *structural* analysis arrived at in P4 for (40) is identical to that shown for (39) in Fig. 6.5, the same 8-level pattern-rule shown in Fig. 6.5 will therefore be matched upon; (ii) however, because the semantics of (40) is different from (39), specifications for the subsequent generation of (40) will differ from that of (39), as is evident in the French translation in (40)(i), below.

(40)   *All representatives of government, such as senators and congressmen, **will now be limited** in their term of service **and their political benefits given to others.***

Translation by Logos Model

(40)(i)   *Tous les représentants du gouvernement, tel que les sénateurs et les membres du congrès, **seront maintenant limités** dans leur terme du service **et leurs profits politiques seront donnés aux autres.***

Commentary

Note in (40)(i) how the ellipsis "... ***and their political benefits given to*** ... " is unelided and made explicit in the French "... ***et leurs profits politiques seront donnés aux*** ... ," just as was done for the parallel construction in (39)(i), shown again in Fig. 6.5. However, in (40)(i) we do not see transformation of the passive construction into the active voice, as was seen in (39)(i). The voice transformation is entirely appropriate in (39)(i) but its absence seems correct in (40)(i).

In all of the other MT systems we tested, target translations for both (39) and (40) strictly conform to the structure of the source sentence, without any of the stylistic transformations shown above. While this fact does not imply anything defective about these other systems, we trust it does indicate something about the translation potential afforded by the computational approach taken in Logos Model, a potential moreover that is achievable without the usual complexity costs.[11]

6.7 Conclusion

From what we have seen thus far of neural MT systems, it seems abundantly clear that the fusion of statistical and neural net technologies exemplified by NMT shows immense promise, especially as these data-driven NMT systems appear to be incorporating linguistic features into their processes. What remains of question is the potential benefit that a symbolic, linguistically-oriented neural net like Logos Model might offer to non-symbolic neural models. For example, what would so-called "deep" NMT look like if the units in their layers were featured by a more abstract, semantico-syntactic ontology like SAL? Wouldn't features at this more abstract semantic-syntactic level add powers of generality to these neural systems, both syntactically and semantically?

The present book was written in the hope that the deep learning and MT communities might find this question interesting and worth considering.

Postscripts

Postscript 6-A

Logos Model translations exhibited below were effected by pattern-rules in SEMTAB, Logos Model's Semantic Table (described earlier in Chap. 6). SEMTAB, we believe, is unique in several respects. First, this Semantic Table is able to contain tens of thousands of context-sensitive pattern-rules affecting translation of verbs, process nouns, and verbal adjectives, which Table is accessed like a dictionary. (At the time development of Logos Model ceased, SEMTAB contained about fifteen thousand context-sensitive pattern-rules for each language pair.) Secondly, SEMTAB is a deep-structure knowledge resource, which means that a single, deep structure pattern-rule can transform a variety of surface structures, as illustrated below in (2)(i) and (3)(i). Logos Model translations here are contrasted with those by other MT systems. Improper transfers are underlined.[12]

---

[11] Note translation of (39) by the University of Montreal LISA Lab's neural MT system, which is basically structure-preserving: *D'autres moyens de stockage, comme les cartes magnétiques et la bande magnétique,* **peuvent également être accessibles** *au moyen de dispositifs facultatifs et* **de leur entrée** *dans le système.* The LISA system however interestingly transforms **can be accessed** to **can be accessible** in the French. The complete mistranslation here of the second clause of (39) is underlined.

[12] See Fig. 4.9 in Chap. 4 for a graphic picture of Semantic Table interaction in Logos Model.

(1)   *We **raised** the children. He **raised** the money. They **raised** questions.*

Logos Model
(1)(i)   **Criamos** *a los niños.* **Reunió** *el dinero.* **Plantearon** *preguntas.*

Google SMT Translate
(1)(ii)   **Levantamos** __*los niños.* **Levantó** *el dinero. Ellos* **hicieron**
           preguntas.

Google GNMT Translate
(1)(iii)   **Criamos***a los niños. Él* **levantó** *el dinero. Ellos* **plantearon**
           preguntas.

Bing NMT Translator
(1)(iii)   **Criamos** *a los niños. Él* **recaudó** *el dinero.* **Plantearon** *preguntas.*

PROMT
(1)(iv)   **Levantamos** *a los niños. Él* **levantó** *el alquiler.*
           Ellos **levantaron** *preguntas.*

SYSTRANet
(1)(v)   **Criamos** *a los niños. Él* **aumentó** *el dinero.* **Plantearon** *preguntas.*

In the French translations below, the verbal concept ***raise*** (in the context of *rent*)
is translated in (2)(i) as a main verb (***augmenté***). In (3)(i) the participial adjective
raising has been rendered as the process noun ***augmentation*** in the context of *rent*
and as ***relèvement*** in the context of *ship*. Note that in (2) and (3), the different
English *surface* structures and consequent French transformations for the concept
raise in the context of *rent* are processed by a single, deep-structure SEMTAB
pattern-rule that links the verbal concept ***raise*** to its semantic object. Without
SEMTAB, the default French transfer for the verb ***raise*** in the context of *rent* would
have been ***lever***, as it was in the context of *ship*.

(2)   *Please **raise** your hand if your rent has been **raised**.*
(2)(i)   *Veuillez **lever** votre main si votre loyer a été **augmenté**.*
(3)   *Rent-**raising** procedures. Ship-**raising** procedures are very complex.*
(3)(i)   *Procédures **d'augmentation** de loyer. Les procédures*
           *de **relèvement** de navire sont très complexes.*

Postscript 6-B

Table 6B.1, below, lists sentences that were translated earlier by the SMT version of
Google Translate. We repeat them now showing output from the SMT version of
Google Translate and, in the second column, out from the new GNMT version of
Google Translate. Translation improvements in the GNMT version of Google

Postscript Table 6B.1 Comparing translations from SMT and GNMT versions of Google translate, Microsoft's NMT Bing translator and Logos Model

John's heart is sound. John's heart sounds healthy. The sound of the heart sounds normal.			
Google SMT	+ + Google GNMT	Bing NMT Translator	Logos Model
Johns Herz ist gesund. Johns Herztöne gesund. Der Klang Herztöne normal.	Johns Herz ist gesund. Johns Herz klingt gesund. Der Klang des Herzens klingt normal.	Das Herz des Johannes ist Klang. John's Heart klingt gesund. Der Klang des Herzens klingt normal.	Johns Herz ist solid. Johns Herz klingt gesund. Das Geräusch des Herzens klingt normal.
The sounds of his heart sound sound.			
Google SMT	+ - Google GNMT	Bing NMT Translator	Logos Model
Die Klänge des Herzens Ton Ton.	Die Klänge seines Herzens klingen ____.	Der Klang seines Herzens Klang klingt.	Die Geräusche seines Herzens klingen solid.
Les sons de son cœur sonnent sonore.	- Les sons de son son du son du cœur.	Les sons de son cœur son ____.	Les sons de son coeur semblent solides.
Strange as it may seem, he did not accept the promotion.			
Google SMT	+ - Google GNMT	Bing NMT Translator	Logos Model
So seltsam es scheinen mag, er wollte nicht akzeptieren, die Förderung.	So seltsam es scheinen mag, er hat die Förderung nicht akzeptieren.	Seltsam, wie es scheinen mag, hat er nicht akzeptieren, die Promotion.	Seltsam, wie es vielleicht scheint, nahm er die Beförderung nicht an.
There are no new methods for revolving credit.			
Google SMT	+ Google GNMT	Bing NMT Translator	Logos Model
Il n'y a pas de nouvelles méthodes de crédit renouvelable.	Il n'y a pas de nouvelles méthodes de renouvellement du crédit.	Il n'y a pas de nouvelles méthodes de crédit renouvelable.	Il n'y a pas de nouvelles façons de faire tourner le crédit.
The individuals who sold their house want to purchase my house.			
Google SMT	++ Google GNMT	Bing NMT Translator	Logos Model
Die Personen, die ihr Haus verkauft möchte mein Haus zu kaufen.	Die Einzelpersonen, die ihr Haus verkauften, wollen mein Haus kaufen.	Die Personen, die Ihr Haus verkauft haben, wollen mein Haus kaufen.	Die Individuen, die ihr Haus verkauften, wollen mein Haus kaufen.
His eldest daughter was married last week.			
Google SMT	+ Google GNMT	Bing NMT Translator	Logos Model
Sa fille aînée était marié la semaine dernière.	Sa fille aînée était mariée la semaine dernière.	Sa fille aînée était mariée la semaine dernière.	Sa fille eldest a été épousée la semaine dernière.
John took the things from the table and put them away.			
Google SMT	+ Google GNMT	Bing NMT Translator	Logos Model
John a pris les choses de la table et de les ranger.	John a pris les choses de la table et les a écartées.	John a pris les choses de la table et les a mis à l'écart.	John a pris les choses de la table et les a fait enfermer.
As he began to recover his health, he realized that his wife had stood by him through difficult times.			

(continued)

Postscript Table 6B.1 (continued)

Google SMT	+ Google GNMT	Microsoft's Bing	Logos Model
Als er begann, seine Gesundheit wiederherzustellen, erkannte er, dass seine Frau von ihm durch <u>schwierig</u> Zeiten gestanden hatte.	Als er begann, seine Gesundheit wiederherzustellen, erkannte er, dass seine Frau von ihm durch schwierige Zeiten gestanden hatte.	Als er anfing, seine Gesundheit zurückzugewinnen, erkannte er, dass seine Frau von ihm durch schwierige Zeiten gestanden hatte.	Als er anfing, seine Gesundheit zurückzubekommen, erkannte er, dass seine Frau ihm durch schwere Zeiten beigestanden hatte.

My eyeglasses are dirty.

Google SMT	+ + Google GNMT	Bing NMT Translator	Logos Model
Meine Brille <u>sind</u> verschmutzt.	Meine Brille ist schmutzig.	Meine Brillen <u>sind</u> schmutzig.	Meine Brille ist schmutzig.

Three eyeglasses.

Google SMT	+ + Google GNMT	Bing NMT Translator	Logos Model
Drei <u>Brille.</u>	Drei Brillen.	Drei Brillen.	Drei <u>Brille.</u>

I prefer a ham or cheese sandwich.

Google SMT	+ + Google GNMT	Bing NMT Translator	Logos Model
Je préfère <u>un jambon ou du fromage sandwich.</u>	Je préfère un sandwich au jambon ou au fromage.	Je préfère un sandwich au jambon ou au fromage.	Je préfère un sandwich <u>de</u> jambon ou <u>de</u> fromage.

The house we are building and that John designed in his earlier days as a young student while he was still in school is very large.

Google SMT	+ Google GNMT	Bing NMT Translator	Logos Model
La maison que nous construisons et que John ___ conçu dans ses premiers jours en tant que jeune étudiant, alors qu'il était encore à l'école est très grande.	La maison que nous construisons et que John a conçue dans ses premiers jours en tant que jeune étudiant alors qu'il était encore à l'école est très grande.	La maison que nous construisons et que John a <u>conçu</u> dans ses premiers jours comme un jeune étudiant alors qu'il était encore à l'école est très grande.	La maison que nous construisons et que John a conçue dans ses plus premiers jours comme un jeune <u>élève</u> pendant qu'il était encore <u>dans</u> l'école est très grande.

The hope that he had was strong.

Google SMT	- Google GNMT	Bing NMT Translator	Logos Model
Die Hoffnung, <u>dass</u> er ___ war stark.	Die Hoffnung, dass er ___ stark war.	Die Hoffnung, <u>dass</u> er <u>___ stark war.</u>	Die Hoffnung, die er hatte, war stark.

The hope that he would win the race was strong.

Google SMT	+ + Google GNMT	Bing NMT Translator	Logos Model
Die Hoffnung, dass er das Rennen <u>zu gewinnen</u> war stark.	Die Hoffnung, dass er das Rennen gewinnen würde, war stark.	Die Hoffnung, dass er das Rennen gewinnen würde, war stark.	Die Hoffnung, dass er das Rennen gewinnen würde, war stark.

John kept the old car. John kept driving the old car. John kept the new car in the garage. He did not try to keep his children from driving the old car. He told them to keep the old car away from the new car in the garage.

Google SMT	+ Google GNMT	Bing NMT Translator	Logos Model

(continued)

Postscript Table 6B.1 (continued)

John hielt den alten Autos. John hielt den Antrieb des alten Autos. John hielt das neue Auto in der Garage. Er versuchte nicht, seine Kinder von der Fahrt der alten Auto zu halten. Er sagte ihnen, das alte Auto vom neuen Auto in der Garage zu halten.	John hielt das alte Auto. John fuhr weiter mit dem alten Auto. John hielt das neue Auto in der Garage. Er hat nicht versucht, seine Kinder davon abzuhalten, das alte Auto zu fahren. Er sagte ihnen, das alte Auto von dem neuen Auto in der Garage zu behalten.	John hielt das alte Auto. John fuhr das alte Auto ___. John hielt das neue Auto in der Garage. Er versuchte nicht, seine Kinder davon zu halten, das alte Auto zu fahren. Er erzählte ihnen, das alte Auto vom neuen Auto in der Garage fernzuhalten.	John behielt das alte Auto. John fuhr das alte Auto weiter. John bewahrte das neue Auto in der Garage auf. Er versuchte nicht, zu verhindern, dass seine Kinder das alte Auto fuhren. Er wies sie an, das alte Auto vom neuen Auto in der Garage fernzuhalten.

The power must be off when putting the cover on, taking it off, or adjusting it.

Google SMT	+ - Google GNMT	Bing NMT Translator	Logos Model
La puissance doit être désactivé lorsque vous mettez le couvercle sur, il décolle, ou ___ ajuster.	L'alimentation doit être éteinte lorsque vous allumez le capot, l'enlevez ou l'ajustez.	L'alimentation doit être éteinte lorsque vous mettez le couvercle, l'enlever ou le régler.	Le pouvoir doit être coupé en mettant la couverture, en la retirant ou en l'ajustant.

Cast iron is apt to break.

Google SMT	+ + Google GNMT	Bing NMT Translator	Logos Model
Gusseisen ist passend, zu brechen.	Gusseisen ist leicht zu brechen.	Gusseisen ist geeignet, zu brechen.	Gusseisen bricht leicht.

They expect all business transactions to be conducted in French.

Google SMT	+ Google GNMT	Bing NMT Translator	Logos Model
Sie erwarten, dass alle Geschäftsvorfälle in Französisch durchgeführt werden.	Sie erwarten, dass alle Geschäftsvorfälle auf Französisch durchgeführt werden.	Sie erwarten, dass alle geschäftlichen Transaktionen auf Französisch durchgeführt werden.	Sie erwarten, dass alle Geschäfts- transaktionen auf französisch geführt werden.

As a final exercise, to illustrate the relative strengths and weakness of each of these systems, we had each of them translate an arbitrarily selected text, choosing for this purpose this very sentence.

Google SMT	- Google GNMT	Bing NMT Translator	Logos Model
Comme un dernier exercice, pour illustrer les points forts et les faiblesses ___ de chacun de ces systèmes, nous avons eu chacun de les traduire un texte choisi arbitrairement, en choisissant à cet effet cette phrase très.	Dans un dernier exercice, pour illustrer les forces et faiblesses relatives de chacun de ces systèmes, nous avons __ chacun __ traduit un texte choisi arbitrairement, en choisissant à cette fin cette même phrase.	Comme un exercice final, afin d'illustrer les points forts et les faiblesses de chacun de ces systèmes, nous avons eu chacun d'eux traduire un texte arbitrairement sélectionné, choisir à cet effet, cette phrase.	Comme un exercice final, pour illustrer les forces et la faiblesse relatives de chacun de ces systèmes, nous avons demandé à chacun d'eux de traduire un texte arbitrairement sélectionné, en choisissant ceci la phrase dans ce but très.

Translate are indicated as follows: + + much improved; + some improvement; + − mixed improvement/degradation; − degradation. Absence of a sign in Google GNMT translations signifies no meaningful change. For comparison purposes, we have added output from the neural net version of Microsoft's Bing Translator, and also from Logos Model. Note that all translations were made in the 2016–2017 time fame and may not represent output of these systems subsequent to that time frame. Indeed, our experience with GNMT in particular has been that, over time, translations by this neural net system have been seen to steadily improve, making it necessary to continually update the second column of the Table above.

References

Juola P (1989) Machine translation and Lojban. Internet blog. http://www.lojban.org/files/why-lojban/mactrans.txt. Accessed 14 Oct 2015
Somers HL (1992/3) Current research in machine translation. Mach Trans 7:231–246

Chapter 7
Some Limits on Translation Quality

Abstract This Chapter examines the extent to which machine translation output is constrained by the structure of source language sentences, i.e., whether MT can enjoy the freedom of the human translator to produce translations that depart in significant ways from the structure of a source sentence. We focus in particular on the issue of clause shifts in the target translation of a source sentence. We describe experiments with Logos Model that both succeeded and failed in this effort to escape from this structure-preserving tendency in MT.

IN TRANSLATIONS PRODUCED BY MT, THE STRUCTURE of a target language sentence is more or less determined by the structure of the source sentence (Somers 1992/3). This is so for a number of reasons, not least of which is that basing target constructions on the syntax of the source sentence, *mutatis mutandis*, is the most straightforward, least complicated way to proceed, and from a methodology perspective it may seem to be the only truly feasible way for a translation machine. Whether this is necessarily the case is what we want to examine here.

Human translators of course suffer from no such constraint, which is why, in human translations, target language sentences not infrequently may entail radical structural shifts away from source language syntax.[1] At times there are good reasons for this shift; target output often sounds foreign if source construction is imitated too closely.

We give some examples of this below, and examine the extent to which MT methodology can imitate the freedom from source constraints that human translators enjoy.

---

[1] There is of course the parallel tendency for translators to adhere more closely than necessary to source language constructions, a tendency called *"translationese"* (Koppel and Odan 2011).

© Springer International Publishing AG, part of Springer Nature 2018   163
B. Scott, *Translation, Brains and the Computer*, Machine Translation:
Technologies and Applications 2, https://doi.org/10.1007/978-3-319-76629-4_7

7.1   First Example

The English sentence in (1), below, contains an infinitive clause that does not work as well in German as it does in English.

(1)   *Cast iron **is apt to break**.*

In (1)(i) we see that a human translator has shifted away from the English construction. Instead, the translator renders the ***be + apt to V*** construction in (1) as ***V + adverb***.

Translation by Professional German Translator

(1)(i)   *Gusseisen **bricht leicht**. (Cast iron **easily breaks**.)*

In contrast to this translation, the two SMT and two linguistic, RBMT systems we have been testing all preserve the infinitive clause in their translations. Here we only show output from Google SMT Translate and SYSTRANet, in (1)(ii) and (1)(iii) respectively. The other SMT and RBMT systems had additional shortcomings and are not shown.

Translation by Google SMT Translate[2]

(1)(ii)   *Gusseisen ist **passend**, zu brechen. (Cast iron is **fit** to break.)*

Translation by SYSTRANet

(1)(iii)   *Roheisen ist **passend** zu brechen. (Pig iron is **fit** to break).*

The German word ***passend*** has the principal meaning of *fitting* or *suitable* rather than *prone* or *likely*, and hence the translations in (1)(ii) and (1)(iii) convey an inapt sense of the English in (1). For reasons we will account for in a moment, Logos Model translation of (1) in (1)(iv), below, is most like the human translation in (1)(i).

Translation by Logos Model

(1)(iv)   *Gusseisen zerbricht **leicht**. (Cast iron **easily** breaks.)*

In the case of (1)(iv), the task of accomplishing this translation was straightforward. Logos linguists had merely to add a single pattern-rule to the thousands of pattern-rules stored in the Semantic Table (SEMTAB). Note that pattern-rule (2) is the B shown in the SEMTAB hidden layer in Fig. 7.1, below. (This Figure alludes to earlier Figs. 4.4, 4.7e, and 4.9 in Chap. 4.)

The SAL pattern-rule that was added to SEMTAB in order to effect the translation in (1)(iv) is shown in (2), expressed in plain English rather than in SAL notation.

---

[2] See Postscript 6-B-1 of Chap. 6 for translations of (1) by Google GNMT Translate and Bing NMT Translator. Translation of (1) by Google GNMT Translate now closely resembles the human translation in (1)(i).

Fig. 7.1 *Figure depicting means by which transformation is effected in translation of sentence (1).* Figure depicts an input string of words in V5 matching on a single pattern-rule in hidden layer P3. This P3 pattern-rule in turn seeks a nested matchup of the V5 pattern with a pattern-rule in SEMTAB. The successful SEMTAB matchup imparts new transfers and constructions to the target equivalent of input string in V5. The SEMTAB pattern-rule in (2) that effects the transformation in (1)(iv) is shown above as **B** in the graphic

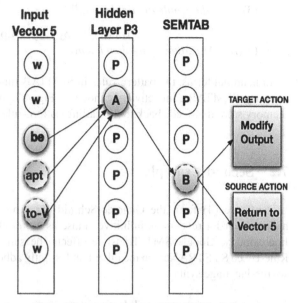

Vector 5 - Input is expressed in SAL (not shown)

HL P3 - Pattern-rule A - Matched pattern is:
be + adj + to-V

SEMTAB - Pattern-rule B - Matched pattern is:
be + apt + to-V

(2)   *BE APT TO-V(INF)* = V*(finite)* **leicht**

Logos Model translated (1) as (1)(iv) in order to prove a point about what Logos Model was potentially capable of. Let us explain.

In the mid-90s, two linguists at Logos began an experiment to see whether underlying Logos Model technology would allow for radical shifts in construction of the sort that often characterize high-quality human translation. In effect, they sought to determine to what extent Logos Model could simulate this freedom from source language construction.

The two Logos linguists focused on the issue of clause shifts such as those exemplified by the human translator in (1)(i), above, and in the other examples that follow.[3]

Note that in example (3), below, the same SEMTAB rule that effected the translation in (1)(iv) now similarly applies to (3)(i).

---

[3] Gdaniec and Schmid (1995). Schmid subsequently further described the experiment in her doctoral dissertation (Schmid 1996) where she relates Logos Model to Langacker's Cognitive Grammar (1991). She observes that the two grammars share basic assumptions about the nature of language as "*general cognitive activity*." She writes (p. 281) that Langacker sees language as "*a*

(3)   *Old people are **liable** to fall.*

Translation by Logos Model

(3)(i)   *Alte Menschen fallen **leicht**.*

In neuronal terms, the pattern-rules in SEMTAB functions like intrinsic or local circuitry. SEMTAB connectivity is shown in Fig. 4.7e of Chap. 4 as a lateral, local memory store that feeds back to the calling pattern-rule.[4]

7.2 Second Example

In senttence (4) from the Gdaniec-Schmid experiment, a single pattern-rule in hidden layer P4 renders an infinitive clause as a *that* clause in the target in (4)(i). Interestingly, Google SMT Translate effects the same structural shift in (4)(ii). Rule-based SYSTRANet, on the other hand, strictly adheres in (4)(iii) to the original source-language syntax.

(4)   *They expect **all business transactions to be conducted** in French.*

Translation by Logos Model

(4)(i)   *Sie erwarten, **dass alle Geschäftstransaktionen** auf französisch **geführt werden**.*

Translation by Google SMT Translate

(4)(ii)   *Sie erwarten, **dass alle Geschäftsvorfälle** <u>in</u> Französisch **durchgeführt werden**.*

Translation by Google GNMT Translate

(4)(iii) *Sie erwarten, **dass alle Geschäftsvorgänge** <u>**durchgeführt werden**</u> <u>Französisch</u>.*

Translation by SYSTRANet

(4)(iii) *Sie erwarten **all Geschäftsvorgänge**, auf französisch **geleitet zu werden**.*

---

psychological and ultimately neurological phenomenon which is acquired through experience." She notes that *"Both theories [Cognitive Grammar and Logos Model] consider neural networks as a valid model of human mental activity...."*

[4] The E-G Semantic Table contains roughly 15,000 pattern-rules that for the most part serve specific semantic purposes, as the name implies. If Logos Model had been allowed to continue development after 2000, the volume of semantically oriented pattern-rules could by now easily exceed double or triple that number. Even as it now stands, it is not unusual for a certain verb to have forty or more SEMTAB rules covering its multiple meanings and the various generalized SAL contexts that trigger these meanings.

Commentary

Google SMT & GNMT Translate both also transform the infinitive construction in (4) into a *dass* clause (but in the GNMT case this is not done without other construction difficulties). Bing NMT Translator also transformed the infinitive clause in (4) into a *dass* clause (unshown). That these SMT and NMT systems all had recourse to the *dass* clause here well illustrates the fact that the basis for their translations is human translator usage.

7.3   Other Translation Examples

The English sentences in (5)–(8), below, were also part of the original 1995 Gdaniec-Schmid experiment, but the pattern-rules that were written for the desired translations had *"unintended consequences"* and had to be modified (Schmid 1996).[5] In example (5), the pattern-rule was deleted entirely because of unanticipated backfirings.

(5)   *The code must not be lost **when the battery is changed**.*

Experimental Logos Model Translation

(5)(i)   *Der Code darf **bei Batteriewechsel** nicht verlorengehen.*

Current Logos Model Translation

(5)(ii)   *Der Code darf nicht verlorengehen, **wenn die Batterie gewechselt wird.***

In (6)–(8), below, we show further translations that now differ from those reported on in the experiment because of needed SEMTAB pattern-rule changes. The modified pattern-rules nevertheless still effect structural shifts in the translations, indicated in bolding.

(6)   *Both geographic and linguistic factors must be taken into account **when looking after the Italian-speaking area**.*

Current Logos Model Translation

(6)(i)   *Geografische und linguistische Faktoren müssen in Betracht gezogen werden, **wenn man den italienisch sprechenden Bereich betreut**.*

(7)   ***Hoping to raise themselves in society**, they decided to collect antique furniture.*

---

[5] Ideally, given time and motivation, the offending pattern-rules presumably could have been constrained sufficiently to avoid the unintended effects.

Current Logos Model Translation

(7)(i)   *Weil sie hofften, sich selbst in Gesellschaft hochzustellen,*
         beschlossen sie, antike Möbel zu sammeln.

(8)   *This problem is remedied **by reducing** the information*
         to smaller categories.

Current Logos Model Translation

(8)(i)   *Dieses Problem wird behoben, **indem man** die Informationen auf*
         *kleinere Kategorien **reduziert**.*

7.4   Balancing the Picture

Throughout this account, we have looked at different MT systems and their ability
to meet various challenges. All have weaknesses and strengths relative to each other.
A good example of strength may be seen in Bing's NMT Translator's (8)(ii) rendition
of (8), achieving what Logos Model failed to accomplish in this sentence.

Translation by Bing NMT Translator

(8)(ii) *Dieses Problem wird behoben, **durch die Reduzierung***
         *der Informationen **zu** kleineren Kategorien.*

Of all the translations of (8) that we tested, that by Google GNMT Translate in
(8)(iii) most preserves the construction of the original English. This does not imply
however that the translation is flawed.

Translation by Google GNMT Translate

(8)(iii) *Dieses Problem wird behoben, **indem** die Informationen*
         *auf kleinere Kategorien **reduziert werden**.*

In Table 7.1, as a final exercise to illustrate relative strengths and weakness, we
had each of these systems translate an arbitrarily selected text, choosing for this
purpose this very sentence. We boldfaced strings of interest in both source and
translation. Only the most egregious errors in translaton are underlined.

---

[6] Tests designed to compare systems are of limited value if they do not correlate testing with the
kinds of texts used to train each system. There will probably never be such a thing as a perfect,
all-purpose system, no more than there are perfect, all-purpose translators, although clearly some
(in either case) approach that ideal more so than others.

Table 7.1 Comparative translations into French of a randomly selected English sentence performed by each of the MT systems being tested in this study

Input Sentence			
*As a final exercise, to illustrate the relative strengths and weakness of each of these systems,**we had each of them translate**an arbitrarily selected text, choosing for this purpose this very sentence.*			
Logos Model	Google GNMT	Bing NMT	SYSTRANet
*Comme un exercice final, pour illustrer les forces et la faiblesse relatives de chacun de ces systèmes, **nous avons demandé à chacun d'eux de traduire** un texte arbitrairement sélectionné, en choisissant <u>ceci la phrase dans ce but très.</u>*	*Dans un dernier exercice, pour illustrer les forces et faiblesses relatives de chacun de ces systèmes, nous avons ___ chacun ___ <u>traduit</u> un texte choisi arbitrairement, en choisissant à cette fin cette même phrase.*	*Comme un exercice final, afin d'illustrer les points forts et les faiblesses de chacun de ces systèmes, <u>nous avons eu chacun d'eux traduire</u> un texte arbitrairement sélectionné, <u>choisir</u> à cet effet, cette phrase.*	*Comme exercice final, pour illustrer les forces et la failblesse relatives de chacun de ces systèmes, nous **avons fait traduire** à chacun d'eux un texte arbitrairement selectionné, choisissant à cet effet cette phrase <u>même</u>.*

7.5   Conclusion

Performance (in the sense of translation quality) is the only way to measure the underlying competence of any system. But performance's value as a measure of competence is bound to be limited. This is so because the underlying competence itself is a dependent variable subject to explanatory factors quite apart from the approach taken, factors such as the financing available for development, the length of time a system has been in (or out of) development, the skills of those who build and maintain the system, and the kinds of texts their system is being trained to handle.[6] And of course, except for Logos Model, all of these systems are still under development. One must keep in mind therefore that the performances sampled here have been taken *in medias res.*

But none of these factors bear on the theoretical question of how good a system's translation quality could eventually become, as a principled matter. It seems undeniable that the ultimate potential of an MT system is going to be a function of one thing alone, the system's technological basis. That technology either has the potential for achieving translation excellence or it does not. And the best way, and per-

---

[7]Xing Shi et al. (2016, web): *"As the [neural] model first encodes the source sentence into a high-dimensional vector, then decodes into target sentence, it is hard to understand and interpret what is going on inside such a procedure."*

haps the only way, to estimate that potential is to examine what would limit it. And as we have been arguing, what limits any translation technology, what brings any MT development effort into stasis, is complexity in all its various forms, especially the complexity that arises as a system attempts to resolve syntactic and semantic ambiguity, and most critically, the effect this complexity is bound to have on the human developers who must effect these disambiguations, i.e., cognitive complexity.

One may be tempted to think that neural MT based on deep machine learning will eventually relieve the problem of cognitive complexity, given that the learning burden is borne by the machine rather than the human. But that is true only up to a point. Machine learning entails trial and error as well. When false predictions persist, developers must tweak the parameters defining the model, and this tweaking may well cause a previously correct prediction to go wrong. This back and forth process must continue until a stasis is reached and further tweaking to improve translation quality either no longer seems necessary or is no longer feasible. One wants to question whether this inevitable point of stasis is ever likely to coincide with the achievement of persistent, high-quality translation.

The paradox of NMT models based entirely on machine learning is that while they are relatively quick and easy to build, once a certain point has been reached they become hard to improve. Indeed, given the black box nature of machine learning technology, it may at times take longer to effect an improvement than it did to build the model in the first place.[7] With linguistic models, the case is generally the opposite: linguistic systems often take a year or more to develop even an initial capability, whereas individual improvements can often be corrected quite quickly, at least until growing complexity issues begin to pose difficulties.

Whatever the MT model, the number of errors that need fixing is virtually limitless. And unless a way has been found around the complexity problem, complexity will always constitute a limiting factor in model development.

One wonders why complexity is not more acknowledged as a fundamental limiting factor in MT. It seems strange that complexity is rarely blamed for output errors of the type exemplified in this book, some of which are extremely rudimentary. Very likely complexity is rarely alluded to because, like entropy, it is considered a fact of life that one simply must accept and learn to live with. But complexity effects do not enter into the brain's normal handling of language, and, as we argue in this book, neither do they need to be a factor limiting the potential of MT.

References

Gdaniec C, Schmid P (1995) Constituent shifts in the logos English-German system. In: Proceedings of the sixth international conference on theoretical and methodological issues in machine translation. Centre for Computational Linguistics, Catholieke Universiteit Leuven, Leuven, pp 311–318

Koppel M, Odan N (2011) Translationese and its dialects. In: Proceedings of the 49th annual meeting of the association for computational linguistics. Portland, Oregon, pp 1318–1326

Schmid P (1996) Clausal constituent shifts: a study in cognitive Grammar and machine translation. Ph.D. dissertation. Georgetown University. UMI Dissertation Services

Somers HL (1992/3) Current research in machine translation. Machs Trans 7:231–246

Shi X, Padhi I, Knight K (2016) Does string-based neural MT learn syntax? In: Proceedings of the 2016 conference on empirical methods in natural language processing. Austin, pp 1526–1534. http://xingshi.me/data/pdf/EMNLP2016long.pdf. Accessed 18 Mar 2017

Chapter 8
Deep Learning MT and Logos Model

Abstract In this Chapter we compare 45-year-old Logos Model with AI's deep learning technology and the neural net translation (NMT) technology that deep learning has given rise to. At a strictly computational level, Logos Model bears zero relationship to NMT, but we point out a number of ways in which Logos Model may nevertheless be seen to have anticipated NMT, specifically at the level of architecture and function. We take note of the fact that NMT has drifted away from interest in the biological verisimilitude of its models, and we note what experts say about the negative effect this has had on so-called *continual* machine learning (where new learning does not interfere with old learning, an obvious, vital requirement in MT). We discuss the related need for generalizations in MT learning, generalizations that are both semantic as well as syntactic, generalizations akin to the function exhibited by the brain in continual learning and processing of language. Our discussion turns on a particular point that experts at Google Deep Mind are making about continual learning, one they say that that AI has overlooked, and that, from our perspective, bears critically on MT. It concerns the way that the declarative, similarity-based operations of the hippocampus complements the more analytical, procedure-based operations of the neocortex to support continual learning. Most telling in this regard is their assertion that hippocampal learning is more than "*item specific*" and that, to the contrary, it exhibits distinct powers of semantic generalization. We note with satisfaction how that assertion about the complementary nature of hippocampal-neocortex learning comports with the analogical/analytical aspects of language processing in Logos Model. The very name and nature of SAL *pattern-rules* in Logos Model suggest this complementarity. We contend that the views of these deep learning experts provide indirect neuroscientific support for an MT methodology that affords continual, complexity-free learning, one that is predicated upon hippocampal/neocortex-like generalizations (viz., semantico-syntactic patterns). The present Chapter concludes with a Logos Model exercise illustrating the effectiveness of these declarative, hippocampal-like processes for MT.

B. Scott, *Translation, Brains and the Computer*, Machine Translation:
Technologies and Applications 2, https://doi.org/10.1007/978-3-319-76629-4_8

In several very obvious respects, the technologies of Logos Model and deep learning translation models could not be more different. For one, all of Logos Model operations are deterministic, not conditional; they seek to find a single, correct translation result, not the most likely one among a weighted distribution of candidates. This means that, for a deterministic translation process like that of Logos Model, ambiguities encountered along the way almost always have to be resolved virtually as soon as the process becomes aware of them. By contrast, statistically grounded, deep learning applications like NMT do not actually resolve a single ambiguity until the very end, when processing results having the highest likelihood can be calculated and output. Until these final calculations, ambiguity resolution remains suspended among an encoded set of candidate solutions. This is doubtless why deep learning and NMT characterize this end procedure as decoding.[1] In Logos Model parlance, decoding the initial unintelligibility of an input sentence is how a deterministic process necessarily begins.[2]

The second essential difference between the two methodologies concerns the related role of formulaic computation. It is clear that Logos Model employs none of the random variable calculations that characterize deep learning at its heart. To effect its translations, Logos Model relies upon the match-up of categorized linguistic patterns, effected in synapse-like fashion.

These critical differences aside, the suggestion that translation technology developed over 45 years ago could in other ways still have anticipated deep learning (and the neural MT models that have emerged from deep learning labs), must strike the reader as an unlikely stretch. And that contrary view certainly has its defenses. Nonetheless, we outline below the non-mathematical elements of deep learning NMT that arguably were anticipated by Logos Model.

8.1 Points of Similarity and Differences

a. In both the wide variety of deep learning translation models (DLTM) and in Logos Model (LM), processing is predicated on the matching of patterns, never on the application of rules. The aptness of pattern-based processing seems self-evident to us today, but it must be remembered that until the turn of the century, rule-driven processing was *de rigueur* in machine translation, as it was in AI generally. Statistical MT was just getting off the ground, and there was as yet only embryonic interest in the serious exploitation of Hebbian learning. Logos Model's pattern-matching technology, while hardly original as a concept, was

---

[1] Koehn (2011, p.155): *"The task of decoding in [statistical] machine translation is to find the best scoring translation."* Cho et al. (2014) speak of NMT models as *"encoding-decoding models."*

[2] Of course, Logos Model could also be seen as starting out with an encoding function (source string → SAL string), and ending with decoding (transformed SAL string → target string).

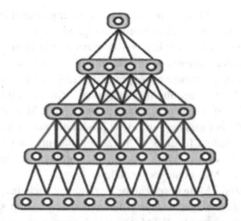

Fig. 8.1 *Graphic of a hierarchical, convolutional neural net.* Units of the input layer at the bottom represent a single feature (e.g., POS) across all words of a sentence. Output layer at the top represents the aggregate value for that feature resulting from net processing. Note how an attention-like principle limits connectivity among layers to the most probable, in contrast to the universal connectivity of early recurrent models (see Fig. 4.2). Also note resemblance to Logos Model (see Fig. 4.4) (Graphic adapted from Kalchbrenner and Blunsom (2013))

    decades ahead of its time as a working, data-driven, MT system predicated entirely on pattern matchups.

b. LM makes no pretense at being an automatic machine-learning application. This is quite clear. In LM, translation know-how is acquired via trial-and-error runs executed entirely under human supervision. Nevertheless, as we shall indicate, learning is an essential part of its translation process.

c. Both DLTM and LM are *exemplar* models that correlate similarity of input sequences with stored experience, a process effected in DLTM by statistical computations, in LM by semantico-syntactic category matching.[3]

d. Both DLTM and LM employ neural network architecture. In both models, all learning achieved about an input sequence (for translation purposes) resides entirely in interunit connectivity. In this, both models mimic the brain, where knowledge of a sentence equates with the sum of incurred synapses.

e. In both DLTM and LM, the networks comprise multiple hidden layers.[4] (See Fig. 8.1). In both DLTM and LM, connectivity can be lateral as well as forward projecting.

---

[3] Kumaran et al. (2016). The authors speak of deep learning processes as *"recurrent similarity computation,"* a term only remotely fitting for Logos Model.

[4] The term *deep* in deep learning refers to the number of hidden layers in the net, as compared to shallower machine learning models like the earlier perceptron and first connectionist models. DLTM can have as many as 10 or more layers (Kumaran et al. 2016). Logos Model has six layers.

f. In both DLTM and LM, units in input layers are engineered to represent features of sentence constituents, such as word class, gender, tense, etc.[5] In hidden layers, features are expanded to include global contextual information, in effect enabling individual units to eventually be translated in the context of entire sentences.[6]

g. In DLTM, units of a sentence are expressed as real-valued vectors (called "word embeddings"). Vectors are multi-dimensional, with each dimension housing a pertinent feature of a given sentence constituent. LM features are based on numbers as well, but numbers in Logos Model are purely symbolic. In DLTM, vector numbers denote features of literal constituents; in LM, numbers denote features of SAL words. Most essentially, numbers are used in DLTM for computations, in LM for category matching.[7]

h. In both DLTM and LM, features can be hierarchical such that, as models proceed from stage to stage (layer to layer), features change from simple to complex, from concrete to abstract. DLTM call this feature aggregation (Zhang and Ye 2010).[8] LM calls it concatenation (Scott 1989, 2003).

i. DLTMs vary in design but generally fall into the class of recurrent networks, recursive networks, or networks that combine both methodologies. Recurrent networks support backpropagation crucial to machine learning and the training of operational NMT systems. Recursive networks provide for full sentence parsing, a principal reason for NMT's superiority over phrase-based SMT. The new NMT version of Microsoft's Bing Translator is an example of a translation model that employs both recurrent and recursive technology, but where machine learning is semi-supervised (Liu et al. 2014). In contrast, LM neural net technology has recursive properties but does not support recurrent backpropagation. In LM, training is entirely supervised.

j. In both DLTM and LM, unit activation accomplishes the entire work of the net. In DLTM, activations entail non-linear transformations (see Fig. 8.2). In LM, by contrast, work is accomplished by the action portion of activated units (i.e., the rule portion of pattern-rules) drawing upon a library of small, highly constrained

---

Google's GNMT Translate has 8 decoding layers and 8 encoding layers, with the top encoding layer connected to the bottom decoding layer.

[5] Sennrich and Haddow (2016). Authors describe modest output improvements for German<->English translation in a recurrent NMT model with experimental linguistic tags attached to input word embeddings. Linguistic tags included POS, lemmas, morphological features, and simple dependency labels (e.g. relating a word in a phrase to its head).

[6] Global context information is technically known as Long Short-Term Memory (LSTM). LSTM was designed to overcome the history-access limitations of n in n-gram processes. Most advanced NMT systems employ LSTM, e.g., Microsoft's Bing Translator, Google Translate.

[7] Logos Model's use of numbers was not a little influenced by the fact that Logos Model was originally implemented in Fortran IV (later re-implemented in C). See Part II Postscript for an illustration of how numerical representation was used, and a brief discussion of why LM use of numbers turned out to be advantageous.

[8] A variant convolutional function is "max-pooling" (see Kalchbrenner et al. 2014).

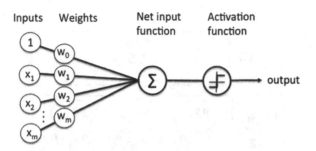

Fig. 8.2 *Processing of multi-unit input in a convolutional neural net.* Graphic shows weights, aggregation, activation and output to the next layer. Functions parallel those of LM. Note that weights in LM are a function of semantico-syntactic specificity. (Based on image by Christoph Bugmer appearing on DeepLearning4j Development Team (2016), web)

program operators. Although very different in implementation, the work of the two models is essentially the same:

- connecting an input sequence to stored experience;
- use of input sequence history in effecting connectivity;
- transforming features;
- concatenating sibling units and projecting to more abstract parent units in the next layer.

k. The most advanced DLTM are recursive and convolutional (Meng et al. 2015). Convolution is a mathematical function that combines an input pattern of features with a relevant set of learned features called a "kernel," also referred to as a "feature map." By contrast, LM processes are non-mathematical but nevertheless entail equivalent recursive and convolutional functions, as described further below. We describe the DLTM process first.

- Convolution mathematically combines input and stored kernel to output a more complex and more abstract representation to the next layer. It accomplishes this by conducting overlapping (convoluted) "sweeps" across the sequence of an input layer, working from left to right. This combining process includes lateral (sideways) connectivity, affording access to previous, long- and short-term history of the sequence.[9] Output of the operation is a child conditionally projected to a parent in the next convolutional layer. This operation is repeated until an output layer is able to conditionally represent original input by a single, complex, abstract value. The subsequent translation task is accomplished by a recurrent neural net that builds upon the hierarchical output of the convolutional operation to produce the ultimate translation. In DLTM, source conditioning and target generation are commonly combined

---

[9] As stated earlier, this is technically known as Long- Short-Term Memory (LSTM), a looping-back function also found in some recurrent NMT models.

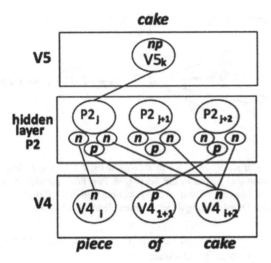

Fig. 8.3 *Detail illustrating middle layer connectivity in LM net.* V4 and V5 are I/O layers. The SAL noun-prep-noun pattern shown has considerably more features than graphic allows. The synapse-like connectivity effected by semantico-syntactic codes mimics the function of neurotransmitters. Note that, because of the *Aspective* SAL code for the noun *piece*, the noun *cake* becomes head of resultant *NP*

seamlessly as a continual task.[10] In LM, source and target handling of increasingly abstract sentence constituents occurs in parallel across the layers until the final, literal translation output takes place.

- LM is not a convolutional net in the mathematical sense, but exercises a form of connectivity productive of similar results, viz., the creation, layer after layer, of a progressively more abstract representation of a sentence, i.e., layered output resembling a bottom-up parse. (See detail in Fig. 8.3, of hierarchical concatenation in LM network.) Arguably, virtually all of the recursive, convolutional functions described above for DLTM were anticipated in LM in non-mathematical ways. We summarize them here:

  – In LM, incremental, so-called "sweeps" of input segments against hidden layers are also overlapped (convoluted). Convolution is achieved in LM by backspacing by one unit of the current search segment before commencing the next sweep.[11] Segment overlapping can be greater than by one unit when called for.
  – LM also supports lateral (sideways) connectivity within a layer, doing so in two respects (only the first of which is shared by DLTM). First, units have

---

[10] Kalchbrenner et al. (2014). Authors describe a convolutional neural net that automatically learns conditional distributions from an aligned, bilingual corpus.

[11] In LM, hidden layer units are indexed on their semantico-syntactic patterns, making sweeps look like longest-match lexical lookup.

access to LM's equivalent of long- short-term memory (LSTM), affording access to history of pertinent connectivity in both current and previous layers.[12] Secondly, and uniquely, lateral connectivity in LM mimics the so-called local or intrinsic circuitry of the brain, allowing for nested searching and matching (see Fig. 4.7 in Chap. 4). Nested connectivity is the principal means for semantic disambiguation in LM. Nested connectivity also serves a great variety of other fine-tuned, analytic purposes affecting both source analysis and target generation.

- As with DLTM, LM input units and hidden layer units (with kernels *qua* feature maps) are combined to produce a more complex, abstract parent that in turn serves as input to the next layer. This operation is repeated layer by layer until further concatenation is no longer possible.
- As with DLTM, LM target generation builds upon the target structures and related data that have been progressively put in place over the network's successive layers.

8.2 Deep Learning, Logos Model and the Brain

Despite their foundation in early connectionist architecture, deep learning models have generally drifted away from connectionism's original concern for cerebral verisimilitude. This may be seen in deep learning models' preference for the term "unit" rather than "neuron," or "neurode." Still, deep learning's original neural inspiration is unmistakable. The very notion of connectivity and the bearing that occurrence frequencies have on deep learning clearly imitate the way learning and memory formation occur in the brain. But there the parallelism seems to end.[13] In deep learning models, occurrence frequencies effect connectivity only conditionally, i.e., with respect to weights. In the brain, occurrence frequencies affecting connectivity seem to function more deterministically. Once learning has occurred, synapse seems selective and deterministic, not distributed and conditional. And this determinism has implications for behavior. Once a student of Farsi, for example, learns that verbs come at the end of Farsi sentences, it must be assumed that that fact gets fixed in memory circuits. When the student composes a Farsi sentence, it does not seem reasonable to think that probability has anything to do with the placement of the verb. It is true that, by virtue of weights, conditional methods can bring about the same result, but never quite so certainly.

---

[12] In LM, this history includes a top-down, structural view of the entire sentence produced by layers R1 & R2 in its initial macro-parse (described in Chap. 6). Being able to view such top-down data at any point in the subsequent micro-parse (layers P1 to P4) has obvious advantages. Bahdanau et al. (2015) describe an NMT model where units are similarly progressively annotated with information about the entire input sequence.

[13] Dettmers (2015, web) notes that it is *"misleading to explain deep learning as mimicry of the human brain."*

There are other features of DLTM that seem to be incongruent with cerebral verisimilitude. We list a few of them here.

• The place of formulaic probability calculation in DLTM has no direct parallel in the brain, and can hardly be the means by which language sequences are handled mentally. One wants to assert this because the resolution of ambiguities associated with these sequences commonly calls for non-formulaic, heuristic searches for contextual clues.

• There is no compelling research data indicating that the brain parses and translates sentences probabilistically.[14] This of course does not mean to suggest that occurrence frequencies are not an important factor in conditioning causal synapses, i.e., that Hebbian learning is not a real factor in learning.

• Backpropagation constitutes a *sine qua non* function in deep learning models, but connectionists acknowledge that automatic feedback to adjust connectivity weights is not biologically plausible. To wit:

Activation signals propagate in one direction, from input to output, and the process of determining the appropriate adjustments to the crucial weights ... depends on a ... biologically implausible backward transmission of a separate error signal across forward-going synapses.[15]

• DLTM as yet has no explicit counterpart to the neuromodulation function that is deemed fundamental to all cerebral processes. In the brain, when a neuron fires, its output is of two distinct kinds, one a postsynaptic transmission that typically gets passed to one or more neuronal partners, the other a neuromodulatory chemical that gets transmitted to a whole population of neurons, thus potentially modulating subsequent synapses. (See Fig. 4.6 in Chap. 4 for a graphic depiction of this.) Logos Model simulates both kinds of synaptic output.[16]

  – Here's how neuromodulation works in LM. Assume a unit in an input layer is an unresolved noun-verb homograph, and that this input unit connects with a unit in a hidden layer whose function is to recognize input units as verbs.[17]

---

[14] Sanborn and Chater (2016, web): "...*that a Bayesian brain must represent all possible probabilities and make exact calculations using these probabilities [is] too complex for any physical system, including brains.*" Authors nevertheless hold for a Bayesian brain but propose that the brain works by "*sampling [just] one or a few [probabilities] at a time.*"

[15] McClelland et al. (1995, p. 25). However, see Hassabis et al. (2017) where authors describe recent AI efforts to find a biologically plausible way around this issue in artificial neural nets, drawing upon dynamic, local information rather than feedback to effect correct connectivity. In LM, local information is also critical in effecting error-free connectivity.

[16] LSTM might be construed as a partial means of simulating neuromodulation in DLTM.

[17] The connection effects this resolution only if all constraints can be satisfied, e.g., that the candidate verb agrees with the subject in number. In LM, data pertaining to the subject will have to have been previously communicated via neuromodulation to the entire hidden layer for this purpose.

When synaptic connection occurs between these units, the activated hidden layer unit effectively resolves the ambiguity. But in addition it will also transmit a signal to all other units in its own hidden layer to the effect that the verb of the present input clause has been established and that, in the instance of this verb's SAL Type, no other verb is called for. Such a signal effectively inhibits the activation of any unit (pattern-rule) in that hidden layer that might want to recognize as verb some other word in the input clause. Thus, for instance, in the sentence *His heart sounds sound,* if the first *sound* gets resolved to a verb, the second *sound* can never be.[18]

• The way DLTM seeks to improve its translation output has no evident parallel in the brain. Because of DLTM's probabilistic basis, it can only learn by tweaking parameters with quasi-educated corrections born of trial and error. Why does this matter? It matters because it is precisely here that cognitive complexity exacts its price. Since DLTM developers are working with what is essentially a black box, parameter tweaking to improve model performance must seem at times like chasing one's tail. A stasis point is apt to be reached beyond which it cannot fix a problem without persistently undoing something else (Dettmers 2015). This weakness is a consequence of the way DLTM learns.

The issue of learning is central to DLTM, but deep learning modality differs significantly from the way neuroscience envisions learning by the brain.[19] Learning is perhaps the most critical of all issues that separate DLTM's processes from both the brain's, and from Logos Model's as well. It will serve our purposes well to focus for a moment on this matter of learning.

8.3 On Learning

Neuropsychologists generally agree that language acquisition entails two distinct but complementary learning functions, the first having to do with imitation, i.e., learning through sociolinguistic exposure, the second with certain cognitive operations that may build on imitation but then go beyond it. This second learning function is invoked at junctures where what has been learned by imitation proves

---

[18] By the same token, a hidden layer unit in LM that recognizes clausal transitions will transmit a neuromodulatory signal that effectively *uninhibits* units whose function is to recognize verbs. (See Fig. 4.6 in Chap. 4 for a neuroscientist's depiction of neuromodulation in the brain.)

[19] Marblestone et al. (2016, web): *"Machine learning and neuroscience speak different languages today."* See also Hassabis et al. (2017). Authors of both papers argue for closer integration between the disciplines, contending that artificial intelligence has always benefited from closer integration with brain processes.

insufficient for some intended language act, whether that act be to express something not said before, or to comprehend something not heard before. In either case, the operation calls upon a cognitive learning function other than imitation.[20,21]

In the Chap. 3 discussion about acquiring a foreign language, we observed that this cognitive learning function has two parts, one analogical, the other analytical. The analogical operation relates things on the basis of similarity, the analytical on the basis either of their distinctness or their connection other than through similarity. To cite an example of the analogical (from an actual experience of the author's), two children are heard discussing a certain event in their young lives. One of the children insists that when this thing happened, the room they were in was empty. The second child disagrees, but the first child persists, saying, *no, nobody was there*, whereupon the second child retorts, *yes, yesbody was there*. The exchange is interesting because the first child's use of the expression *nobody* has imitation as its basis; the first child is merely repeating a word he or she has heard enough times to have learned its meaning and use. The second child has never heard the term, *yesbody*, so obviously this child's use has as its basis some function other than imitation. We would term that function "analogical." *No* is to *nobody* as *yes*, by analogy, ought to be to *yesbody*. Of course, the child's cognitive operation in this particular instance is faulty and will eventually be corrected by imitation in subsequent sociolinguistic exposure. The point here is that analogical operations make these associations not through imitation but through a distinct cognitive function.

Analytical operations, by contrast, are based on the perception of a relationship involving distinctions and connections whose basis is other than similarity. The novelty of associating two unrelated concepts that are normally never linked can at times be somewhat striking, as in oxymorons like *organized chaos*, or in metaphors like the title of Ferlingetti's poem, *Coney Island of the Mind*.

What, you may ask, do oxymorons and metaphors have to do with learning? We are using the notion of "learning" here in the widest sense of seeing something not seen before, of discerning a hitherto unrecognized or unexpected connection between things, concepts or events that are gleaned not by empirical exposure but by some cognitive operation. These cognitive operations do not have to be striking. Their essential property is simply that their product is unpredicted, unforetold by anything in prior experience, i.e., that something new is being learned. The learning for the most part is utterly commonplace, present in trivial linguistic acts that may be forgotten virtually as soon they occur. The words in these language acts have all

---

[20] Neuroscience first became aware that the brain had two entirely different learning and memory regions when trauma to the hippocampus caused memory loss of recent experience, leaving remote, long-term memory intact (McClelland et al. 1995).

[21] We use "learning" here in the broadest, everyday sense of seeing/hearing something not seen/ heard before, or saying something that had to be learned to say because it was never said before. The knowledge, for example, that 79 is a prime number was not learned directly from experience but by virtue of a learned cognitive act.

been learned from exposure and imitation, but the way these words are put together in a communicative act is almost always novel, and for that reason must be learned (in our broad sense of learning) for the language act to be complete (or decoded, to use our term for language acts *qua* comprehension).

Another way of seeing these different aspects of learning is in the distinction between usage and rules, between learning something because we have been exposed to it, i.e., learning through imitation, and learning something we may have never heard or seen before, i.e., learning through cognitive function. For example, most of us are far more apt to ask, *Who did you see?* than, *Whom did you see?* We do this following common usage, even though we may appreciate that the latter expression alone is grammatical. Yet some do observe the rule of grammar. They learned a rule in school to the effect that pronoun objects of verbs and prepositions have to be inflected, a rule learned independently of popular usage and applied in novel circumstances not by imitation but by a cognitive operation applying a rule.

There is another fundamental aspect of learning that we have yet to mention, one already implicit in the cognitive operations described above. This has to do with the notion of generality and the cognitive ability to generalize (Goldberg 2009; Kumaran and McClelland 2012). For example, if we come to learn that something is generally true, like for instance the general fitness of athletes, such learning is based only indirectly on individual, empirical observations of particular athletes. The generality of the observation comes directly from the cognitive operations we have been describing, only indirectly from experience. And this is no less true about the grammar lessons learned in school or the insights that gifted language students figure out on their own. Generalities and rules are not objects of experience, and can only be learned through acts of cognition, not imitation. Why does this matter for MT? Models based entirely on usage, without benefit of cognitive function (i.e., something akin to rules) will suffer lack of generality. We see this deficiency in SMT and why its developers have been looking to linguistic rules for help (Koehn 2011). How NMT for its part might achieve generality in its processes is a question we seek in part to answer in this book.

A related aspect of learning that concerns us is the notion of abstraction and how abstraction relates to generality. The two notions seem close but are clearly not the same. Abstraction differs from generality in the way that specificity differs from concreteness. Generality and its opposite, specificity, imply number, as in the major and minor premises of a syllogism, e.g., *All men are mortal, Socrates is a man*, etc. On the other hand, abstraction and its opposite, concreteness, have to do with degree. If one were to complain, for example, that a certain statement was too general and too abstract, the generality would have to do with the *number* the statement applies to, and in the latter case, with its *degree* of abstractness, its lack of concreteness. That is why notions of second-order abstractions are meaningful whereas second-order generalities are not, and why parse trees depict degrees of abstraction, not degrees of generality.

What's interesting about the above is that rules seem to partake of both generality and abstraction, particularly so with rules of grammar. Take, for example, the rule that declarative sentences in Farsi are SOV constructs. The rule applies generally to all sentences and at the same time could not be more abstract; both number and degree are implicated in learning this rule. Interestingly, too, this SOV rule is both descriptive and prescriptive, relating to both usage and principle. This in turn suggests that the two principles of learning we have been discussing both contribute to a student's acquisition of this Farsi rule, i.e., that both imitation and the two analytical and analogical cognitive functions all get involved in some complementary fashion, much as our discussion in Chap. 3 suggests.

What does this have to do with machine translation? It is fairly obvious that machine translation could never have been conceived of as a possibility were it not for the existence of grammar rules that were both abstract and general in nature. How else, for instance, could a machine cope with the multiplicity of words if not by the abstractions of word class that in effect reduce their number? And how could a machine handle the infinitude of possible constructions if not by the simplifying generalizations of syntax, or in other words by the rules that prescribe these constructions in their countless instantiations?

It is clear from this why Chomsky's turn to syntax helped form the original grounds for machine translation. His theory of syntax provided both the generality and the abstraction that machines needed in order to cope with natural language. Through syntax, immense lexicons could be manipulated by means of a dozen symbols, and through syntax the infinite variety of literal sentences could be handled via the finite set of rules that purportedly generates them. This reduction of literal sentences to abstract, generalized syntactic strings made MT possible. But as we argue, the process of decoding in syntactically oriented models inevitably runs into a wall of ambiguity and attendant complexity, a wall that eventually proves difficult if not impossible to surmount. How else are we to explain present limitations of rule-based MT systems after nearly five decades of effort?

These limitations are why MT developers began attributing their difficulties to these rules of syntax themselves. Even Chomsky is said to have abandoned rules and turned to the lexicon (Palmer 2006).[22] Statistical machine translation did the same thing, eschewing rules and turning instead to the mining of raw language. Neural Net systems have generally been built upon this statistical grasp of literal language. But despite all that statistically oriented, rule-free NMT technology has accomplished, the need for linguistics has not been eliminated. To witness this,

---

[22] Chomsky abandoned his formalisms (Chomsky 1990) but never his theory that syntax was separate and distinct from semantics. His theory of syntax however has not held up well, e.g., (Palmer 2006, 267): *"Chomsky's current theory has reallocated the explanatory burden from … the syntactic module to the lexicon, with no advance in plausibility. My own exploration and evaluation of Chomsky's theories … led me to predict that his work will ultimately be seen as a kind of scientific flash flood, generating great excitement, wreaking havoc, but leaving behind only an arid gulch."*

observe how two NMT systems mishandle agreement in the translations of (4), below. Errors are underlined.

(4)   *Nations who accepted the refugees were honored today by the United Nations.*

Translation by Google GNMT Translate

(4)(i)   *Les nations qui ont accepté les réfugiés ont été **honorés** aujourd'hui par les Nations Unies.*

Translation by LISA Lab NMT

(4)(ii)   *Les nations qui ont accepté les réfugiés ont été **honorés** aujourd'hui par l'ONU.*

Translations by Logos Model, SYSTRANnet, PROMT

(4)(iii)   *Les nations qui ont accepté les réfugiés ont été **honorées** aujourd'hui par les Nations Unies.*

Commentary

Given the feminine gender of the subject *nations*, the passive English construction *were **honored*** should be rendered *ont été **honorées*** in French, as the linguistic systems have done in (4)(iii).[23]

Data-driven systems of whatever stripe need linguistics if they are to produce high-quality translations in a consistent way. SMT developers readily acknowledge this and are currently working to bring rules of syntax back into the translation process (Koehn 2011, 337*ff*). Deep learning has sought to overcome SMT's limitations chiefly through the power of abstraction (aggregation). As we have noted in DLTM's more advanced, recursive models, sentences are treated not as a sequence of word patches but as an aggregate whole, giving the translation process the benefit of an aggregate, global view of the entire source string. Global data are what enables a model to insure that subject and predicate agree in number, and so on.

There still remains the question of generality, however. Non-linguistic, usage-based models commonly suffer from a lack of generality, i.e., from reduced ability to handle text different from the corpora they have been trained on. The problem is that non-linguistic models are trained on the basis of only one of the learning principles we are discussing, viz., the *empirical* principle, the principle of learning from usage, which leaves them open to the problem of sparseness. Given the essentially black box nature of NMT processes, it is unclear how NMT models plan to compensate for the unavailability of generalized linguistic information in these processes.

To put this in terms of our discussion, one cannot pass from the confines of the literal to the openness of the general, from the strictly empirical to broad, underlying

---

[23] In its translation of (4), Microsoft's Bing NMT Translator most interestingly (and quite legitimately) transformed the passive voice of the English sentence into the active voice in French: *Les Nations Unies ont honoré aujourd'hui les pays qui ont accepté les réfugiés.* For some reason, in a subsequent run of (4) through Bing MNT Translator, the French output reverted to the passive voice.

principles and rules, without requisite cognitive function, i.e., without analytical and analogical operations. For example, one cannot learn anything in general about the placement of French adjectives just by learning how scores of specific French adjectives happen to be placed, not without a cognitive operation that effectively formulates generalized knowledge from such data. Non-linguistic systems will be powerless when confronted with a French adjective they have not been trained to deal with. Decisions based on probability will help, but never invariably, which is why NMT still has problems to solve.

Rules are a key way of formulating generalized knowledge, but the dilemma for MT is that rules themselves become a mixed blessing. Without them, MT models inevitably exhibit shortcomings in linguistic competence, and with them, MT models all experience complexity effects that eventually limit their potential.

These observations bring us back to the question of how the brain processes language, and whether MT might glean something from the brain about linguistic competence that is utterly free of complexity effects. For help in this, we turn to a recent study on learning by key pioneers of Deep Mind technology. What is most intriguing about their reflection is the authors' evident desire to recapture a degree of cerebral likeness in deep learning machines.

8.4   The Hippocampus and Continual Learning

A recent paper by three authors associated with Google Deep Mind (Kumaran et al. 2016)[24] has something very interesting to say about learning in the brain, and what this might mean for AI's deep learning models. Given our own perspectives on this, the paper strikes us as significant because it seeks to restore a degree of cerebral resemblance to machine learning. The authors do not discuss translation, and they touch on language only obliquely, but what they have to say nevertheless seems quite relevant to the topic of our book. We briefly summarize key postulates of their paper.

- The authors state that intelligent agents must of necessity possess two distinct but complementary systems of learning, one that is instance-based and that serves the rapid acquisition of the specifics of experience, and another that performs the more slowly learned consolidation of that experience into long-term memory and understanding. Different circuitries of the brain are known to be recruited for each type of learning: the hippocampus for recording the immediate specifics of experience, and neocortex for effecting more reflective

---

[24] Kumaran et al. (2016, web). One of the authors, Demis Hassabis, was the founder of Deep Mind Technologies, a British-based AI enterprise acquired by Google in 2014 as Google Deep Mind. The study's principal author, Dharshan Kumaran, is a senior research scientist at Google Deep Mind. Most interestingly, the third author is James McClelland, co-originator of connectionism in the mid-80s. His presence as author signals Google Deep Mind's interest, in their words, in *"high-lighting the connection between neuroscience and machine learning."*

learning. Neocortex includes the inferior prefrontal gyrus (general Broca area), the language region of the brain that neuropsychologists and neurolinguists have commonly referred to as rule-oriented.

- The authors recognize that AI has traditionally equated machine learning exclusively with procedure-driven, neocortical learning.[25] Declarative, hippocampal learning was deemed too superficial, too instance-based to produce meaningful knowledge. A specific experiential item acquired by the hippocampus does not become knowledge in the AI sense until that item is grounded structurally in what surrounds it. For example, in the discussion in our Introduction about the morpheme *sound*, AI would have assigned no role to the hippocampus in learning its form and function. The hippocampus can assemble the letters of this morpheme and recognize it as a legitimate word, but it takes the procedure-driven operations of neocortical learning (working memory) to ground its form and meaning in the context of a sentence. It is thought that instance-based hippocampal learning lacks the generality to do this, which is why the brain must turn to neocortex, and why in effect AI has traditionally done so as well.[26]

- These authors do not agree with this commonly held view about learning, and they are working to revise AI's traditional position on it, clarifying it for neuroscience as well. The key point in their revision concerns the hippocampus and this matter of generality. As we have repeatedly noted, hippocampal representation was traditionally thought, in their words, to only "*support memory of specifics, leaving generalizations to the complementary neocortical system*," a neuroscience orthodoxy these authors seek to challenge. In support, they cite a recent study where subjects were shown to "*rapidly ... create links among a set of experiences*" even after only one such exposure. In their view, the sparseness of the exposure and the rapidity of the learning implicate the hippocampus, not neocortex (Kumaran et al. 2016, web). Their position here has significance for machine translation and is worth outlining (for one because it supports the views of our book having to do with continual learning).

- If the brain had but a single learning system, these authors argue, the connectivity being formed by new learning could easily conflict with the connectivity of previously acquired, long-term learning. We have seen this already in the marble-dropping problem prevalent in MT development, where translation improvements are often accompanied by unintended degradations. To avoid such interference,

---

[25] In Kumaran et al. (2016, web), authors observe that deep networks "*share the characteristics of the slow-learning of the neocortical system ...; they achieve an optimal parametric characterization of the statistics of the environment by learning gradually through repeated, interleaved exposure to large numbers of training examples.*" Multi-layered neural networks "*gradually learn to extract features when trained by adjusting weights to minimize errors in network output.*"

[26] As we saw in Chap. 5, this perception of hippocampal learning as specific and superficial has been common among virtually all neuropsychologists, and doubtless explains why hippocampal role in language processes had remained unrecognized for so long. In this view, language acquisition calls for the generalities of grammar (neocortex), not just the specifics of lexicon (hippocampus).

the accretion of new knowledge to established knowledge has to be gradual and regulated. Whatever the learning agent, man or machine, there has to be a way of accommodating the new with the old without risk of undoing something already learned, and a single learning system with its tendency to forget does not seem to afford that protection.

• Single-learning systems trained to deal with a fixed set of features will have trouble learning input exhibiting new features without risking interference with previous learning. Complementary learning on the other hand supports continual learning, doing so by virtue of its adaptability. Complementarity allows the two brain areas to collaborate both in supplementing and in exploiting each other's learning methods. This is why new learning rarely confuses the brain.

Much of what is said in the above paragraphs can apply to MT. For MT learning to be unlimited (continual), new learning (e.g., fixes) must cause no disruptions in current capability (i.e., marble dropping must be negligible and manageable). In short, MT learning also needs to be complementary. Complementary learning would free MT from the unintended disruptions that new learning typically causes in both data-driven, usage-based models and in linguistically driven, rule-based models, each of which seems to be predicated on a single learning principle.

We have offered Logos Model as evidence of this freedom from disruptions to new learning. In its long history, Logos Model has never run up against the problem of unmanageable degradation in connection with new learning, and all that such degradation implies for an MT model's potential, a freedom we attribute to the complementary nature of Logos Model learning. Complementarity is embodied in the very pattern-rules that constitute Logos Model's translation know-how. As their very name suggests, pattern-rules combine both empirically derived data patterns and cognitive, linguistic know-how (rules) into individual stored memory units. These units in turn are organized into two complementary collections (as described in Chap. 6), the first of which accomplishes an abstract, macro overview of a sentence, and the second of which ramifies this sentence structure into micro-linguistic detail sufficient for the needs of translation.

It is tempting to think that one of these pattern-rule collections functions is like hippocampus, the other like Broca, that one is lexical and semantic, the other syntax-oriented. But in truth the two collections are altogether too complementary to be separated in this way, just as semantics and syntax are no longer separable in the semantico-syntactic SAL symbology that Logos Model uses to process language in this complementary way. The distinction between syntax and semantics is undeniable, certainly, but they differ only in the way that thumb and forefinger differ as together they pick up a marble. But the fact that Logos Model integrates the neocortical function (essentially syntactic and analytical) and the hippocampal function (essentially semantic and analogical) and does so in this complementary fashion, suggests Logos Model has close kinship to the brain, closer than traditional AI's deep learning with its neocortex-oriented, single-learning principle.[27]

---

[27] As stated in Chap. 6, Logos Model was depicted over two decades ago as a fortuitous implementation of hippocampal declarative, associative, pattern-based learning (Scott 1990, 2003).

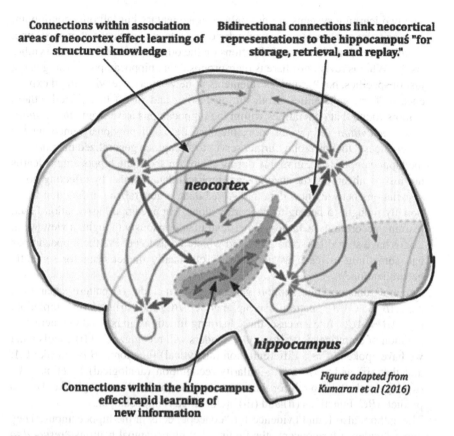

Fig. 8.4 *Bidirectional connectivity between neocortex and hippocampus.* Connectivity within hippocampus learns the specifics of immediate experience, connecting these with stored experience. Neocortex connectivity embeds that experience in wider context and structure. The learning of each is supplemented by feedback from the other. (Figure adapted from Kumeran et al. (2016))

The two-sided, complementary learning that these Deep Mind authors advocate is not new. Two decades ago, co-author James McClelland described learning as complementary interaction between the hippocampus and the neocortex. (See Fig. 8.4). What is new concerns the authors' assertions regarding the hippocampus's hitherto unrecognized capacity for generalization, and the vastly increased importance that they attach to hippocampal learning because of that capacity for generalization. They challenge the notion that generalized, structured knowledge representation is housed in neocortical circuitry alone. Below are some of the key points in the authors' revision to complementary learning system (CLS) theory.[28]

---

[28] McClelland et al. (1995, web*):* Authors propose that *"memories are first stored via synaptic changes in the hippocampal system; that these changes support reinstatement of recent memories in the neocortex; that neocortical synapses change a little on each reinstatement; and that remote*

- The two learning systems are not only complementary but fall on a continuum, ranging from semantic memory of individual facts of experience at one extreme, to inferences and stored generalizations on the other, in effect forming a synthesis.[29,30] What is revisionist here is their proposal that hippocampal learning is not just of specifics, but *"combines"* elements of new experience with stored experience to form generalities. Both during testing and in off-line periods, these authors found that generalities within the hippocampus arise from *"the simultaneous activation"* of two or more memory traces of previously unconnected experiences. Off-line replay further serves to strengthen generalized memories in the hippocampus (e.g., in replay during sleep). In short, the hippocampus learns not just by absorbing the specifics of empirical data but also by effecting novel associations between new data and stored data, a generalization function traditionally thought to belong to neocortex alone. Hippocampal, association-based learning accordingly is far less superficial than previously thought, a view we at Logos have shared for some time, and which led us to believe the hippocampus had something to teach us about MT's classically unmet need for semantic generalization.[31]
- Cerebral functions that support generalization include: (i) pattern separation, e.g., *AB vs. CA*; (ii) pattern overlap, e.g., *AB BC*; and (iii) pattern completion, e.g., *AB* ➔ *ABC*. In each case, these learning functions go beyond the mere registration of empirical data. Hopefully, readers will recognize that (i) entails what we have spoken of as a differentiation (analytical) function: *AB* is not like *CA*; and that (ii) and (iii) entail similarity-recognition (analogical) functions: *AB* overlaps with *BC* enough for them to be similar, and *AB* is enough like *ABC* to predict *ABC*. Functions (ii) and (iii) are distinctly hippocampal.
- The authors also found evidence for "concept" cells in the hippocampus. They cite as evidence for concepts the finding that hippocampal neurons *"respond to common features across many events."* As example, they speak of identical cells

---

memory is based on accumulated neocortical changes. Models that learn via adaptive changes to connections help explain this organization ... The hippocampal system permits rapid learning of new items without disrupting this structure."

[29] As noted in Chap. 5, constructionist linguists would clearly agree with this.

[30] See related paper on complementary learning by Guise and Shapiro (2017) where, in a study of spatial learning among rats, the authors propose that prior knowledge in medial prefrontal cortex (mPFC) interacts with the CA1 component of the hippocampus, teaching the latter to *"retrieve distinct representations of similar circumstances,"* thus supporting new learning in the hippocampus. Evidence for this is seen in the fact that when mPFC is inactivated, new learning by CA1 is interfered with.

[31] In Chap. 2 we asked whether there might not be some unrecognized cerebral function that accounts for the brain's freedom from complexity in processing language, a function that might be simulated to the benefit of MT. What Kumaran, Hassabis and McClelland assert about semantic generalizations in the hippocampus might be said to identify that unrecognized function. Logos Model may be said to have demonstrated it.

firing at varied pictures or mentions of some famous individual. We would add to this that semantic exemplars, fundamental to hippocampal learning, might also be construed as concepts. Indeed, it may be no exaggeration to assert that cortical operations at the more abstract, conceptual level constitute the brain's most distinguishing characteristic, and that in the cerebral treatment of language, this process of abstraction begins with the hippocampus.

MT processing, if it is to enjoy generality, must also be able to operate conceptually. Certainly, MT would not be able to function if it did not see commonalities among different language strings. But these commonalities in MT to date have been exclusively syntactic. MT linguists generally do not seem to know of any other grounds for conceptual generality but syntax.[32] The only meaningful thing that words like *book* and *newspaper* traditionally have had in common for MT is their part of speech, and that they are both count nouns (even though the reader has very likely already unconsciously classified them in some semantically more abstract way, such as print media, for example). And neuropsychologists too commonly equate the generalities of language exclusively with syntax (and morphology). We saw ample evidence of this bias in our discussion in Chap. 5.

We call this equating of generality exclusively with syntax unfortunate because it does not seem at all likely that the brain ever operates at an exclusively syntactic level, certainly not in its normal, moment-by-moment handling of language. This fact alone might explain why the brain never suffers from complexity in processing language. Judging from the experience of syntax-first processing in MT, if the brain were to process sentences syntactically to satisfy its need for generality, it could hardly avoid complexity effects. By the same token, to the extent that MT satisfies the need for generality with syntax alone, its run-in with complexity is unavoidable. And in the measure that MT models eschew syntactic abstraction so as to become free of complexity, this freedom is enjoyed at the price of generality. In short, one cannot have effective generality without abstract conceptuality, but to avoid the downside of complexity, abstract conceptuality must be other than purely syntactic. Logos Model suggests this processing should be semantico-syntactic, as illustrated by the SAL representation language elaborated in Part II of this book.

We argue that the brain cannot be processing language simply at either the strictly syntactic level or at the purely lexical level, as if these were the only possible processing levels. Another linguistic level seems called for in order to explain cerebral processes with language. Unfortunately, the Google Deep Mind authors do not discuss language but they do briefly note that the hippocampus also supports the

---

[32] In academic linguistics, semantic field theory fully understands that semantics has an abstract, generalized aspect, no less than syntax. For example, terms like *batter, pitcher, catcher, fielder* all bring to mind the more general concept of *baseball*. However, I'm not aware of any MT model that knows how to exploit this aspect of semantics. Logos Model's SAL comes closest but is far less concerned with semantic abstractions (and hypernymy *per se*) than with the interaction of meaning with syntax, i.e. with their mutual complementarity. Semantic field theory does not concern itself with the interactions of semantics and syntax.

Fig. 8.5 *Second-order noun categories excerpted from the SAL taxonomy.* SAL semantico-syntactic abstraction language allows Logos Model to deal in categorical abstractions that are semantic as well as syntactic

learning of semantic "categories."[33] What these categories would look like representationally, or how they are used in learning they do not say. But it is well established that the hippocampus associates new words with stored exemplars, and that this association is how words of new input are acquired semantically. To our knowledge, no one has suggested that these exemplars might be second-order words, like those suggested in Fig. 8.5 above.[34] But it seems a reasonable conjecture, for example, that if an individual knows that the French translation of the English preposition *in* differs according to whether the object of the proposition is a city versus a country (*à Paris, en France*), that individual will also know to make the same distinction when translating *in London* and *in England.* The individual will do so because in the back of the mind is the notion not that *London* and *England* are like *Paris* and *France*, but that they are a city in one case and a country in another. This is how Logos Model operates, and it seems not unreasonable to assume that the brain operates with similar semantic categories as well.[35]

To sum up this discussion, a learning machine is only going to be capable of *continual* learning if it can: (i) simulate these notions about the *complementary* character of cerebral learning; and (ii) exercise powers both of abstraction and generality. With respect to natural language processing, this means that the machine must, like the brain, synthesize semantics and syntax, lexicon and grammar, patterns and rules. For a translation machine, more particularly, this means that MT models

---

[33] The authors cite a 1993 study in their bibliography (Knowlton and Squire 1993) to the effect that *"category knowledge"* can be acquired *"cumulatively from multiple examples,"* but we note that this dated study characteristically, and very specifically, excludes the hippocampus from category learning.

[34] However, see discussion on second-order language by two constructionists in Postscripts 5-F and 5-G in Chap. 5.

[35] The neurolinguist Pulvermüller (2013, web) reports on neuroimaging studies designed to identify and locate processes and regions responsible for *"symbolic semantics."* Though he does not cite hippocampus directly, he identifies multiple temporal and parietal areas linked in *"combinatorial learning."* Interestingly, Pulvermüller speaks of *"correlated learning"* that takes place between circuits that handle new words, for example, and *"previously learning circuits,"* a correlation he says that *"leads to the emergence of semantic categories."*

must simulate the associative, pattern-based, semantically-driven methods of the hippocampus as the brain's front line in dealing with language input, with the more analytic aspects of neocortex being drawn into that decoding process exactly where and when it needs to be.[36]

Authors Kumaran, Hassabis and McClelland argue that without these virtues of the hippocampus, one would be hard pressed to account for the brain's ability to absorb the specifics of new experience so rapidly and effortlessly, without conflict with older knowledge. And for the same reason, it seems most unlikely that language translation by the brain could be handled chiefly by logic-driven processes of the neocortex. The brain eventually tires of solving puzzles, playing chess, summing numbers, the kinds of activities the neocortex is recruited for, but the brain never tires of language. A bi-lingual Englishman living in Paris hardly wearies of switching back and forth between languages all through the day. There is a reason for this. As Hayakawa and Hayakawa (1991) have aptly put it, language is to humans the way water is to fish. Although these authors do not say so, one conjectures they too would locate the brain's ordinary facility with language in the immediate, non-procedural, pattern-driven processes of the hippocampus, processes not too unlike those we sought to place in Logos Model.

The authors of this study never directly allude to the problems of complexity and how their interpretation of the hippocampus might mitigate the effects of complexity on machine learning. It seems that the matter of complexity relief has never been a focus of interest to them. But from our perspective, the hippocampus recommends itself precisely for this reason. Freedom from complexity has been the unique experience of Logos Model, chiefly (we reason) because of its hippocampus-like functioning. As we have argued throughout this book, if this is how the brain handles language, it is hard to imagine a better course for MT, especially given the history of difficulties with complexity in all other approaches. Indeed, can anyone offer a better way to cope with the richness and unpredictability that natural language poses to the machine, a richness and unpredictability no artificial, cerebrally-indifferent process has ever been able to master without eventually running into obstacles of its own making?

8.5 Conclusion

This book might seem to be raising doubts about MT's future, but that is far from its intent. The various linguistically-driven and data-driven models have all undeniably made progress and the improvements are significant and not a little impressive. But

---

[36] Neuroscientists like Pothos (2007) identify these patterns with hippocampal exemplars. Pothos concurs that semantic patterns far more than syntactic rules form the deeper basis of language learning.

the question how far these efforts can go does remain a legitimate one. Is there reason to believe that rules on the one hand or that data-driven computations on the other will eventually bring MT output to Turing's sought-after goal of human-quality translation? These methods have not done so thus far; one sees that models of every stripe, even after decades of effort, generally arrive at a plateau of competence beyond which they cannot seem to rise. Rules were once rejected but the need for the linguistic competence and generality that rules provide is undeniable. Yet, rules bring their own set of problems. MT developers of every stripe acknowledge this paradox and the problems it poses.

Listen to their voices.

It is simply hopeless to write an exhaustive set of rules for translating a source sentence into a correct translation (Cho 2015, web).

Of particular note is the remark by Philipp Koehn (2011) about introducing syntactic rules into the statistical processes of SMT:

The problem of the complexity of ... rules (or the complexity of models) will continue to emerge throughout our search for more syntactically informed modes of translation (Koehn 2011, 307).

Nowadays, hope for the future of MT is increasingly shifting to deep learning models like rule-free neural networks, but NMT's ultimate prospects still remain in question.[37] One group of NMT developers, for example, speaks openly about "*the curse of long sentences.*"[38]

We show that the neural machine translation performs relatively well on short sentences without unknown words, but its performance degrades rapidly as the length of the sentence and the number of unknown words increase (Cho et al. 2014, web).

Interestingly, these same NMT workers blame their troubles on the weakness of their representation language (Toral and Sánchez-Cartagena 2017). Logos Model's developers would be sympathetic to this; the SAL representation language, described in Part II of this book, has always been regarded as a key contributor to Logos Model's freedom from complexity. But we have alluded in this work to still deeper causes for MT's difficulties, most of which seem largely unrecognized. Let us briefly summarize them.

- Behind all these problems lies the dichotomy that (we argue) was mistakenly erected between syntax and semantics, between grammar and the lexicon, thanks chiefly to Chomsky's syntax-first theory and the negative complexity effects this theory brought about. Palmer (2006, 267) rightly observes, "*As [Chomsky's]*

---

[37] Koehn and Knowles (2017, web). Authors note that the quality of NMT output generally degrades (i) where input text is out-of-domain, and/or (ii) where training resources were scant. Authors also note that the internal processes of NMT systems are difficult to interpret given that "*specific word choices are based on large matrices of real-numbered values.*"

[38] Toral and Sánchez-Cartagena (2017) report that phrase-based SMT significantly outperforms NMT on sentences greater than 40 words in length in a wide variety of languages.

models increased in complexity, they became less plausible psychologically," and we would add, less tractable computationally. No truly effective MT model was ever built embodying syntax-first theory, although a number had been attempted.

- Dictionaries are still being built comprising literal words characterized by syntactic symbols. To our knowledge, apart from SAL, there is still no fully developed, representational middle ground between the literalness of semantics and the abstractions of syntax, not even among constructionists. (See discussion at the end of Chap. 5, and Postscripts 5-F and 5-G.) MT developers have had to choose whether to process language at the literal level, as in usage-driven SMT and NMT models, or to devise a way of manipulating syntactic symbols, as in rule-driven, linguistic models. Few opt for rule-driven technology any longer, very likely for the reasons we have been adducing. Rule-based systems that have survived, like SYSTRANet and PROMT Translator, have largely done so through hybridization with usage statistics. But as everyone acknowledges, usage-based models have their problems as well. Statistics-based models trained on countless billions of sentences can still be confounded by the simplest of sentences. That's because it is easy enough to write a sentence that has never been seen before in the history of the world. SMT and NMT models accordingly need the power of generality, and for that they need rules. All of which seems to place MT models of every kind squarely between the horns of a dilemma.

- The solution to this dilemma, we argue, is fairly straightforward: do as we speculate the brain is doing. This means to represent language in an integrated, semantico-syntactic manner. The SAL representation language shown in Part II of this book offers an illustration of what such a language might look like. However imperfect, SAL proved effective because it was developed inductively to resolve in a principled way the down-to-earth structural and semantic ambiguities developers encountered day after day. Moreover, it does not seem possible to explain how the brain can be free of complexity in any other way than by processing language in a manner that integrates syntax and semantics. One would be hard pressed to otherwise account for the brain's freedom from complexity effects. Just where syntax alone would normally give rise to the complexity of multiple interpretations, some semantic clue has to be available to cut through that ambiguity. Language would not be an efficient and effective means of communication if this were not so. This need for semantics during structural analysis is what SAL supplied to Logos Model. Can anyone demonstrate another way for brain or machine to process language effectively in a generalized way?

- Process language with language itself, declaratively, not procedurally, i.e., not with logic. By this we mean that new input should be processed by associating it with semantico-syntactic patterns of language previously learned and stored in memory, by having these stored patterns react to the input to interpret it, and by letting the input stream itself drive this process. But this will only work if input sentence and stored patterns are both represented semantico-syntactically (at levels of abstraction that afford generality), so that processing is neither purely lexical nor purely syntactic, but rather, as we keep noting, processing at the level of meanings that have syntactic effect.[39]

8.6 A Final Demonstration

The sentence in (5), below, contains a relative clause nested inside a relative clause. This moderately complicated sentence structure posed problems for all but Logos Model, as evident in the translations reproduced below. Sentence (5) was intentionally formed to resemble the semantic domain most SMT and NMT systems have been trained on, to give them every advantage, a domain for which, by contrast, Logos Model had had no training. Errors are underlined.

(5)   *The nations who signed the agreement our country offered have changed their mind.*

Translation by Google GNMT Translate
(5)(i)   *Les nations qui ont signé l'accord offert ___ notre pays ont changé leur esprit.*

Translation by Bing SMT Translator[40]
(5)(ii)   *Les nations qui ont signé l'accord ___ notre pays offerts ont changé d'avis.*

Translation by Hybridized, Rule-based PROMT
(5)(iii) *Les nations qui ont signé l'accord ___ notre pays offert ont changé d'avis.*

Translation by Hybridized Rule-based SYSTRANet
(5)(iv)   *Les nations qui ont signé l'accord ___ notre pays offert ont changé d'avis.*

Translation by Logos Model
(5)(v)   *Les nations qui ont signé l'accord que notre pays a offert ont changé leur esprit.*

---

[39] In this respect SAL can be seen as a considerably more refined elaboration of Case grammar (Fillmore 1968) and Valency grammar (Fischer and Ágel 2010). That these grammars traditionally speak of their verb classifications as *syntactic subdivisions* conceals the fact that these verb subdivisions have their basis in semantics, i.e., that they are really semantico-syntactic subdivisions.

[40] Microsoft's Bing NMT Translator turned out the best translation among all systems: *Les Nations qui ont signé l'accord que notre pays offrait ont changé d'avis.* We elected to show its SMT output for (5) only to demonstrate the point of this exercise.

Commentary

Except for Logos Model with its powers of generality, none of the shown
models correctly handle the nested relative clause in (5), viz.,
our country offered. Google GNMT Translate seems to have tried eliding
this relative clause in its translation. A correct elision would have
been *offert **par** notre pays*. Both Logos Model and GNMT translate
the English phrase *changed their mind* literally in French. The other systems
rendered this expression more idiomatically as *changé d'avis*, which is much
to be preferred.

Translation by LISA Lab NMT

(5)(vi)   *Les nations signataires de l'accord de notre pays ont changé d'avis.*

Commentary

LISA Lab's NMT translation in (5)(vi) is quite remarkable in that both relative
clauses in the source have been eliminated in the French rendition.
Note that the first relative clause is reduced to the adjective
signataires (*signatories*). Such transformations of style mimic what one
might expect a human translator to do with (5), and reflect this NMT model's
training on aligned, bi-lingual corpora.

Note, however, the difficulty the LISA Lab model has with sentence (6), below.
This sentence has essentially the same syntax as (5) but has vocabulary that lies in
an entirely different semantic domain. The output in (6)(i) well illustrates the
endemic shortcomings of usage-based NMT systems, which is their lack of
generality.

(6)   *The man who drove the car my brother owns has left.*

Translation by LISA Lab NMT

(6)(i)   *L'homme qui a __UNK__ la voiture____ a quitté.*

Translations by Logos Model

(6)(ii)   *L'homme qui a conduit la voiture que mon frère possède est parti.*

That Logos Model is shown as having translated (5) and (6) correctly is not a
sign Logos Model is a better translator; often enough its output may be inferior to
that of others. Rather what we seek to demonstrate is that Logos Model is based on
sounder technology and that its translations could, in theory, eventually begin to
approach the quality of human output (for texts concerned with the transfer of information rather than with aesthetic effect). The powers of generality afforded by its
underlying technology may be seen in the fact that the 45-year old model was
trained almost exclusively on the domains of commerce and technology, yet translates reasonably well domains it has not been exposed to (except for inevitable

shortcomings in domain-specific word selection). This cannot be said of usage-based models that lack powers of generality.

* * *

We would like to end this book on a light note of irony. As everyone knows, there are abundant instances where a machine can outperform the brain, as for example in playing chess or Go, in retrieving data or solving equations, etc. The list could go on almost endlessly. Given this, is it conceivable that a machine fashioned to mimic the brain's handling of language could also outperform the brain? We offer an ironic example of this in the translation of sentence (7). Most of our readers will stumble over (7) at first reading, indicating the difficulty the brain itself has in coping with the elisions involved. Yet, despite its utter unlikeliness usage-wise, (7) is perfectly grammatical and, except for the elisions, is not very different syntactically from the sentences in (5) and (6).

The note of irony alluded to above is this: because of the factual grammaticality of sentence (7) and despite its departure from usage, Logos Model, alone among all translation agents including the brain, experienced no trouble at all in handling (7).

(7)   *The cat the dog we owned chased belonged to our neighbor.*

Translation by Logos Model[41]
(7)(i)   *Le chat **que** le chien **que** nous avons possédé a chassé a appartenu à notre voisin.*

Commentary
Logos Model accomplished source analysis of (7) and target generation of (7)(i) purely on the basis of brain-like, synaptic responses to an input language stream.

Let us briefly review Logos Model's process one final time, keeping sentence (7) in mind.

- In the macro-parse conducted by the first two hidden layers of Logos Model, synapses between input patterns and stored patterns brought about recognition of (i) applicable parts of speech, (ii) clause transitions and (iii) clause types. In the case of (7), transitions to elided relative clauses were seen to occur after both the noun *cat* and the noun *dog*. Notations were made to this effect, but no concatenation occurs as yet in the macro-parse.
- In the subsequent micro-parse performed over the next four hidden layers, a complete, deterministic, bottom-up parse of (7) is performed. The two elided

---

[41] If (7) had been formed with no elisions, e.g.,: *The cat **that** the dog **that** we owned chased belonged to our neighbor,* readers presumably would have had somewhat less difficulty with it.

relative clauses are extracted and left as traces (t1) and (t2) in the resultant kernel sentence, as shown below:

> (kernel) – *cat* (t1) (t2) *belonged-to neighbor.*

The extracted relative clauses identified by traces (t1) and (t2) are then processed separately:

> (trace1) – (*that*) *dog* (t2) *chased*
> (trace2) – (*that*) *we owned*

- Parallel target work over these last four hidden layers entailed generation of a target parse showing (i) target word order, (ii) notations for word transfers along with potential insertions and deletions, and (iii) notations for relevant morphology.
- In target action of the final hidden layer, target parse is instantiated with literal words, morphological notations are implemented, and the target sentence (7)(i) is output. In effect, the elided relative clauses in the English are unelided in the French and restored to their proper place in the main clause, along with the insertion of the relative pronoun *que*.
- Finally, it should be noted that each hidden layer of Logos Model presently contains as many as four thousand generalized pattern-rules, ordered by their semantico-syntactic features in dictionary-like fashion. Because these stored units are content-addressable, input units in (7) were able to seek synapsis directly (and exclusively) with stored units that best corresponded semantico-syntactically. Critically, because of content-addressability, the practical size and comprehensiveness of the hidden layers can keep growing endlessly, with strictly sublinear impact on throughput performance, making Logos Model's translation potential seemingly unlimited.

For all the claims made in this book about what a translation machine can be made to do, we must admit that there are bound to be upper limits to these possibilities. It is unlikely a machine will ever match the human translator in coping with the wordplay, rhythms, and assonances of creative prose, or indeed with any text where matters of style are paramount. Not that translation machines cannot be expected to do exceptionally well, given suitable prose, i.e., prose whose purpose is information transfer, but it is hard to imagine we could ever devise a machine to more than approximate to some interesting degree the matchless faculty of gifted human translators for handling prose whose intent is to charm or entertain with the magic of language itself. True, not all AI workers would agree that machine intelligence has any inherent limits (Kurzweil 2013).[42] Time alone will tell whether they are right. To all such visionaries, one recommends the translation of unconstrained natural language as a fitting measure of how far a computer can be brought relative to the powers of the brain. Such a measure will tell us whether the

---

[42] Google's Ray Kurzweil, for one, believes that machines in the future will not only emulate the human neocortex but will actually extend it.

hallowed Turing test can ever be fully met, where machine translation in effect is no longer distinguishable from human translation.

It's true that Turing's early dream is rarely alluded to anymore, but one senses that the new developments in deep neural net translation may have opened a door to fresh possibilities. Neural MT has serious unsolved problems, but the exciting promise of NMT lies precisely in the fact that it is data-driven and neural-like, akin to the brain to some degree at least. As the claims of this book imply (and seek to demonstrate), the more that artificial neural nets learn to absorb from the genuine cerebral model (i.e., the more deep learning pursues genuine cerebral verisimilitude), the less will NMT's current problems block its prospects. Already NMT's accomplishments, limited though they be, nonetheless suggest that neural net technology has already begun to usher in an exciting new period in MT. One hopes that readers and MT developers will consider the contributions to that end that have been offered and elaborated in these pages.

***

All Logos Model translations were executed on an OpenLogos website at INESC-ID, Portugal: http://www.l2f.inesc-id.pt/openlogos/demo.html
OpenLogos is available for downloading free of charge from The German Research Center for Artificial Intelligence (DFKI) in Germany: http://logos-os.dfki.de
Further information about Logos Model technology is available at: http://www.logosinstitute.org/LOGOS-TECHNOLOGY.html
Organizations interested in obtaining OpenLogos source programs and data for development purposes should contact DFKI for further information.

Readers interested in contacting the author (Bud Scott) may reach him at logos.institute@gmail.com

References

Bahdanau D, Cho K, Bengio Y (2015) Neural machine translation by jointly learning to align and translate. In: Oral presentation at the 3rd international conference on learning and representation (ICLR 2015). San Diego. http://www.iclr.cc/lib/exe/fetch.php?media=iclr2015:bahdanau-iclr2015.pdf. Accessed 26 Nov 2016

Cho K (2015) Introduction to neural machine translation with GPUs (part 1). https://devblogs.nvidia.com/parallelforall/introduction-neural-machine-translation-with-gpus. Accessed 24 June 2016

Cho K, von Merriënboer B, Bahdanau D, Bengio Y (2014) On the properties of neural machine translation: encoder-decoder approaches. In: Proceedings of the eighth workshop on syntax, Semantics and Structure in Statistical Translation (SSST-8), Doha, pp 103–111. https://arxiv.org/pdf/1409.1259.pdf

Chomsky N (1990) On formalization and formal linguistics. Nat Lang Linguist Theory 8:143–147

Deeplearning4j Development Team (2016) Introduction to deep neural networks. https://deep-learning4j.org/neuralnet-overview. Accessed 14 Aug 2016

Dettmers T (2015) Deep learning in a Netshell: core concepts. Internet Blog. https://devblogs. nvidia.com/parallelforall/deep-learning-nutshell-history-training. Accessed 8 June 2016

Fillmore C (1968) The case for case. In: Bach E, Harms RT (eds) Universals in linguistic theory. Holt/Rinehart and Winston, New York/London, pp 1–88

Fischer K, Ágel V (2010) Dependency grammar and valency theory. In: The Oxford handbook of linguistic analysis. Oxford University Press, Oxford, pp 223–255

Goldberg AE (2009) The nature of generalization in language. Cogn Linguist 20(1):93–127

Guise KG, Shapiro M (2017) Medial prefrontal cortex reduces memory interference by modifying hippocampal encoding. Neuron 94(1):183–192

Hassabis D, Kumaran D, Summerfield C, Botvinick M (2017) Neuroscience-inspired artificial intelligence. Neuron 95(2):245–258

Hawakawa SI, Hayakawa AR (1991) Language in thought and action, 5th edn. Houghton Mifflin Harcourt, New York

Kalchbrenner N, Blunsom P (2013) Recurrent convolutional neural networks for discourse compositionality. In: Proceedings of the 2013 workshop on continuous vector space models and their compositionality, Sofia, pp 119–126

Kalchbrenner N, Grefenstette E, Blunsom P (2014) A convolutional neural net for modeling sentences. In: Proceedings of the 52nd annual meetings of the association for computational linguistics, Baltimore, pp 655–665

Knowlton BJ, Squire LR (1993) The learning of categories: parallel brain systems for item memory and category knowledge. Science 262(5140):1747–1749

Koehn P (2011) Statistical machine translation. Cambridge University Press, Cambridge

Koehn P, Knowles R (2017) Six challenges for neural machine translation. In: Proceedings of the first workshop on neural machine translation, Vancouver, pp 26–39. http://arXiv: 1706.03872v1. Accessed 13 Dec 2017

Kumaran D, McClelland JL (2012) Generalization through the recurrent interaction of episodic memories: a model of the hippocampal system. Psychol Rev 119(3):573–616

Kumaran D, Hassabis D, McClelland JL (2016) What learning systems do intelligent agents need? complementary learning systems theory updated. Trends Cogn Sci 20(7). https://doi. org/10.1016/j.tics.2016.05.004. Accessed 12 Jan 2017

Kurzweil R (2013) How to create a mind: the secret of human thought revealed. Penguin Books, New York

Liu S, Yang N, Li M, Zhou M (2014) A recursive recurrent neural network for statistical machine translation. In: Proceedings of the 52nd annual meeting of the association for computational linguistics, Baltimore, pp 1491–1500

Marblestone AH, Wayne G, Kording KP (2016) Toward an integration of deep learning and neuroscience. Front Comput Neurosci 10(19). https://doi.org/10.3389/fncom.2016.00094

McClelland JL, McNaughton BL, O'Reilly RC (1995) Why there are complementary learning systems in the hippocampus and neocortex: insights from the successes and failures of connectionist models of learning and memory. Psychol Rev 102(3):419–457. https://www.ncbi. nlm.nih.gov/pubmed/7624455

Meng F, Lu Z, Wang M, Li H, Jiang W, Liu Q (2015) Encoding source language with convolutional neural network for machine translation. In: Proceedings of the 53rd annual meeting of the association for computational linguistics and the 7th international joint conference on natural language processing, vol 1, Long Papers, Beijing, pp 20–30

Palmer DC (2006) On Chomsky's appraisal of Skinner's verbal behavior: a half-century of misunderstanding. Behav Anal 29(2):253–267

Pothos EM (2007) Theories of artificial grammar learning. Psychol Bull 133:227–244

Pulvermüller F (2013) How neurons make meaning: brain mechanisms for embodied and abstract-symbolic semantics. Trends Cogn Sci 17(9):458–470. http://www.sciencedirect.com/science/article/pii/S1364661313001228. Accessed 13 Dec 2015

Sanborn AN, Chater N (2016) Bayesean brains without probabilities. Trends Cogn Sci 20(121):883–893.   http://www.sciencedirect.com/science/journal/13646613/20/12?sdc=1. Accessed 6 Feb 2017

Scott B (1989) The logos system. In: Proceedings of MT summit II, Munich, pp 137–142

Scott B (1990) Biological neural net for parsing long, complex sentences. Logos Corporation Publication

Scott B (2003) Logos model: an historical perspective. Mach Transl 18(1):1–72

Sennrich R, Haddow B (2016) Linguistic input features improve neural machine translation. arXiv:1606.02892v2 [cs.CL]. Accessed 15 Aug 2017

Toral, Antonio and Victor M. Sánchez-Cartagena. 2017. A multifaceted evaluation of neural versus phrase-based machine translation for 9 language directions.In: Proceedings of the 15th conference of the european chapter of the association for computational linguistics, vol 1, Long Papers, Valencia, pp 1063–1073. arXiv:1701.02901 [cs.CL]

Zhang J, Ye L (2010) Series feature aggregation for content-based image retrieval. Comput Electr Eng 36(4):691–701

Part II

Chapter 9
The SAL Representation Language

Abstract SAL stands for Semantico-syntactic Abstraction Language, a symbolic, second-order language to which natural language readily maps. SAL is organized as a taxonomy (ontology) of supersets, sets and subsets, allowing it to represent virtually any expressed thought, any sentence, at multiple levels of abstraction. To date, SAL has been developed for English and German languages only. In what follows we show only the English language variant. SAL is not a metalanguage but approaches one. Because nouns denote things and concepts that are virtually universal, SAL codes for nouns are generally applicable to any natural language. For the other open-class parts of speech (verbs, adjectives and adverbs), SAL is apt to be metalinguistic only at the SAL superset level.

9.1 Overview of SAL

AS AN ACTUAL LANGUAGE, SAL has about 1000 elements, which makes it very roughly two orders of magnitude richer than pure syntax and two orders of magnitude leaner than literal language. Except when literal treatment is needed, Logos Model deals with language principally at this more abstract SAL level. This dealing with language at a midpoint between pure syntax and pure literalness constitutes the defining characteristic of Logos Model.

SAL was developed inductively in the 1970s, in response to particular needs of analysis as these needs affected translation. It was not conceived of as an academic exercise and therefore at times may be found to lack the internal consistency and tidiness that might be expected of an ontology developed for academic reasons. One must also bear in mind that compressing something as rich as natural language into a second order language must necessarily entail a degree of arbitrariness in the mapping, an arbitrariness that one can always question.

Below we list all SAL parts of speech for both open and closed classes. For each of the open class parts of speech, taxonomic charts for each POS then immediately follow.

© Springer International Publishing AG, part of Springer Nature 2018   205
B. Scott, *Translation, Brains and the Computer*, Machine Translation:
Technologies and Applications 2, https://doi.org/10.1007/978-3-319-76629-4_9

9.2   SAL Parts of Speech

SAL comprises 15 parts of speech, divided into open and closed classes.

9.2.1   Open Classes (Table 9.1)

Table 9.1 SAL open classes

Numeric code	Mnemonic code	Part of speech
WC 1	N	Noun
WC 2	VT & VI	Verb
WC 4	ADJ	Adjective
WC 3 & 6	ADV	Adverb

9.2.2   Closed Classes (Table 9.2)

Table 9.2 SAL closed classes

Numeric code	Mnemonic code	Part of speech
WC 11 & 13	PREP	Preposition
WC 12	AUXMO	Auxiliary/modal
WC 14 & 15	DET	Determiner
WC 16	AR	Arithmate
WC 17	NEG	Negative
WC 18	INTREL	Relative/interrogative
WC 19	CONJ	Conjunction
WC 20	PUNC	Punctuation

All natural language elements, including punctuation, are encoded in SAL via the triplet WC TYPE FORM (WC T F). Triplet codes are expressed numerically internal to the system.[1] Thus, for example, the WC T F triplet for plural functional nouns (such as, e.g., *screws, doors, pencils*, etc.) would be represented internally as 1 34 2, where 1 stands for the word class (1 = nouns), 34 stands for the type of noun (34 = concrete functional nouns), and 2 stands for the noun's morphology (2 = plural).[2] Type codes lower in the taxonomy inherit the higher taxonomic type codes. Thus set code 34 inherits the superset code 3 for concrete nouns (see Concrete

---

[1] See Part II Postscript for discussion and illustration regarding Logos Model use of numbers. Note that SAL mnemonics are employed strictly for documentation purposes.

[2] Mnemonically 1 34 2 would be expressed as *N(COfunc; pl)*.

Nouns chart). In inflected languages like German, the Form field would express case as well as number. Both WC and Form codes are also taxonomic, allowing for respective WC and Form code grouping. These POS and morphology groupings are expressed internally via negative numbers in WC and Form field positions.[3]

Although the use of numbers like this is quite foreign to linguistic convention, the practice has proven to have many advantages computationally, especially with respect to the storing, accessing, and matching of patterns when expressed numerically in this way.[4]

Moreover, the range that a number falls within itself conveys meaning. For example, numbers ranging from 2 to 16 signify superset codes, 17 to 99 stand for set codes, and 100–997 represent subset codes.[5] The advantages of this arrangement are hardly trivial. For example, in matching an input pattern against a body of stored patterns, the system first looks at patterns whose initial codes lie within the subset range, then at the set range, and finally at the superset range, in effect insuring that more specific patterns are afforded a chance to fire before more general patterns. Also, linguists find they can access and navigate among numerical patterns quite easily. This is important, given the many thousands of stored patterns in this Model. And new patterns submited to the system find their own place in storage automatically, much the way new words and phrases do in a dictionary (Table 9.3).

Table 9.3 Numeric ranges for SAL open class codes

POS	Supersets	Sets	Subsets
Nouns	2–12	21–99	100–997
Verbs	2–12	21–99	100–997[a]
Adjectives	13–16	80–89	100–997
Adverbs	10–23		100–997

[a]Verb subset codes with their set code are used to identify individual verbs

The SAL taxonomic charts on the following pages are for the SAL open word classes for English source, beginning with nouns.

9.3 SAL Nouns (WC 1)

SAL nouns comprise ten supersets. An eleventh superset is reseved for unfound words, which is treated by default as an undifferentiated noun (Fig. 9.1).

---

[3] The negative number −1 represents the universal case, i.e., any WC, Type or Form. Thus, −1 −1 −1 would represent any element whatsoever. Negative numbers below −1 in the Type field function differently. They are addresses pointing to an array containing an ad hoc set of Type codes for the given element.

[4] See Postscript Part II for typical diagnostic output showing use of numbers.

[5] Some slight variation in SAL superset ranges occurs for certain WCs.

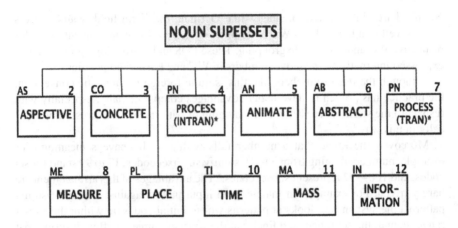

Fig. 9.1 SAL superset taxonomy for nouns

Superset 1 is reserved for words of text unfound in the dictionary (UF 1). Subset codes within Superset 1 reflect orthography, e.g., initial cap, all cap, etc., helpful in detecting proper names, among other things.

*Intransitive and Transiive Process Nouns (PN 4 and PN 7) share the Type codes of their corresponding verbs and hence do not have separate noun charts of their own.

The effect of these codes may be seen in the way that the preposition **by** is handled (or not handled) in sentences (1)–(3) below. The error in sentence (3(i)) is underlined.

(1)   *She will have come back* **by** *Monday.*
(2)   *The citation was referred to* **by** *John.*
(3)   *The box is* **by** *the door.*
(1)(i)   *Elle sera revenue* ***d'ici*** *lundi.*
(2)(i)   *John s'est reporté à la citation.*
(3)(i)   *La boîte est* ***par*** *la porte.*

In its handling of (3), Logos Model lacked a pattern-rule to make use of the SAL code for *door* and hence translates the preposition **by** incorrectly. Of all systems tested, Microsoft's Bing Translator alone translates (3) correctly: *La boîte est* ***près de*** *la porte.*

9.3.1   Aspective Nouns

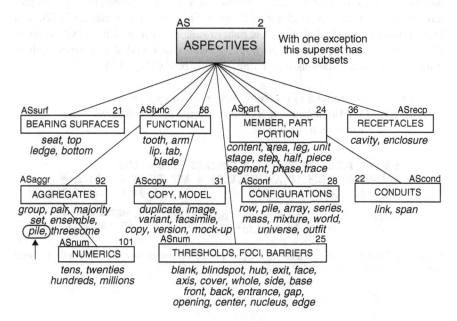

Fig. 9.2 SAL taxonomy for aspective nouns

Translations of Fig. 9.2 Sentences by Logos Model

(4)   She **raised** a pile of children. He **raised** the flag.

(4)(i)   Sie **zog** einen Haufen von Kindern **auf**. Er **hob** die Fahne **hoch**.

In the above translation, note that the noun phrase **pile** of children has been parsed as *NP* with the singular morphology of the aspective noun **pile** but with the semantics of the animate noun *children*. This hybrid coding for *NP* has allowed the input elements *raise children* to match a SEMTAB pattern-rule (shown below) designed to render *raise* into German as **aufziehen** whenever *raise* has an animate object, like *children* in the above example, or *geese* in sentence (5) below. Without a SEMTAB pattern-rule to see *raise* in the context of an animate object, the transfer for *raise* would have been the dictionary's default transfer, **hochheben**.

In the SEMTAB pattern-rule illustrated below, note that the first element in the pattern is always used for indexing purposes only. In the example, the relevant pattern begins with the second element, 0 318 0. The zeros in this element's WC and Form positions signify that this same pattern-rule will also match on POS variants of the verb *raise*, such as process noun, gerund and/or verbal adjectives. This is illustrated in the translations shown immediately below (Fig. 9.3).

(5)   *The **raising** of chickens; Geese **raised** by farmers.*

(5)(i)   *Das **Aufziehen** von Hühnern; Gänse, die von Bauern*
         ***aufgezogen** werden.*

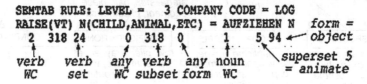

Fig. 9.3 SEMTAB pattern-rule showing the pattern-rule's comment line and below it the numeric representation of the specified SAL pattern

9.3.2   Concrete Nouns

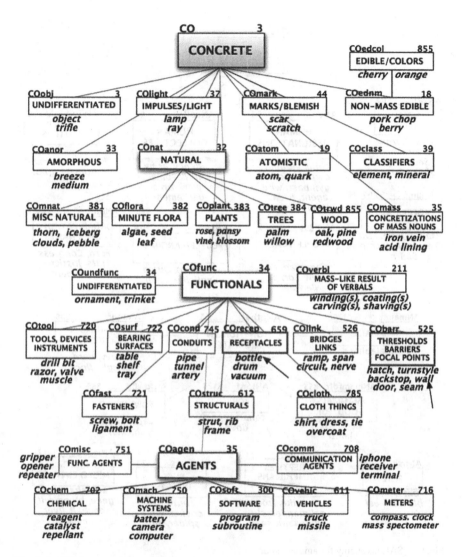

Fig. 9.4 SAL taxonomy for concrete nouns

Translations of Fig. 9.4 Sentences by Logos Model

(6)   *from the bottle, from the wall.*
(6)(i)   *aus der Flasche, von der Wand.*
(7)   *He runs the machine. They run the company.*
(7)(i)   *Il fait marcher la machine. Ils dirigent la compagnie.*

9.3.3   *Animate Nouns*

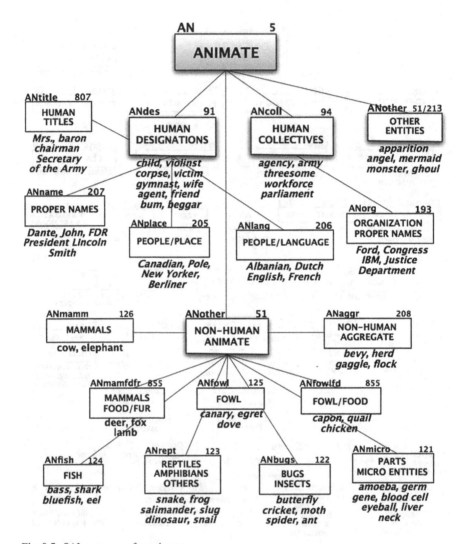

Fig. 9.5   SAL taxonomy for animate nouns

Translations of Fig. 9.5 Sentences by Logos Model

(8)   *flesh eating insects; insects eating flesh.*

(8)(i)   *insectes qui mangent de la chair; insectes qui mangent la chair.*

(9)   *a moth-eaten coat.*

(9)(i)   *eine von Motten gegessene Jacke.*

9.3.4   Abstract Nouns

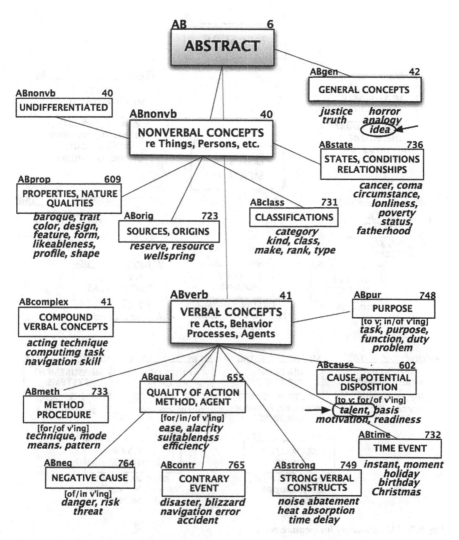

Fig. 9.6   SAL taxonomy for abstract nouns

Translations of Fig. 9.6 Sentences by Logos Model

(10)   *Talent for **baking** bread; ideas for **baking** bread.*

(10)(i)   *Talent, Brot zu **backen**; Ideen zum **Backen** von Brot.*

(11)   *Kinds of **baking** flour; Methods of **baking** bread.*

(11)(i)   *Arten von **Backmehl**; Methoden des **Backens** von Brot*

9.3.5 *Measure Nouns*

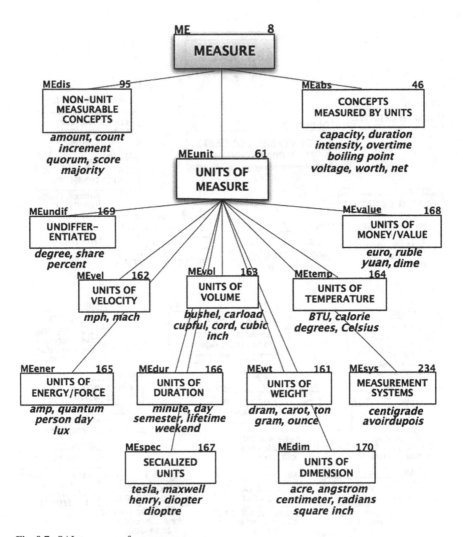

Fig. 9.7 SAL taxonomy for measure nouns

Translations of Fig. 9.7 Sentences by Logos Model

(12)   *An increase of* **resistance to** *disease.*

(12)(i)   *Eine Steigerung von* **Schutz vor** *Krankheit.*

(13)   *An increase of* **length to** *five inches.*

(13)(i)   *Eine Steigerung der* **Länge zu** *fünf Zoll.*

9.3.6   Place Nouns

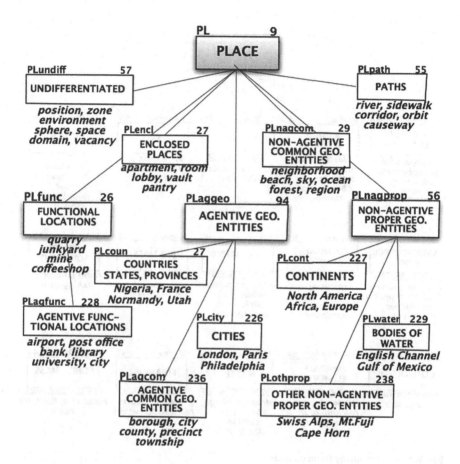

Fig. 9.8 SAL taxonomy for place nouns

Translations of Fig. 9.8 Sentences by Logos Model

(14)   *The **city plans** to renovate its parks. The **city plans** to renovate*
          were never approved of by the governor.

(14)(i)   *La **ville a l'intention** de rénover ses parcs. Le gouverneur*
          *n'a jamais approuvé les **plans de ville** à rénover.*

(15)   *The things the **city plans**. They came out against the **city plans**.*

(15)(i)   *Les choses que la **ville prévoit**. Ils se sont déclarés*
          *contre les **plans de ville**.*

(16)   *The weather is pleasant **in** Paris. The weather is pleasant **in** France.*

(16)(i)   *Le temps est plaisant **à** Paris. Le temps est plaisant **en** France.*

(17)   *He **turned into** a driveway. He **turned into** a pumpkin.*

(17)(i)   *Il **a tourné dans** une allée. Il **s'est changé en** une citrouille.*

9.3.7 Mass Nouns

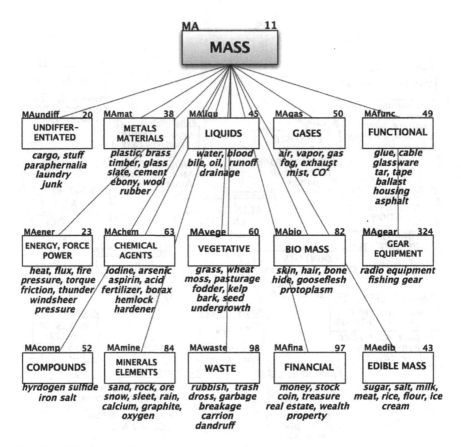

Fig. 9.9 SAL taxonomy for mass nouns

Translation of Fig. 9.9 Sentence by Logos Model

(18)   *Before any planting is done he is going to **clear rubbish** out from the garden.*

(18)(i)   *Avant que tout planter soit fait, il va **débarrasser les détritus** du jardin.*

9.3.8 Information and Time Nouns (Fig. 9.10)

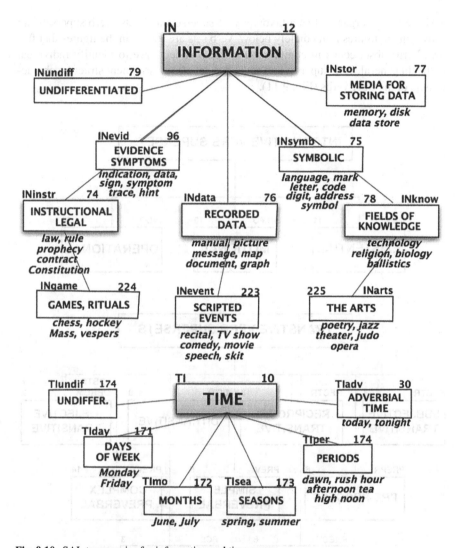

Fig. 9.10 SAL taxonomies for information and time nouns

<u>Translations by Logos Model</u>

(19)   *Documents **about** the war; Flowers **about** the place.*

(19)(i)   *Dokumente **über** den Krieg; Blumen **um** den Platz.*

(20)   *He wants to learn to **play chess**.*

(20)(i)   *Il veut apprendre à **jouer aux échecs**.*

(21)   *All signs **point to a happy end**.*

(21)(i)   *Tous les signes **indiquent une fin heureuse**.*

9.4   SAL Verbs (WC 2)

SAL verbs are organized as a taxonomy of supersets and sets. Verb supersets are shown in the figures immediately below. Verb sets are shown in the figures that follow. Verb subset codes in conjunction with set codes serve to identify individual verbs. In general, verb superset and set codes denote the argument structure characteristic of member verbs (Fig. 9.11).

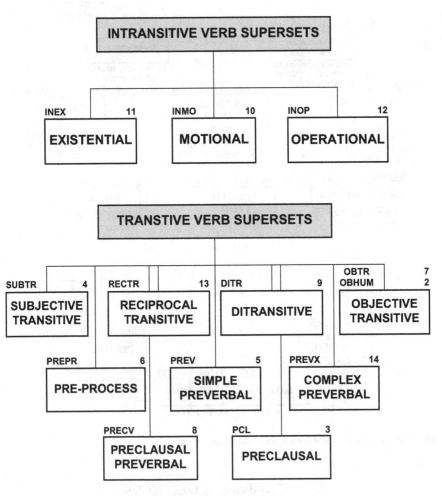

Fig. 9.11 SAL verb supersets

9.4.1 The Intransitive-Transitive Verb Spectrum

The SAL codes for verbs reflect the degree of transitivity that member verbs exhibit, i.e., the degree to which a verb's subject is engaged with something outside of itself. This is illustrated in the verb circle diagram immediately below. As one proceeds around the circle, from the EXISTENTIAL at the top to the OBJECTIVE TRANSITIVE down at the bottom, and thence up to the PRECLAUSAL back near the top, note that there is a progression from intransitive to transitive and then back up again to the near intransitive. In the paragraphs that follow, we explain the point of all this (Fig. 9.12).

Fig. 9.12 Transitivity wheel for verbs

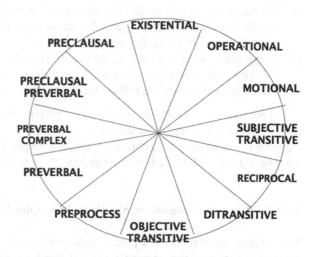

9.4.1.1 Intransitives (Overview)

Verbs that take no direct object are intransitive and therefore do not place their subjects in a direct relationship to something outside themselves, e.g., *John is cold, John eats well, John runs fast*. On the other hand, intransitive verbs often place their subjects in an indirect relation to something external to themselves and thus often convey a degree of implicit transitivity. For example:

(i). Existential Intransitive: *John is at school* ➔ *John attends school*.

(ii). Operational Intransitive: *John speaks to his teacher* ➔ *John addresses his teacher*.

(iii). Motional Intransitive: *John goes home* ➔ *John enters his house*.

9.4.1.2 Simple Transitives (Overview)

Verbs that take direct (and indirect) objects are transitives, and transitive verbs with restricted complementation are called simple transitives. Simple transitive verbs reflect degrees of transitivity, ranging from weak to strong. This degree of transitivity concerns the extent to which the verbal action affects the subject instead of, or as well as, the object. For example:

  (i). Subjective Transitive: *John studies French.* Here the verb's effect is entirely on the subject.
 (ii). Reciprocal Transitive: *John fought his opponent.* Here the verb's effect is on both subject and object.
(iii). Ditransitives: *John gives his daughter a car.* Here the verb's effect is chiefly on the direct and indirect objects, but the action also affects the subject (e.g., who no longer has what has been given away).
 (iv). Objective Transitive: *John fixes the engine.* Here the verb's subject is involved with the action merely as its agent. The verb's action has no implicit affect on the subject, and therefore reflects the strongest possible degree of transitivity.

Simple transitive verbs may also require a prepositional phrase to complement the verb in order to complete its meaning. For example: in *John takes the car out of the garage*, the prepositional phrase beginning with *out of* complements *takes* and the intended sense of the verb is incomplete without its complementation.

9.4.1.3 Preverbal Transitives, Simple and Complex (Overview)

Verbs whose direct object is a process noun, verbal construction, or another verb constitute a verb class that, in itself, is not sufficiently transitive to effect the intended action. They help other verbs do that. We call such verbs preverbals, of which there are three basic kinds:

  (i). Pre-process: *John **carried out** repairs on the car.*
 (ii). Preverbal (Simple): *John **finished** repairing the engine.*
(iii). Preverbal (Complex): *John **helped** Henry repair the car.*

9.4.1.4   Preclausal Transitives (Overview)

Verbs whose main action is to introduce a new subject and verb (i.e., introduce a new clause) are preclausal. They are of two basic kinds, Preverbal Preclausals and Simple Preclausals, illustrated in (i) and (ii), respectively.

(i). Preverbal Preclausal: *John **told** Henry to repaint the car.*
(ii). Preclausal (Simple): *John **said** he was tired.*

The Transitivity Wheel for Verbs shown above terminates the circle with simple Preclausal verbs, suggesting that this class of transitive verb begins to approach intransitivity. To illustrate, note that in sentence (20), below, the transitive verb *dream* would be coded as a Preclausal transitive verb, and the intransitive verb *dream* in (21) would be coded as Preclausal within the Operational intransitive superset. The close association of these the two classes of verbs may be seen from the fact that they are positioned diametrically opposite each other near the top of the Wheel.

(20)   *John dreams that he was there.*
(21)   *John hardly ever dreams.*

In what follows we display taxonomic charts of the various SAL supersets and sets for verbs. Beneath each chart are translations that reflect some aspect of the verb relevant to the verb's taxonomy. The translations are not necessarily optimal but nevertheless faithfully reflect how Logos Model was making use of the SAL language at the time development ceased in 2000. It is not difficult to find constructions that Logos Model has not yet been equipped to handle. It seems reasonable to assume, however, that had a model of this kind been allowed to continue development until the present time, utter collapses such as the one illustrated in (22)(i) below might have been far more uncommon.[6]

(22)   *For the last sixteen or seventeen years ...*
(22)(i)   **Ou les seize dernières dix-sept années ...*

---

[6]All of the other systems tested handled this construction correctly.

9.4.2   Intransitive Verbs

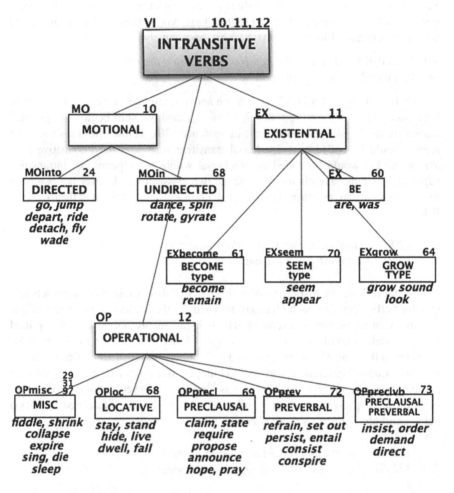

Fig. 9.13 SAL taxonomy for intransitive verbs

Translations of Fig. 9.13 Sentences by Logos Model
(23)   *He **should never have become** our President.*
(23)(i)   *Il **n'aurait jamais dû devenir** notre président.*
(24)   *They **swam across** the lake.*
(24)(i)   *Ils **ont traversé** le lac **à la nage**.*
(25)   *He **held out for** more money.*
(25)(i)   *Il **a tenu bon pour** plus d'argent.*
(26)   *He **holds onto** his money.*
(26)(i)   *Il **se cramponne à** son argent.*

9.4.3 Subjective Transitive Verbs

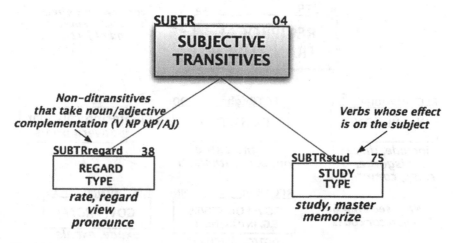

Fig. 9.14 SAL taxonomy for subjective transitive verbs

<u>Translations of Fig. 9.14 Sentences by Logos Model</u>

(27)   *He **takes after** his father.*
(27)(i)   *Il **tient de** son père.*
(28)   *We did not **mind the cost.***
(28)(i)   *Nous ne nous sommes pas **occupés du coût.***
(29)   *The actor **had difficulty memorizing** his lines.*
(29)(i)   *Der Schauspieler **hatte Schwierigkeiten dabei**, sich seine Zeilen **einzuprägen.***

9.4.4 *Reciprocal Transitive Verbs*

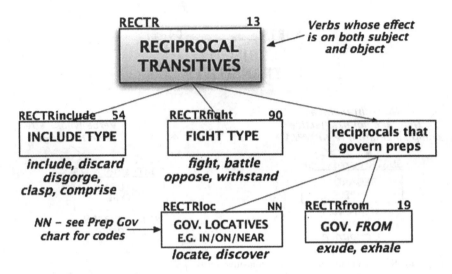

Fig. 9.15 SAL taxonomy for reciprocal transitive verbs

Translations of Fig. 9.15 Sentences by Logos Model

(30)   *The two **fought** all night.*

(30)(i) *Les deux **se sont battus** toute la nuit.*

(31)   *Social Security Numbers **need not be included**.*

(31)(i) *Les numéros de sécurité sociale **ne doivent pas être inclus**.*

9.4.5 *Ditransitive Verbs*

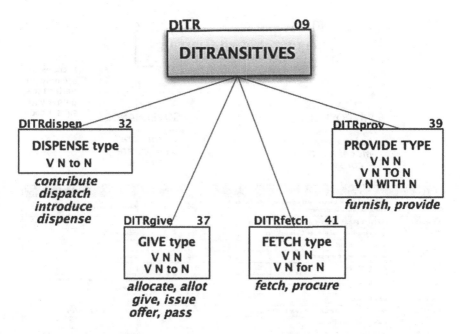

Fig. 9.16 SAL taxonomy for ditransitive verbs

Translations of Fig. 9.16 Sentences by Logos Model

(32)   *They **provided** John a new car.*

(32)(i)   *Ils **ont fourni** une nouvelle voiture à John.*

(32)(ii) *Sie **stellten** John ein neues Auto **bereit**.*

(33)   *Each employee **was allotted** an extra vacation day.*

(33)(i)   ***On a attribué** un jour de vacances supplémentaire
          à chaque employé.*

(33)(ii) *Jedem Angestellten wurde ein zusätzlicher Ferientag verteilt.*

(34)   ***The man we were introduced to** became a good friend.*

(34)(i)   ***L'homme à qui nous avons été présentés** est devenu un bon ami.*

(34)(ii) *Der Mann, dem wir vorgestellt wurden, wurde ein guter Freund.*

9.4.6   Objective Transitive Verbs

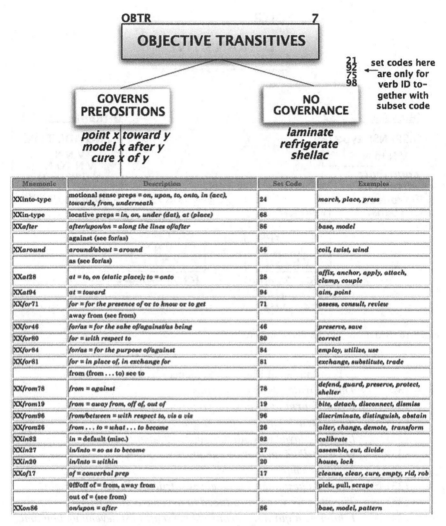

Fig. 9.17 SAL taxonomy for objective transitive verbs
Note that the above preposition governance list is only a partial list.

Translations of Fig. 9.17 Sentences by Logos Model

(*35*)   They **modeled** the new car **on** an older version.

(35)(i)   *Ils* **ont calqué** *la nouvelle voiture* **d'après** *une plus vieille version.*

(36)   He **exchanged** the old computer **for** a new one.

(36)(i)   *Il* **a échangé** *le vieil ordinateur* **contre** *un nouveau.*

9.4.7   Pre-process Verbs

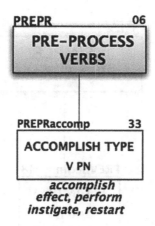

Fig. 9.18 SAL taxonomy for pre-process verbs

Translations of Fig. 9.18 Sentences by Logos Model

(37)   *A program review **was called for by the supervisor**.*
(37)(i)   ***Le supérieur a réclamé** une revue de programme.*
(38)   *The process restart procedure **could not be performed**.*
(38)(i)   ***On ne pourrait pas faire fonctionner** la procédure de relance de processus.*

9.4.8 Simple Preverbal Verbs

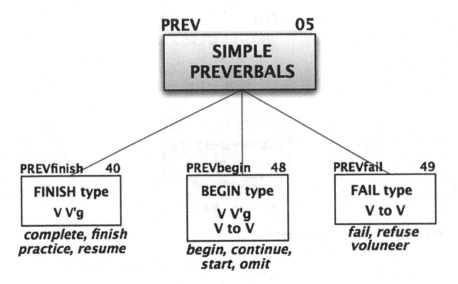

Fig. 9.19 SAL taxonomy for simple preverbal verbs

Translations of Fig. 9.19 Sentences by Logos Model

(39)   *He **practices playing** the piano every day.*
(39)(i)   *Il **s'exerce à jouer** du piano chaque jour.*
(40)   *He **volunteered to take** on the project.*
(40)(i)   *Il **s'est proposé pour entreprendre** le projet.*
(41)   *He **omitted mentioning** that he was unemployed.*
(41)(i)   *Il **a oublié de mentionner** qu'il était sans travail.*

9.4.9 Preverbal Complex Verbs

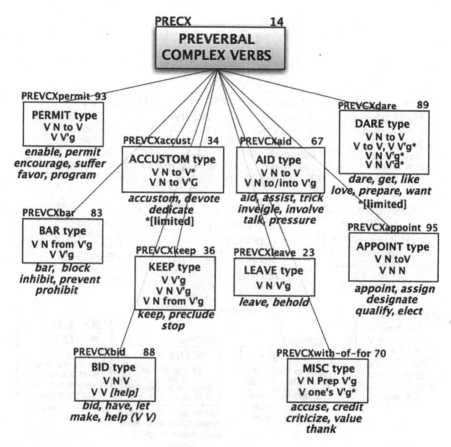

Fig. 9.20 SAL taxonomy for preverbal complex verbs

Translations of Fig. 9.20 Sentences by Logos Model

(42)   *We are no longer **accustomed to working** overtime.*

(42)(i)   *Nous ne sommes plus **habitués à travailler** des heures supplémentaires.*

(43)   *Illness **prevented them from carrying on with** their work.*

(43)(i)   *La maladie **les a empêché de continuer** leur travail.*

(44)   *A sudden weakness **kept the runner from keeping up with** the others.*

(44)(i)   *Une faiblesse soudaine **a empêché le coureur de se maintenir au niveau** des autres.*

(45)   ***Warm** milk before bedtime **helps** you to sleep.*

(45)(I)   ***Réchauffez-vous** le lait avant **les aides** d'heure du coucher pour dormir.*[7]

---

[7] Sentence is an extreme example of POS misresolutions by Logos Model.

9.4.10   Preverbal-Preclausal Verbs

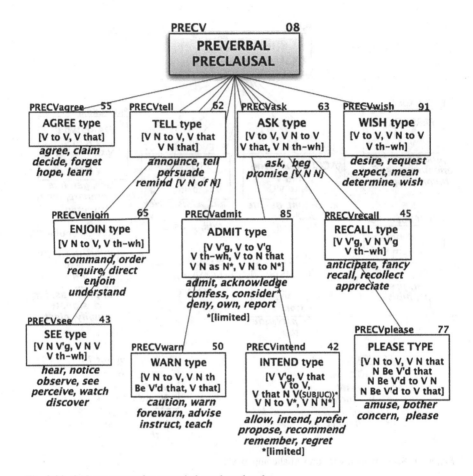

Fig. 9.21 SAL taxonomy for preverbal preclausal verbs

Translations of Fig. 9.21 Sentences by Logos Model

(46)   *The perpetrator **had been warned** not to do that.*

(46)(i)   ***On avait conseillé** au coupable de ne pas faire cela.*

(46)(ii)   *Der Täter **war gewarnt worden**, das nicht zu machen.*

(47)   *They **reminded their boss he** had promised them a raise in salary.*

(47)(i)   *Ils **ont rappelé à leur patron qu'il** leur avait promis une augmentation de salaire.*

(47)(ii)   *Sie **erinnerten ihren Chef, dass er** sie eine Gehaltserhöhung versprochen hatte.*

(48)   *The request not to show any sign of annoyance **was ignored by the chief**.*

(48)(i)   *Le chef n'a pas tenu compte de* la demande de ne pas montrer
de signe de l'irritation.

(48)(ii)   *Die Bitte, kein Zeichen von Ärgernis zu zeigen,* **wurde vom
Leiter ignoriert**.

9.4.11   Preclausal Verbs

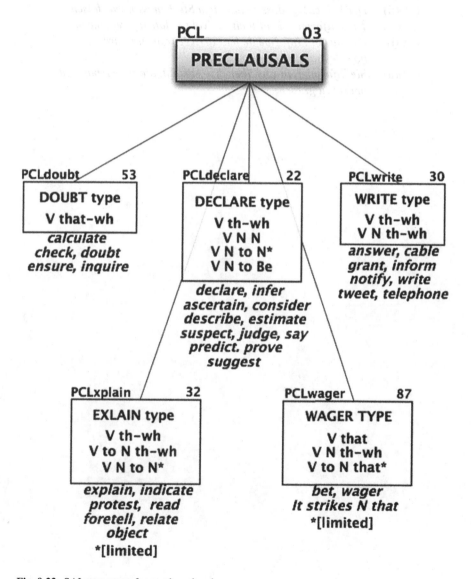

Fig. 9.22 SAL taxonomy for preclausal verbs

Translations of Fig. 9.22 Sentences by Logos Model

(49)   *The expenses **were objected to***.

(49)(i)   ***On a objecté aux** dépenses.*

(50)   *There was a lot of **doubt over what** he told them.*

(50)(i)   *Il y avait beaucoup de **doute sur ce qu**'il leur a dit.*

(50)(ii)   *Es gab viel **Zweifel daran, was** er ihnen sagte.*

(51)   *The **suggestion he** was **on the verge of dying** was false.*

(51)(i)   *La **suggestion** qu'il était **sur le point de la mort** était fausse.*

(51)(ii)   *Der **Vorschlag, dass** er **nah dem Sterben** war, war falsch.*

(52)   ***They informed us of** their arrival too late to greet them.*

(52)(i)   ***Ils nous ont informé de** leur arrivée trop en retard*
            pour les saluer.

(52)(ii)   ***Sie informierten uns über** ihre Ankunft, die zu verspätet <u>ist</u>,*
            um sie zu grüßen.

9.5   SAL Adjectives (WC 4)

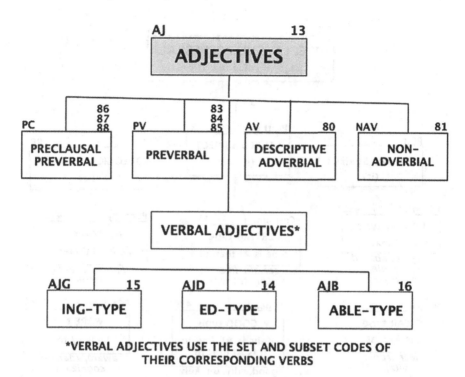

*VERBAL ADJECTIVES USE THE SET AND SUBSET CODES OF
THEIR CORRESPONDING VERBS*

Fig. 9.23   SAL adjective sets

Non-verbal adjectives are descriptive adjectives and are organized into a single SAL superset, with sets and subsets. Note that descriptive adjectives whose predicate adjective function introduces *that* clauses (like *feasible* in *feasible that*) or *infinitive* clauses (like *ready* in *ready to act*) are always coded for the most complex function they exhibit. The third category of adjectives in the above diagram, Descriptive Adverbial, denotes descriptive adjectives whose only distinguishing feature is their convertibility to adverbs (e.g., *rapid* ➔ *rapidly*). In Logos Model lexicons, descriptive adjectives and process nouns have what are called an *alternate word class* so that they can be converted to verb and adverb respectively, e.g., *rapid movement* ➔ *move rapidly*. The fourth adjectival category shown in Fig. 9.23 denotes adjectives that are not convertible to adverbs (e.g., *bridal*).

Verbal adjectives have three distinct supersets (for the *-ing*, *-ed*, and *-able* forms, respectively), but otherwise use the set and subset codes of their corresponding verbs.

9.5.1 Preclausal/Preverbal Adjectives

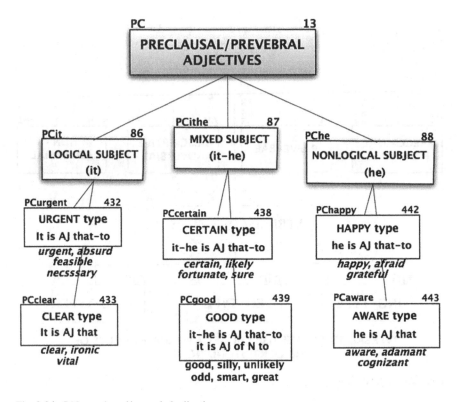

Fig. 9.24 SAL preclausal/preverbal adjectives

Translations of Fig. 9.24 Sentences by Logos Model

(53)   *It is not **necessary** that everyone **agree**.*

(53)(i) *Il n'est pas **nécessaire** que tout le monde **soit d'accord**.*

(54)   *It was **absurd to** say something like that.*

(54)(i) *Il était **absurde de** dire quelque chose comme cela.*

(55)   *It's quite **clear he** doesn't regret what he did.*

(55)(i) *Il est tout à fait **clair qu'il** ne regrette pas ce qu'il a fait.*

(56)   *She was **lucky her** illness was cured so easily.*

(56)(i) *Elle était **heureuse que sa** maladie ait été guérie si facilement.*

(57)   *They are fully **aware these** issues must be looked into.*

(57)(i) *Ils sont entièrement **conscients qu'on** doit examiner ces questions.*

9.5.2   Preverbal Adjectives

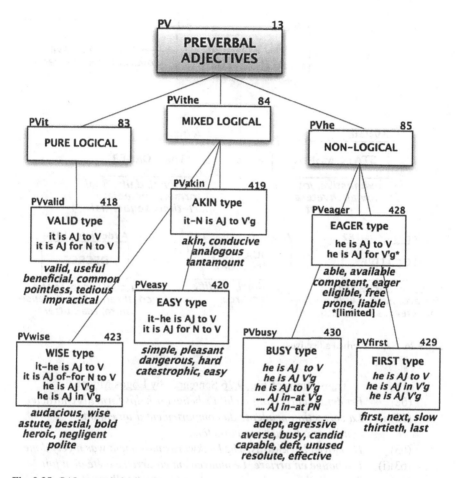

Fig. 9.25 SAL preverbal adjectives

Translations of Fig. 9.25 Sentences by Logos Model

(58)   *Such help is not **conducive to solving** the difficulty.*

(58)(i)   *Telle aide n'est pas **contribuante à la résolution** de la difficulté.*

(59)   *John is **eager to please** his friends. **Pleasing** his friends*
           *is **easy** for him.*

(59)(i)   *John est **impatient de faire plaisir** à ses amis. **Faire plaisir***
           *à ses amis **est facile** pour lui.*

(60)   *Is it **wise** to do that?*

(60)(i)   *Est-il **sage** de faire cela?*

(61)   *She is quite **adept at playing** the cello.*

(61)(i)   *Elle est tout à fait **experte à jouer** du violoncelle.*

9.5.3 *Adverbial Adjectives*

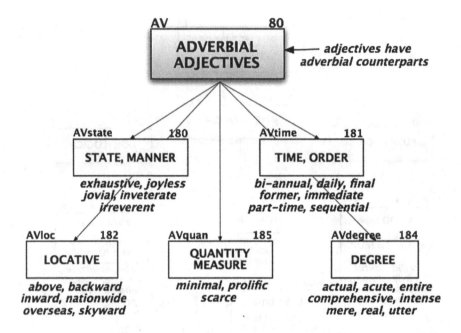

Fig. 9.26 SAL adverbial adjectives

Translations of Fig. 9.26 Sentences by Logos Model

(62)   ***Prudently correcting*** *a child's behavior helps form his character.*

(62)(i)   ***La correction prudente*** *du comportement d'un enfant*
          contribue à former son caractère.

(63)   *He moved **backwards**. The **backwards** movement was nicely done.*

(63)(i)   *Il a bougé **en arrière**. Le mouvement **en arrière** a été bien fait.*

(64)   *The **part-time** workers were rehired to work **full-time**.*

(64)(i)   *Les travailleurs **à mi-temps** ont été réembauchés pour*
          *travailler **à plein temps**.*

(65)   ***Faithfully*** *fulfilling the tasks he was asked to do,*
        *John won a **faithful** worker's reward.*

(65)(i)   *En remplissant **fidèlement** les tâches qu'on lui a demandé*
          *d'accomplir, John a gagné la récompense d'un travailleur **fidèle**.*

9.5.4 Non-adverbial Adjectives

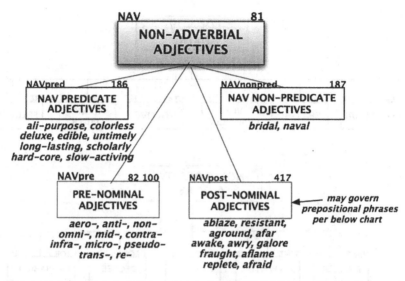

Fig. 9.27 SAL non-adverbial adjectives. Post-Nominal adjectives may govern prepositions as per Chart

Preposition	Mnemonic	Numeric	Examples
Locative prepositions (at, on, in, under, above, etc.)	AVloc	13 68 180/417	asleep (on), submersible (in)
for	AVfor	13 46 180/417	ineligible, avid, famous, suitable (for)
from	AVfrom	13 26 180/417	distinct, inseparable, remote (from)
in (non-locative) = e.g., with respect to	AVin	13 20 180/417	active, deficient, fluent, foremost, methodical, prevalent, well-versed (in)
of	AVof	13 17 180/417	apprehensive, devoid, envious, intolerant, suspicious (of)
about/over/on (non-locative)	AVabout	13 90 180/417	jittery, joyous, jumpy, obdurate (about/over), reliant, conditional (on)
to	AVto	13 57 180/417	adjacent, detrimental, extraneous (to)
with	AVwith	13 59 180/417	consistent, familiar, incompatible (with)

Translations of Fig. 9.27 Senttences by Logos Model

(66)   *They designed a fabric that is **resistant** to water.*

(66)(i)   *Ils ont conçu un tissu qui est **résistant** à l'eau.*

(67)   *The police have been provided **anti-rioting** gear.*

(67)(i)   *On a fourni l'équipement **anti-manifestant** à la police.*

(68)   *It is not wise to be too **afraid** about the future.*

(68)(i)   *Il n'est pas sage d'être trop **effrayé** au sujet du futur.*

9.6   SAL Adverbs (WC 3 and WC 6)

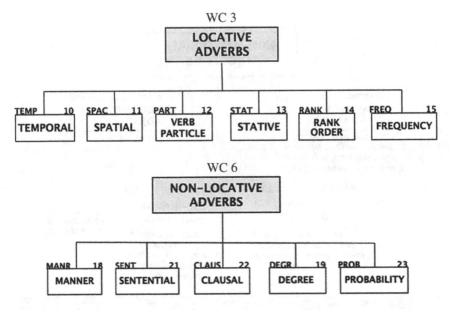

Fig. 9.28   SAL taxonomies for locative and non-locative adverbs

9.6.1   *Locative Adverbs have the Following Supersets*

(a) TEMPORAL adverbs express concepts of time, including sets (not shown) for
    past, present and future time, e.g. *formerly, now, soon,* etc.
(b) SPATIAL adverbs express concepts of place or direction, e.g., *here, there-
    abouts,* etc.
(c) VERB PARTICLES give meaning to verbs but can act as adverbs, e.g., *put
    aside, such matters aside,* etc.
(d) STATIVE adverbs express states, conditions, e.g., *alone, OK,* etc.
(e) ORDER/RANK adverbs express concepts like *last, first of all, thirdly,* etc.
(f) FREQUENCY adverbs express concepts like *often, always,* etc.

9.6.2 Non-locative Adverb have the Following Supersets

(a) MANNER adverbs express how something is done, e.g., *smoothly*.
(b) SENTENTIAL adverbs tend to modify entire sentences, e.g., *basically, generally, as a rule*, etc.
(c) CLAUSAL adverbs function as collapsed clauses, e.g., *as follows, where indicated*, etc.
(d) DEGREE adverbs are intensifiers that modify other adverbs and express their degree, e.g., *very, more, too, less*, etc.
(e) PROBABILITY adverbs express concepts like *maybe, for sure*.

All of these adverbial supersets have sets and subsets, affording a fairly elaborate taxonomy for the word class. A number of adverbs, especially the verb particles, have been given unique subset codes to allow for handling at the explicit word level.

In sentence (69), below, we see how the adverb-verb sequence *systematically classifying* is translated into an adjective-process noun construction in (69)(i).

Translations of Fig. 9.28 Sentences by Logos Model

(69)   *We spent time doing tasks such as **systematically**
        classifying documents.*

(69)(i) *Nous avons passé le temps à accomplir les tâches telles que
        la classification systématique des documents*

In sentence (70), below, we highlight the presence of various kinds of adverbs. The example is from a text translated by Logos Model while under contract to the office of the Canadian Secretary of State. Translations are given in (70)(i) for French and in (70)(ii) for German.

(70)   *Let me **also** note that because of the **relatively** close movement
        of the Canadian dollar with the U.S. dollar, our currency has
        declined along with the U.S. dollar against these other currencies
        this past year, removing much of the exchange rate distortion that
        was hampering the ability of Canadian firms to compete with
        producers **overseas**.)*

(70)(i)   *Permettez-moi **également** de noter qu'à cause du mouvement*
           ***relativement** proche du dollar canadien avec le dollar américain,*
           *notre monnaie a décliné **cette année dernière** avec le dollar*
           américain contre ces autres monnaies, en enlevant beaucoup
           de la distorsion de taux de change qui gênait la capacité des
           compagnies canadiennes de faire concurrence aux producteurs
           ***outre-mer**.*

(70)(ii)   *Erlauben Sie mir **auch**, zu bemerken, dass wegen der **relativ***
           nahen Bewegung des kanadischen Dollars mit dem US Dollar,
           *unsere Währung **dieses letzte Jahr** mit dem US Dollar gegen*
           diese anderen Währungen gesunken ist, was viel von der
           Wechselkurs-Verzerrung entfernt, die die Fähigkeit kanadischer
           Firmen behinderte, mit Herstellern nach <u>Übersee</u> zu konkurrieren.

Postscript

Postscript 9-A

Although Logos Model's use of numbers is foreign to linguistic convention, the practice has proven to have many advantages computationally, especially with respect to the storing, indexing, accessing, and matching of patterns when expressed numerically. In SAL for example, superset codes generally range from 1 to 17 set codes from 18 to 99, and subset codes from 100 to 997. The benefit of this is that these numbers allow developers to instantly recognize a pattern's place in the taxonomy, i.e., its degree of semantico-syntactic specificity. This number arrangement facilitates the internal practice of matching SAL input against stored patterns first on the basis of subset codes, then on sets, and finally on supersets, thus insuring priority to more specific pattern-rules. Finally, this arrangement allows pattern-rules to be self-organizing and rationally indexable. Developers do not need to ponder where to place a pattern-rule or where to look for it.

Figure 9.29, is an extract from a Logos Model diagnostic showing use of numbers. The diagnostic shown becomes available at the end of the second of Logos Model's six processing stages, i.e., at the end of the macro-parse.

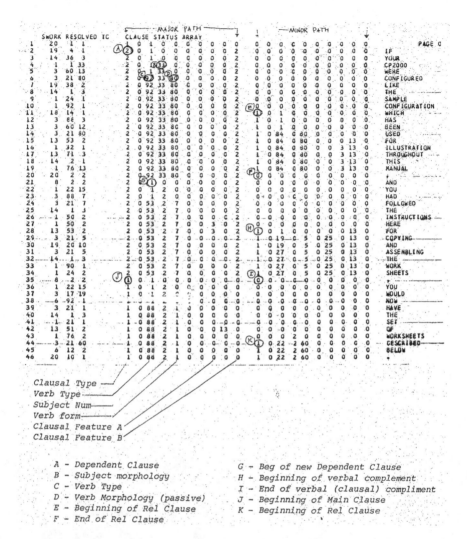

Clausal Type
Verb Type
Subject Num
Verb form
Clausal Feature A
Clausal Feature B

A - Dependent Clause
B - Subject morphology
C - Verb Type
D - Verb Morphology (passive)
E - Beginning of Rel Clause
F - End of Rel Clause

G - Beg of new Dependent Clause
H - Beginning of verbal complement
I - End of verbal (clausal) compliment
J - Beginning of Main Clause
K - Beginning of Rel Clause

Fig. 9.29 *Extract from Logos Model diagnostic showing use of numbers.* Diagnostic is output at end of RES2 module

Printed in the United States
By Bookmasters